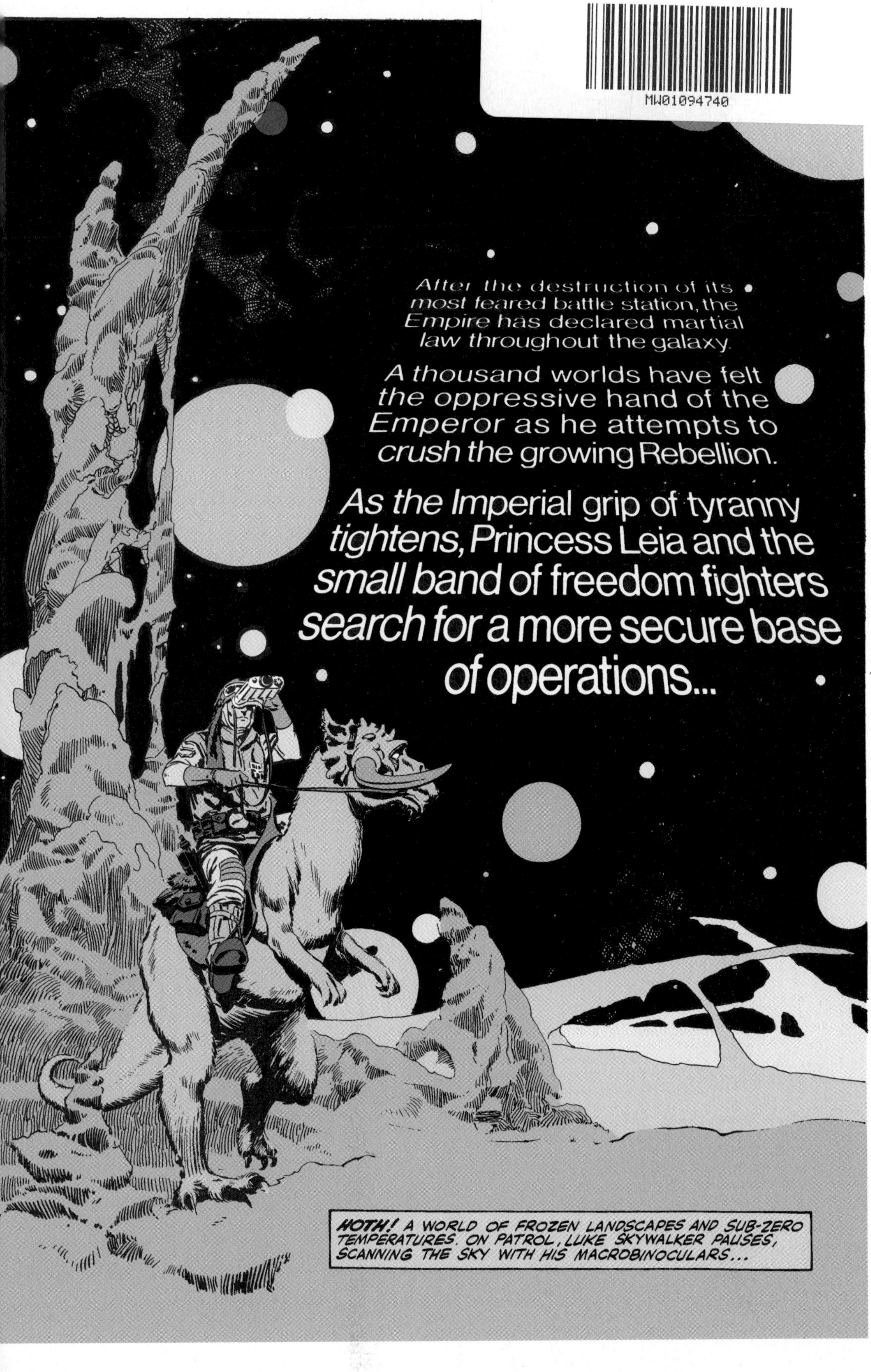
After the destruction of its most feared battle station, the Empire has declared martial law throughout the galaxy.
A thousand worlds have felt the oppressive hand of the Emperor as he attempts to crush the growing Rebellion.
As the Imperial grip of tyranny tightens, Princess Leia and the small band of freedom fighters search for a more secure base of operations...
HOTH! A WORLD OF FROZEN LANDSCAPES AND SUB-ZERO TEMPERATURES. ON PATROL, LUKE SKYWALKER PAUSES, SCANNING THE SKY WITH HIS MACROBINOCULARS...

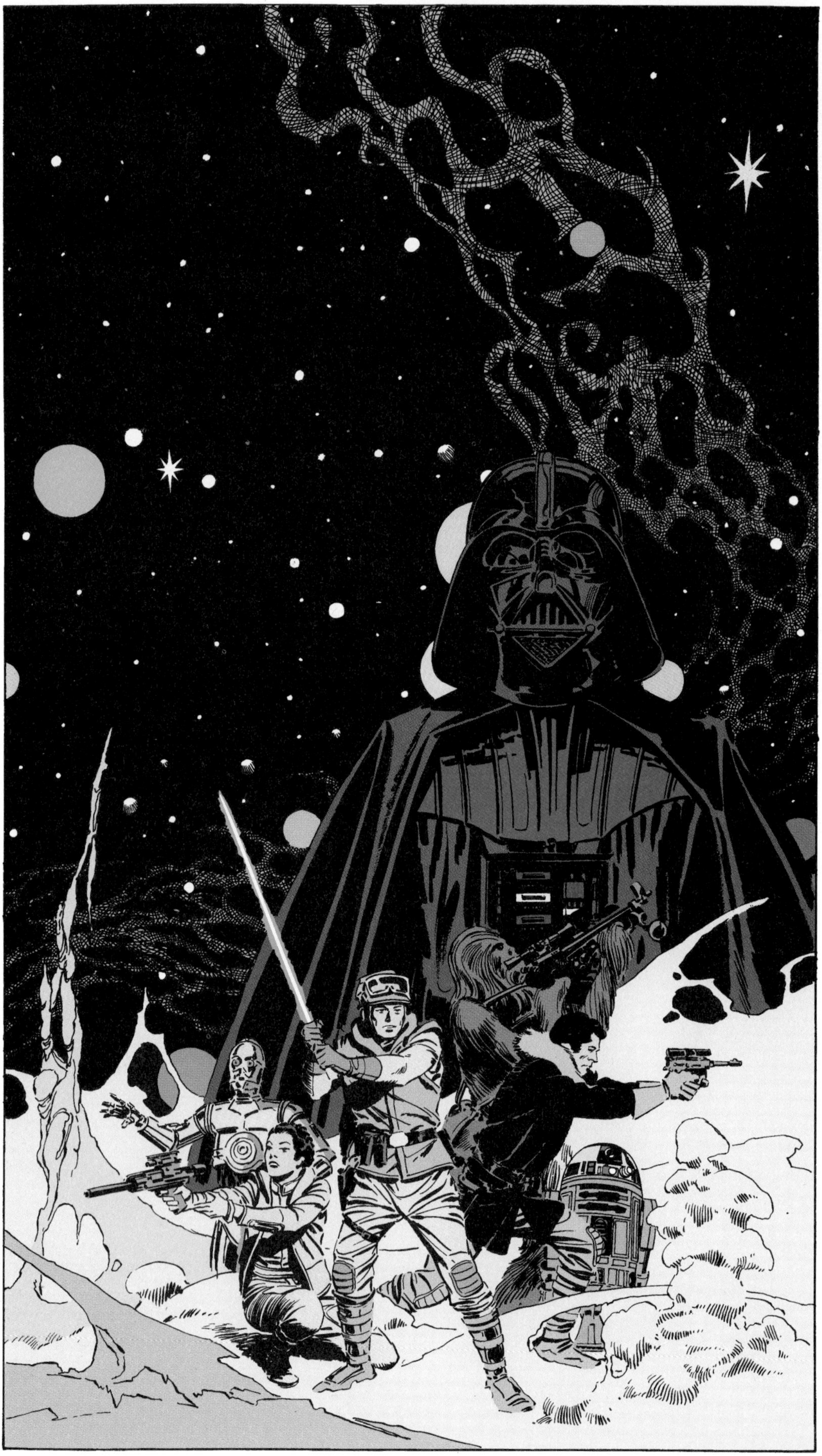

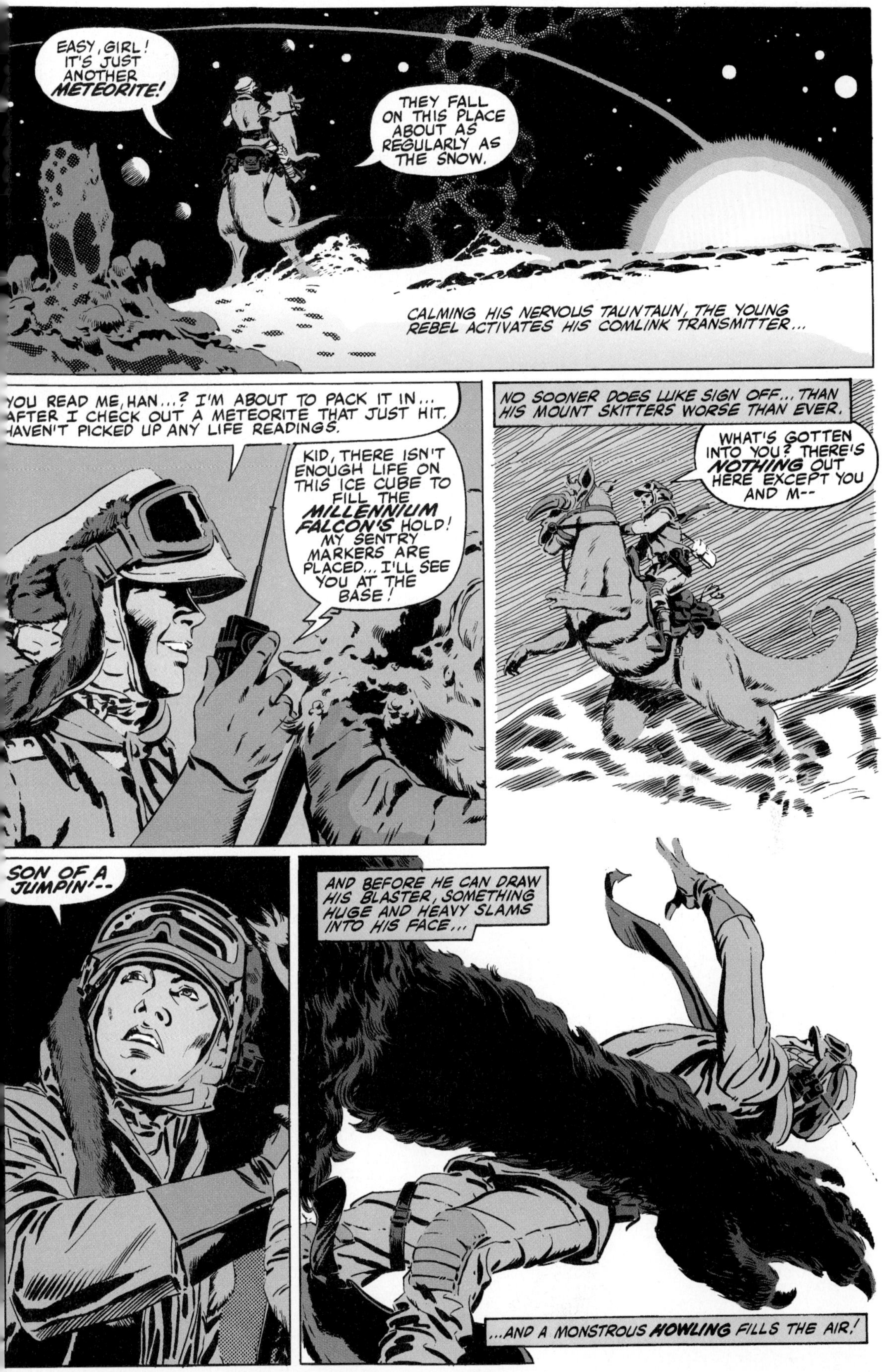
EASY, GIRL! IT'S JUST ANOTHER METEORITE!
THEY FALL ON THIS PLACE ABOUT AS REGULARLY AS THE SNOW.
CALMING HIS NERVOUS TAUNTAUN, THE YOUNG REBEL ACTIVATES HIS COMLINK TRANSMITTER...
YOU READ ME, HAN...? I'M ABOUT TO PACK IT IN... AFTER I CHECK OUT A METEORITE THAT JUST HIT. HAVEN'T PICKED UP ANY LIFE READINGS.
KID, THERE ISN'T ENOUGH LIFE ON THIS ICE CUBE TO FILL THE MILLENNIUM FALCON'S HOLD! MY SENTRY MARKERS ARE PLACED... I'LL SEE YOU AT THE BASE!
NO SOONER DOES LUKE SIGN OFF... THAN HIS MOUNT SKITTERS WORSE THAN EVER.
WHAT'S GOTTEN INTO YOU? THERE'S NOTHING OUT HERE EXCEPT YOU AND M--
SON OF A JUMPIN'--
AND BEFORE HE CAN DRAW HIS BLASTER, SOMETHING HUGE AND HEAVY SLAMS INTO HIS FACE...
...AND A MONSTROUS HOWLING FILLS THE AIR!

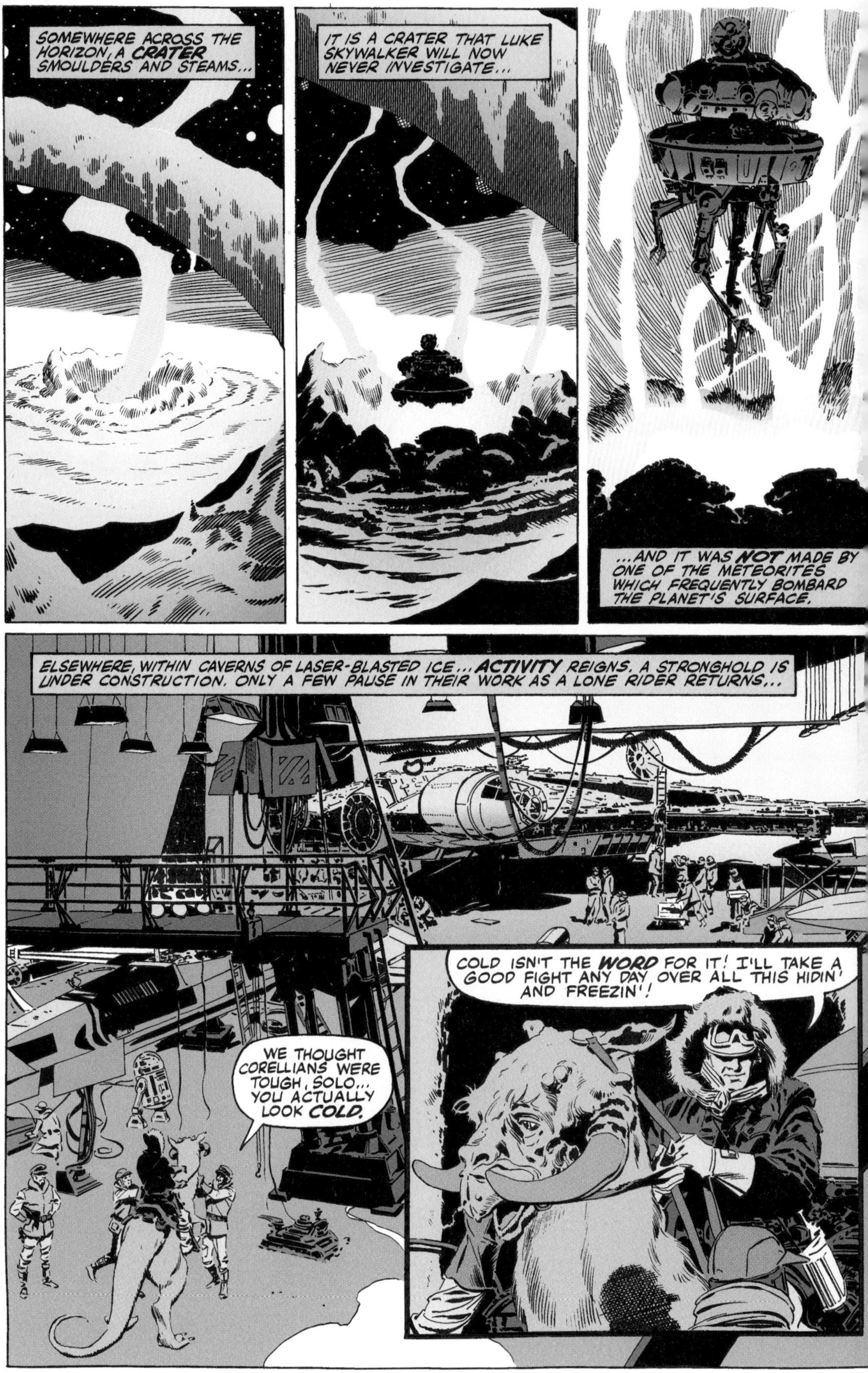
SOMEWHERE ACROSS THE HORIZON, A CRATER SMOULDERS AND STEAMS...
IT IS A CRATER THAT LUKE SKYWALKER WILL NOW NEVER INVESTIGATE...
...AND IT WAS NOT MADE BY ONE OF THE METEORITES WHICH FREQUENTLY BOMBARD THE PLANET'S SURFACE.
ELSEWHERE, WITHIN CAVERNS OF LASER-BLASTED ICE... ACTIVITY REIGNS. A STRONGHOLD IS UNDER CONSTRUCTION. ONLY A FEW PAUSE IN THEIR WORK AS A LONE RIDER RETURNS...
WE THOUGHT CORELLIANS WERE TOUGH, SOLO... YOU ACTUALLY LOOK COLD.
COLD ISN'T THE WORD FOR IT! I'LL TAKE A GOOD FIGHT ANY DAY OVER ALL THIS HIDIN' AND FREEZIN'!

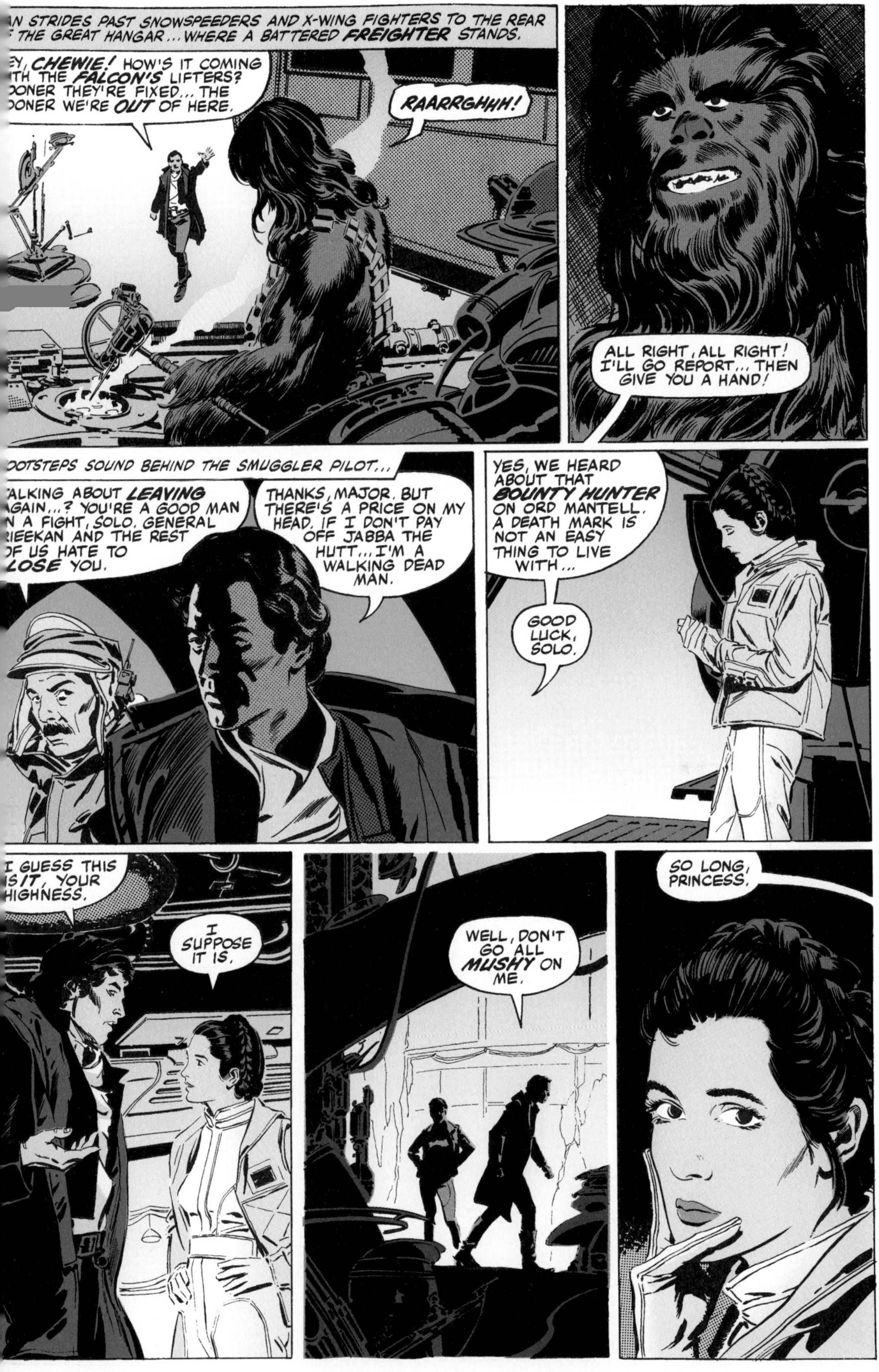
AN STRIDES PAST SNOWSPEEDERS AND X-WING FIGHTERS TO THE REAR
F THE GREAT HANGAR... WHERE A BATTERED FREIGHTER STANDS.
EY, CHEWIE! HOW'S IT COMING
ITH THE FALCON'S LIFTERS?
OONER THEY'RE FIXED... THE
OONER WE'RE OUT OF HERE.
RAARRGHHH!
ALL RIGHT, ALL RIGHT! I'LL GO REPORT... THEN GIVE YOU A HAND!
OOTSTEPS SOUND BEHIND THE SMUGGLER PILOT...
ALKING ABOUT LEAVING AGAIN...? YOU'RE A GOOD MAN N A FIGHT, SOLO. GENERAL RIEEKAN AND THE REST OF US HATE TO LOSE YOU.
THANKS, MAJOR, BUT THERE'S A PRICE ON MY HEAD. IF I DON'T PAY OFF JABBA THE HUTT... I'M A WALKING DEAD MAN.
YES, WE HEARD ABOUT THAT BOUNTY HUNTER ON ORD MANTELL. A DEATH MARK IS NOT AN EASY THING TO LIVE WITH...
GOOD LUCK, SOLO.
I GUESS THIS IS IT, YOUR HIGHNESS.
I SUPPOSE IT IS.
WELL, DON'T GO ALL MUSHY ON ME.
SO LONG, PRINCESS.

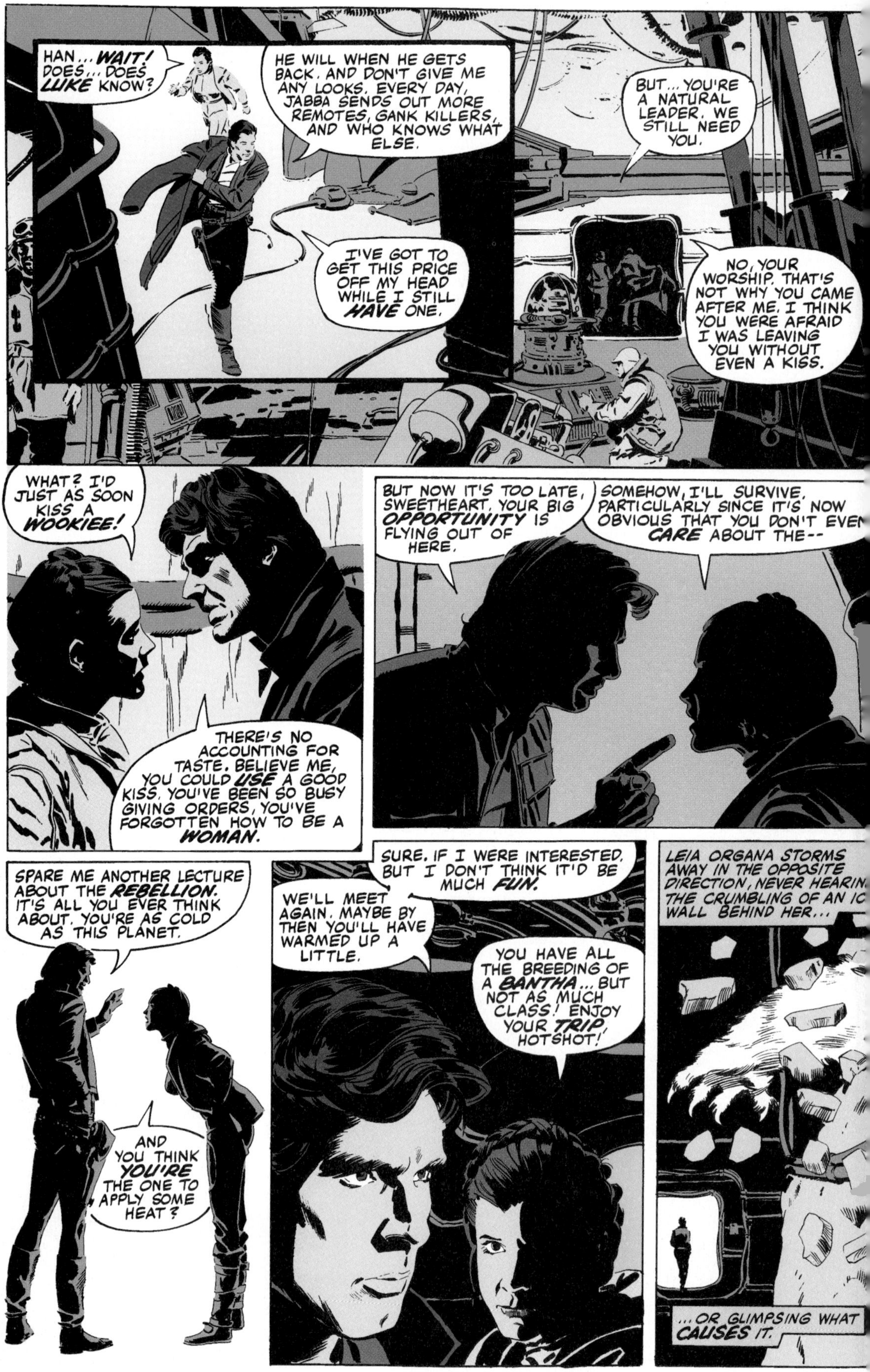
HAN... WAIT! DOES... DOES LUKE KNOW?
HE WILL WHEN HE GETS BACK. AND DON'T GIVE ME ANY LOOKS. EVERY DAY, JABBA SENDS OUT MORE REMOTES, GANK KILLERS, AND WHO KNOWS WHAT ELSE.
I'VE GOT TO GET THIS PRICE OFF MY HEAD WHILE I STILL HAVE ONE.
BUT... YOU'RE A NATURAL LEADER. WE STILL NEED YOU.
NO, YOUR WORSHIP. THAT'S NOT WHY YOU CAME AFTER ME. I THINK YOU WERE AFRAID I WAS LEAVING YOU WITHOUT EVEN A KISS.
WHAT? I'D JUST AS SOON KISS A WOOKIEE!
THERE'S NO ACCOUNTING FOR TASTE. BELIEVE ME, YOU COULD USE A GOOD KISS. YOU'VE BEEN SO BUSY GIVING ORDERS, YOU'VE FORGOTTEN HOW TO BE A WOMAN.
BUT NOW IT'S TOO LATE, SWEETHEART. YOUR BIG OPPORTUNITY IS FLYING OUT OF HERE.
SOMEHOW, I'LL SURVIVE. PARTICULARLY SINCE IT'S NOW OBVIOUS THAT YOU DON'T EVEN CARE ABOUT THE--
SPARE ME ANOTHER LECTURE ABOUT THE REBELLION. IT'S ALL YOU EVER THINK ABOUT. YOU'RE AS COLD AS THIS PLANET.
AND YOU THINK YOU'RE THE ONE TO APPLY SOME HEAT?
SURE. IF I WERE INTERESTED. BUT I DON'T THINK IT'D BE MUCH FUN.
WE'LL MEET AGAIN. MAYBE BY THEN YOU'LL HAVE WARMED UP A LITTLE.
YOU HAVE ALL THE BREEDING OF A BANTHA... BUT NOT AS MUCH CLASS! ENJOY YOUR TRIP, HOTSHOT!
LEIA ORGANA STORMS AWAY IN THE OPPOSITE DIRECTION, NEVER HEARING THE CRUMBLING OF AN ICE WALL BEHIND HER...
...OR GLIMPSING WHAT CAUSES IT.

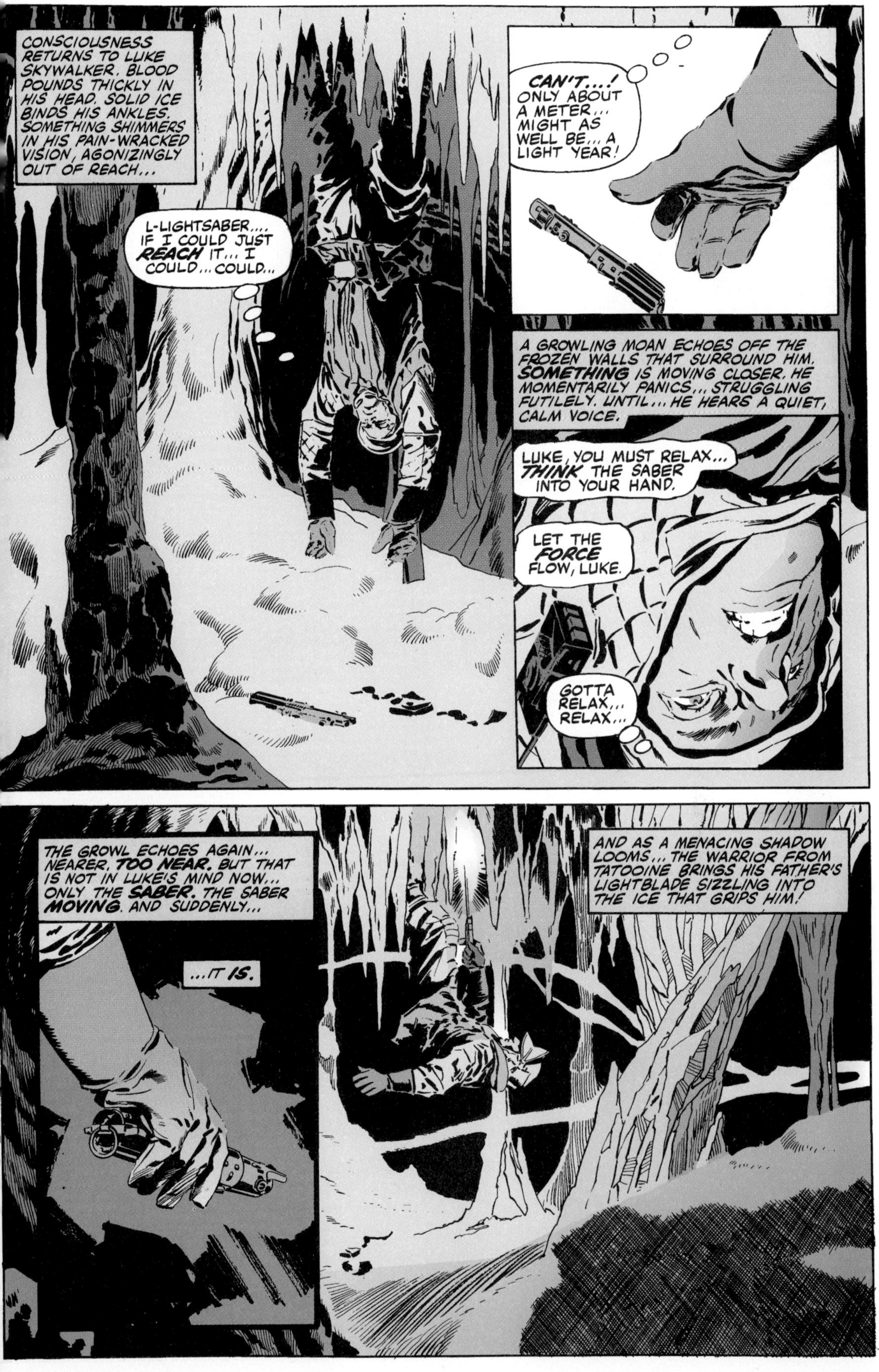
CONSCIOUSNESS RETURNS TO LUKE SKYWALKER. BLOOD POUNDS THICKLY IN HIS HEAD. SOLID ICE BINDS HIS ANKLES. SOMETHING SHIMMERS IN HIS PAIN-WRACKED VISION, AGONIZINGLY OUT OF REACH...
L-LIGHTSABER... IF I COULD JUST REACH IT... I COULD... COULD...
CAN'T...! ONLY ABOUT A METER... MIGHT AS WELL BE... A LIGHT YEAR!
A GROWLING MOAN ECHOES OFF THE FROZEN WALLS THAT SURROUND HIM. SOMETHING IS MOVING CLOSER. HE MOMENTARILY PANICS... STRUGGLING FUTILELY. UNTIL... HE HEARS A QUIET, CALM VOICE.
LUKE, YOU MUST RELAX... THINK THE SABER INTO YOUR HAND.
LET THE FORCE FLOW, LUKE.
GOTTA RELAX... RELAX...
THE GROWL ECHOES AGAIN... NEARER, TOO NEAR. BUT THAT IS NOT IN LUKE'S MIND NOW... ONLY THE SABER. THE SABER MOVING. AND SUDDENLY...
...IT IS.
AND AS A MENACING SHADOW LOOMS... THE WARRIOR FROM TATOOINE BRINGS HIS FATHER'S LIGHTBLADE SIZZLING INTO THE ICE THAT GRIPS HIM!

LUKE **FALLS**, CRASHING HEAVILY INTO THE SNOW... AS SOMETHING **HUGE** RUSHES TOWARD HIM!

HE **ROLLS**, SLASHING OUT WITH HIS LIGHTBLADE...

...AND A SCREAM OF **PAIN** FILLS THE ICY GORGE.

IT STILL ECHOES IN HIS MIND AS HE SOMEHOW STAGGERS TO SAFETY...

...LIMPING INTO THE GATHERING GRAYNESS THAT HERALDS THE APPROACH OF SUB-ZERO **NIGHT** ON HOTH.

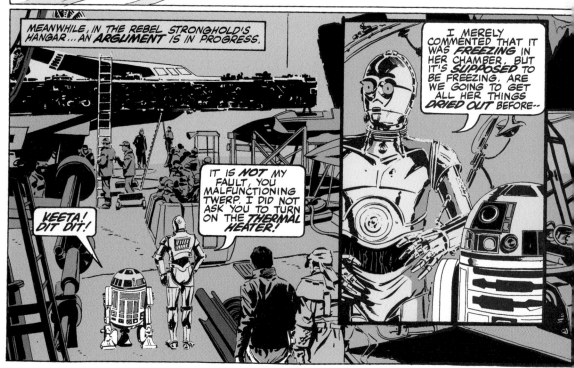

MEANWHILE, IN THE REBEL STRONGHOLD'S HANGAR... AN **ARGUMENT** IS IN PROGRESS.

I MERELY COMMENTED THAT IT WAS **FREEZING** IN HER CHAMBER, BUT IT'S **SUPPOSED** TO BE FREEZING, ARE WE GOING TO GET ALL HER THINGS **DRIED OUT** BEFORE--

IT IS **NOT** MY FAULT, YOU MALFUNCTIONING TWERP. I DID NOT ASK YOU TO TURN ON THE **THERMAL HEATER**!

KEETA! DIT DIT!

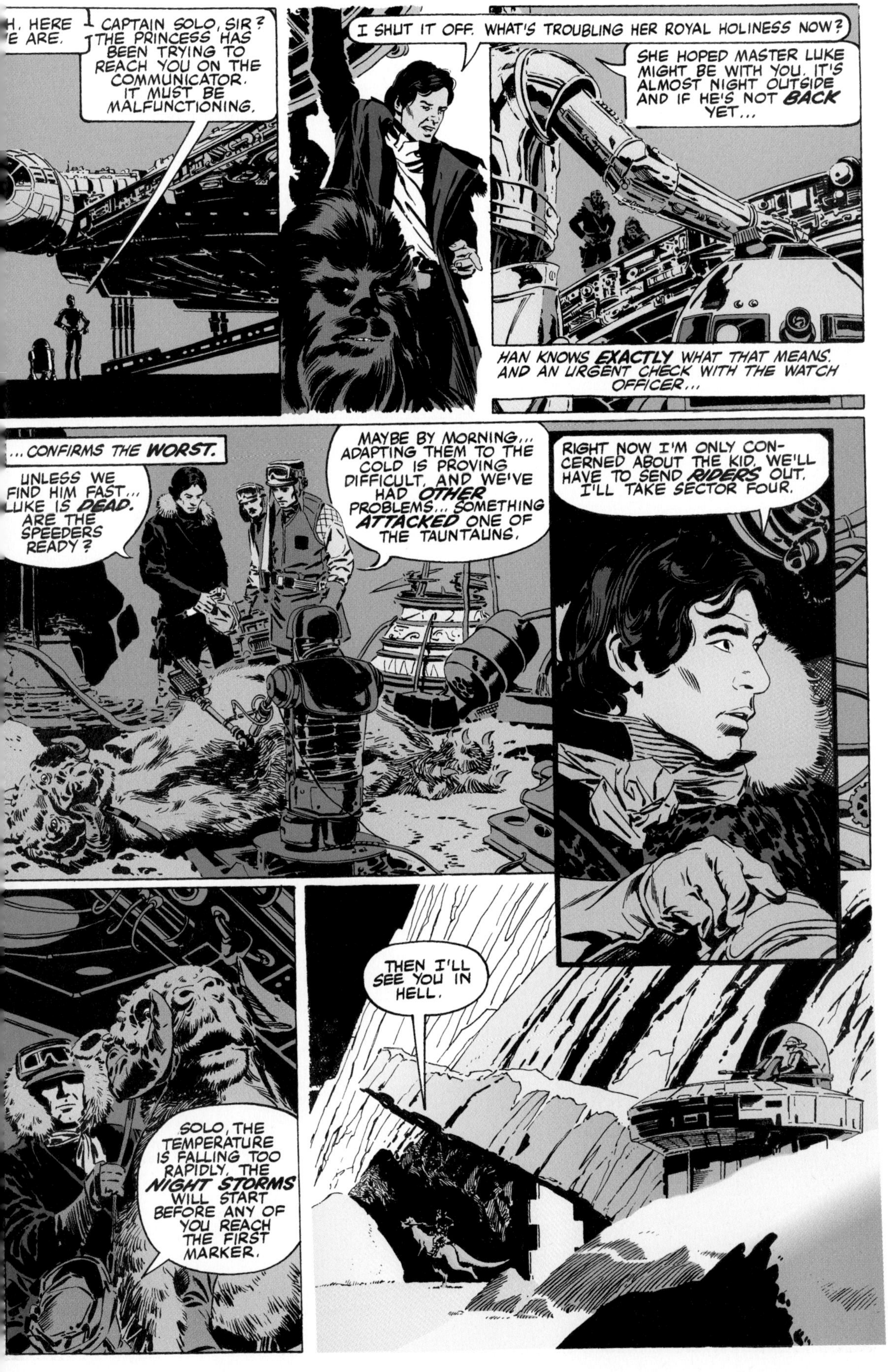
H, HERE
E ARE.
CAPTAIN SOLO, SIR? THE PRINCESS HAS BEEN TRYING TO REACH YOU ON THE COMMUNICATOR. IT MUST BE MALFUNCTIONING.
I SHUT IT OFF. WHAT'S TROUBLING HER ROYAL HOLINESS NOW?
SHE HOPED MASTER LUKE MIGHT BE WITH YOU. IT'S ALMOST NIGHT OUTSIDE AND IF HE'S NOT BACK YET...
HAN KNOWS EXACTLY WHAT THAT MEANS. AND AN URGENT CHECK WITH THE WATCH OFFICER...
...CONFIRMS THE WORST.
UNLESS WE FIND HIM FAST... LUKE IS DEAD. ARE THE SPEEDERS READY?
MAYBE BY MORNING... ADAPTING THEM TO THE COLD IS PROVING DIFFICULT, AND WE'VE HAD OTHER PROBLEMS... SOMETHING ATTACKED ONE OF THE TAUNTAUNS.
RIGHT NOW I'M ONLY CONCERNED ABOUT THE KID. WE'LL HAVE TO SEND RIDERS OUT. I'LL TAKE SECTOR FOUR.
SOLO, THE TEMPERATURE IS FALLING TOO RAPIDLY. THE NIGHT STORMS WILL START BEFORE ANY OF YOU REACH THE FIRST MARKER.
THEN I'LL SEE YOU IN HELL.

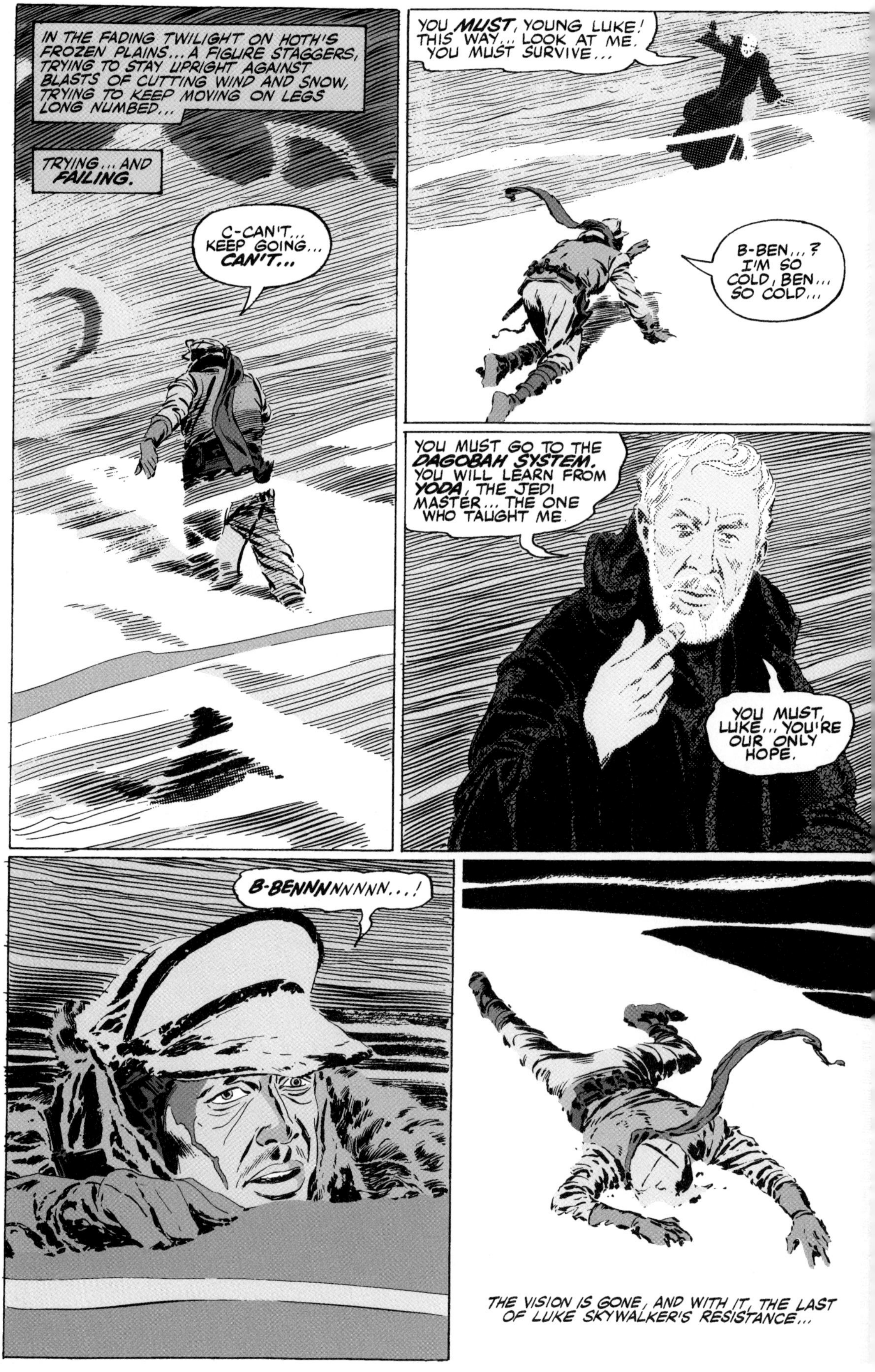
IN THE FADING TWILIGHT ON HOTH'S FROZEN PLAINS... A FIGURE STAGGERS, TRYING TO STAY UPRIGHT AGAINST BLASTS OF CUTTING WIND AND SNOW, TRYING TO KEEP MOVING ON LEGS LONG NUMBED...
TRYING... AND FAILING.
C-CAN'T... KEEP GOING... CAN'T...
YOU MUST, YOUNG LUKE! THIS WAY... LOOK AT ME. YOU MUST SURVIVE...
B-BEN...? I'M SO COLD, BEN... SO COLD...
YOU MUST GO TO THE DAGOBAH SYSTEM. YOU WILL LEARN FROM YODA, THE JEDI MASTER... THE ONE WHO TAUGHT ME.
YOU MUST, LUKE... YOU'RE OUR ONLY HOPE.
B-BENNNNNNNN...!
THE VISION IS GONE, AND WITH IT, THE LAST OF LUKE SKYWALKER'S RESISTANCE...

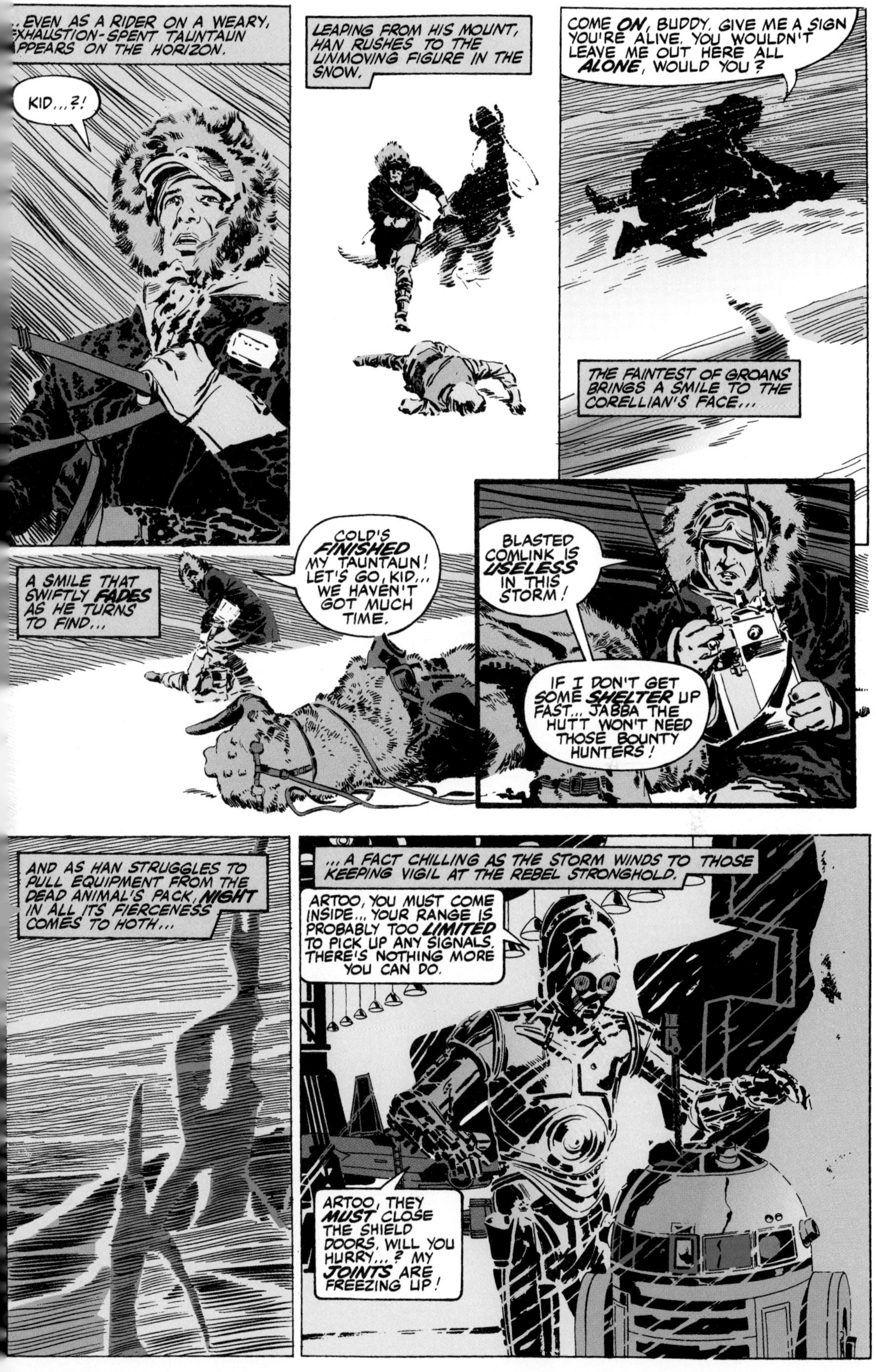
...EVEN AS A RIDER ON A WEARY, EXHAUSTION-SPENT TAUNTAUN APPEARS ON THE HORIZON.
KID...?!
LEAPING FROM HIS MOUNT, HAN RUSHES TO THE UNMOVING FIGURE IN THE SNOW.
COME ON, BUDDY, GIVE ME A SIGN YOU'RE ALIVE. YOU WOULDN'T LEAVE ME OUT HERE ALL ALONE, WOULD YOU?
THE FAINTEST OF GROANS BRINGS A SMILE TO THE CORELLIAN'S FACE...
A SMILE THAT SWIFTLY FADES AS HE TURNS TO FIND...
COLD'S FINISHED MY TAUNTAUN! LET'S GO, KID... WE HAVEN'T GOT MUCH TIME.
BLASTED COMLINK IS USELESS IN THIS STORM!
IF I DON'T GET SOME SHELTER UP FAST... JABBA THE HUTT WON'T NEED THOSE BOUNTY HUNTERS!
AND AS HAN STRUGGLES TO PULL EQUIPMENT FROM THE DEAD ANIMAL'S PACK, NIGHT IN ALL ITS FIERCENESS COMES TO HOTH...
...A FACT CHILLING AS THE STORM WINDS TO THOSE KEEPING VIGIL AT THE REBEL STRONGHOLD.
ARTOO, YOU MUST COME INSIDE... YOUR RANGE IS PROBABLY TOO LIMITED TO PICK UP ANY SIGNALS. THERE'S NOTHING MORE YOU CAN DO.
ARTOO, THEY MUST CLOSE THE SHIELD DOORS. WILL YOU HURRY...? MY JOINTS ARE FREEZING UP!

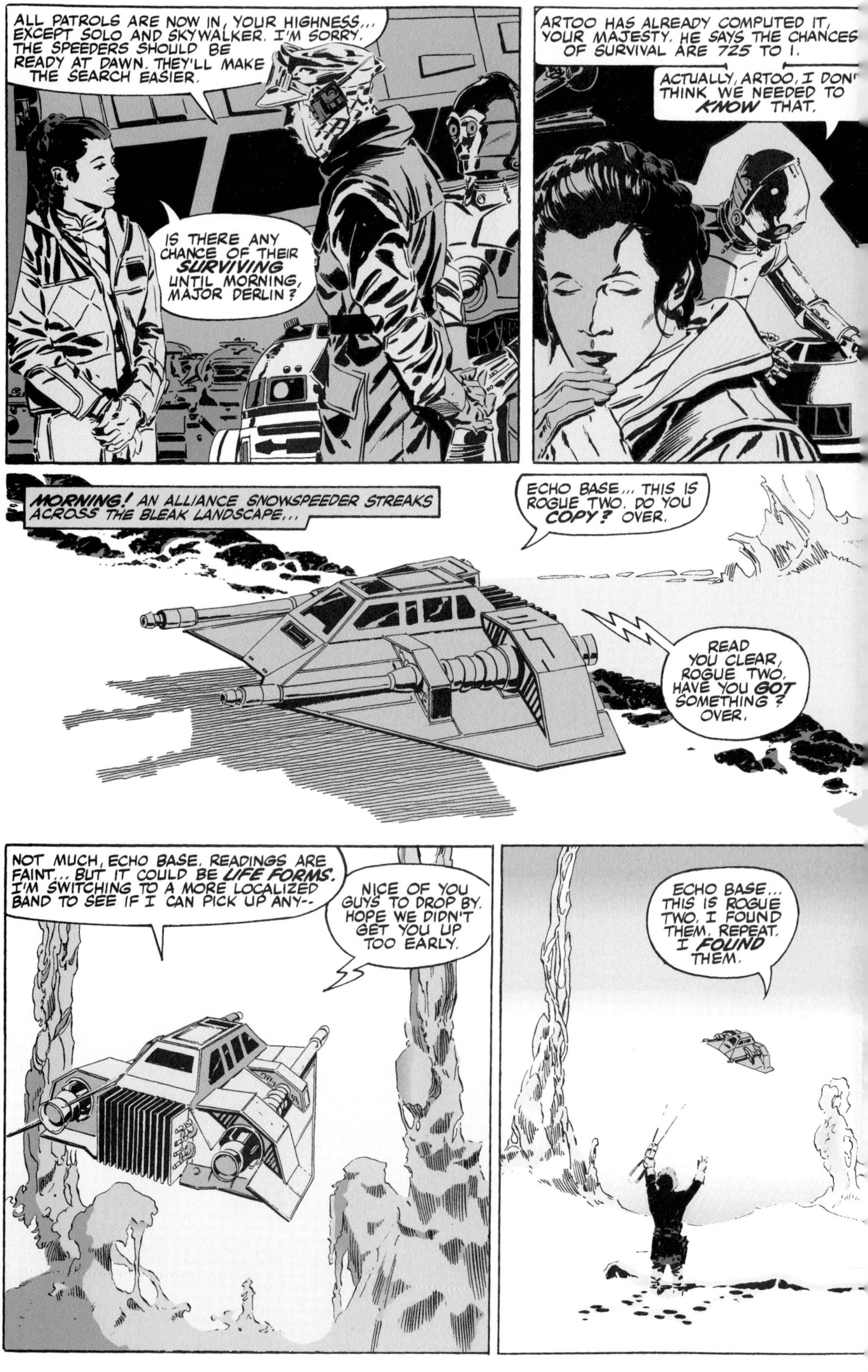
ALL PATROLS ARE NOW IN, YOUR HIGHNESS... EXCEPT SOLO AND SKYWALKER. I'M SORRY. THE SPEEDERS SHOULD BE READY AT DAWN. THEY'LL MAKE THE SEARCH EASIER.
IS THERE ANY CHANCE OF THEIR SURVIVING UNTIL MORNING, MAJOR DERLIN?
ARTOO HAS ALREADY COMPUTED IT, YOUR MAJESTY. HE SAYS THE CHANCES OF SURVIVAL ARE 725 TO 1.
ACTUALLY, ARTOO, I DON' THINK WE NEEDED TO KNOW THAT.
MORNING! AN ALLIANCE SNOWSPEEDER STREAKS ACROSS THE BLEAK LANDSCAPE...
ECHO BASE... THIS IS ROGUE TWO. DO YOU COPY? OVER.
READ YOU CLEAR, ROGUE TWO. HAVE YOU GOT SOMETHING? OVER.
NOT MUCH, ECHO BASE. READINGS ARE FAINT... BUT IT COULD BE LIFE FORMS. I'M SWITCHING TO A MORE LOCALIZED BAND TO SEE IF I CAN PICK UP ANY--
NICE OF YOU GUYS TO DROP BY. HOPE WE DIDN'T GET YOU UP TOO EARLY.
ECHO BASE... THIS IS ROGUE TWO. I FOUND THEM. REPEAT. I FOUND THEM.

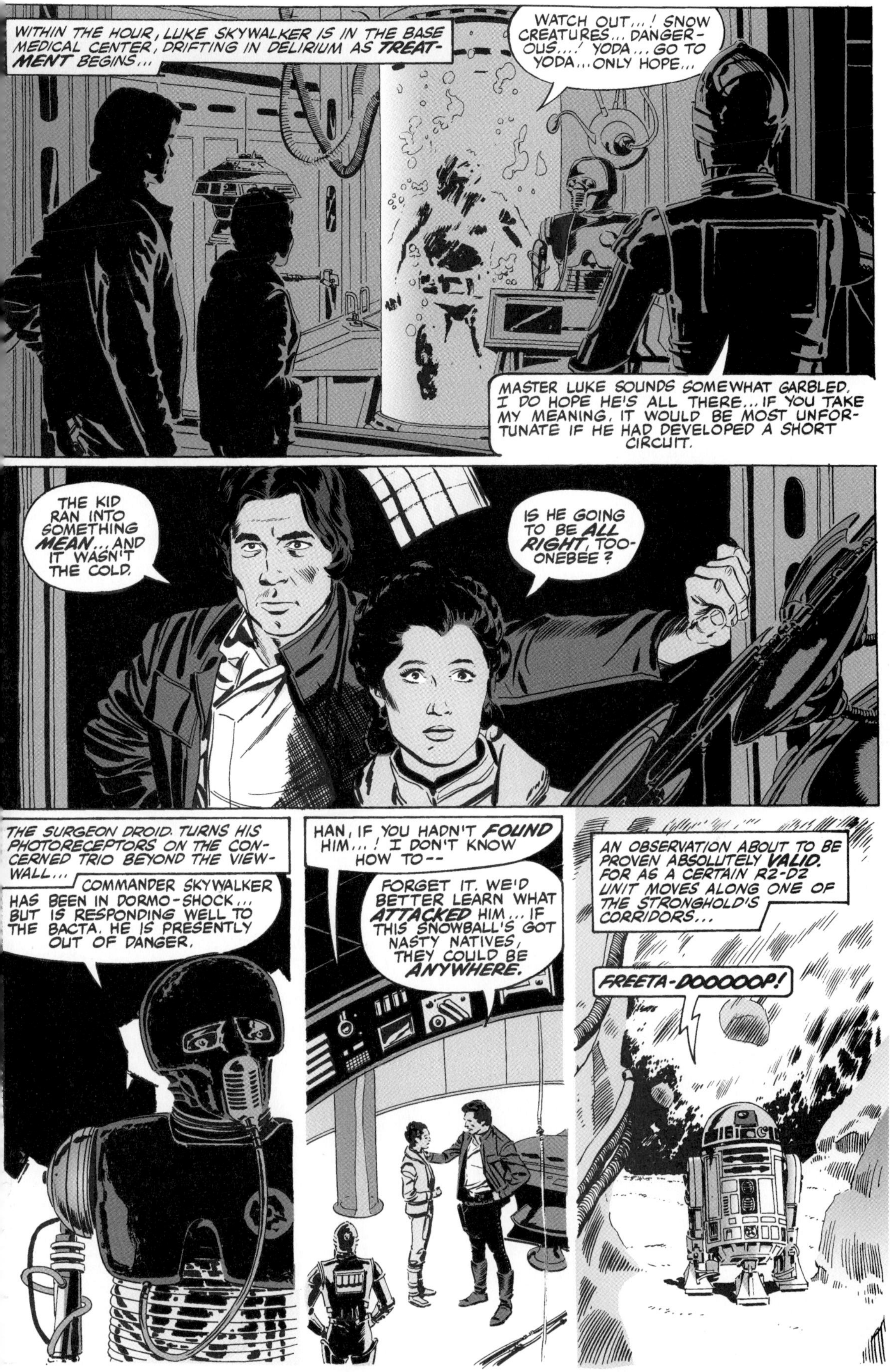

WITHIN THE HOUR, LUKE SKYWALKER IS IN THE BASE MEDICAL CENTER, DRIFTING IN DELIRIUM AS TREATMENT BEGINS...
WATCH OUT...! SNOW CREATURES... DANGEROUS...! YODA... GO TO YODA... ONLY HOPE...
MASTER LUKE SOUNDS SOMEWHAT GARBLED. I DO HOPE HE'S ALL THERE... IF YOU TAKE MY MEANING. IT WOULD BE MOST UNFORTUNATE IF HE HAD DEVELOPED A SHORT CIRCUIT.
THE KID RAN INTO SOMETHING MEAN... AND IT WASN'T THE COLD.
IS HE GOING TO BE ALL RIGHT, TOO-ONEBEE?
THE SURGEON DROID TURNS HIS PHOTORECEPTORS ON THE CONCERNED TRIO BEYOND THE VIEW-WALL...
COMMANDER SKYWALKER HAS BEEN IN DORMO-SHOCK... BUT IS RESPONDING WELL TO THE BACTA. HE IS PRESENTLY OUT OF DANGER.
HAN, IF YOU HADN'T FOUND HIM...! I DON'T KNOW HOW TO--
FORGET IT. WE'D BETTER LEARN WHAT ATTACKED HIM... IF THIS SNOWBALL'S GOT NASTY NATIVES, THEY COULD BE ANYWHERE.
AN OBSERVATION ABOUT TO BE PROVEN ABSOLUTELY VALID. FOR AS A CERTAIN R2-D2 UNIT MOVES ALONG ONE OF THE STRONGHOLD'S CORRIDORS...
FREETA-DOOOOOOP!

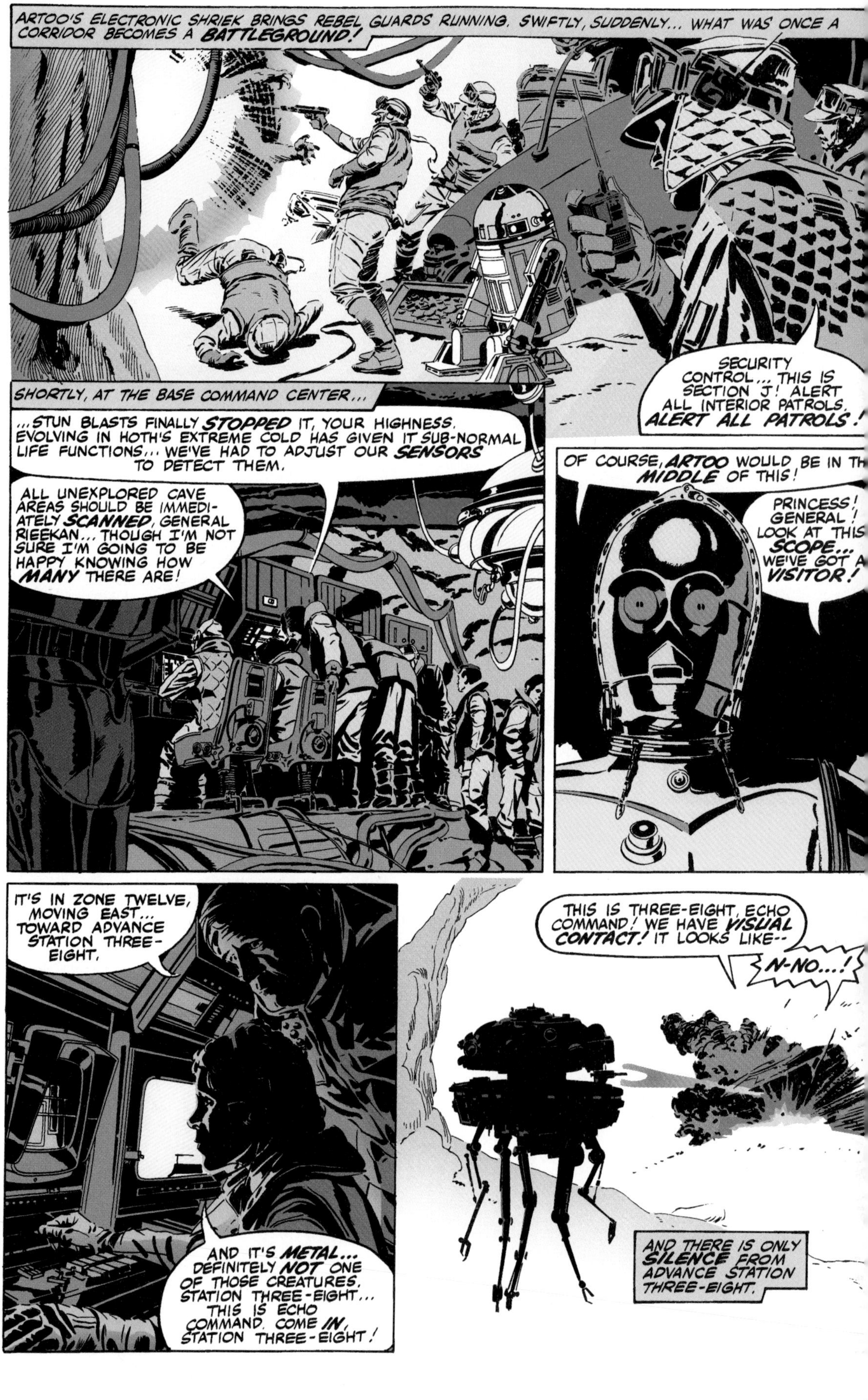
ARTOO'S ELECTRONIC SHRIEK BRINGS REBEL GUARDS RUNNING. SWIFTLY, SUDDENLY... WHAT WAS ONCE A CORRIDOR BECOMES A BATTLEGROUND!
SECURITY CONTROL... THIS IS SECTION J! ALERT ALL INTERIOR PATROLS. ALERT ALL PATROLS!
SHORTLY, AT THE BASE COMMAND CENTER...
...STUN BLASTS FINALLY STOPPED IT, YOUR HIGHNESS. EVOLVING IN HOTH'S EXTREME COLD HAS GIVEN IT SUB-NORMAL LIFE FUNCTIONS... WE'VE HAD TO ADJUST OUR SENSORS TO DETECT THEM.
ALL UNEXPLORED CAVE AREAS SHOULD BE IMMEDIATELY SCANNED, GENERAL RIEEKAN... THOUGH I'M NOT SURE I'M GOING TO BE HAPPY KNOWING HOW MANY THERE ARE!
OF COURSE, ARTOO WOULD BE IN TH MIDDLE OF THIS!
PRINCESS! GENERAL! LOOK AT THIS SCOPE... WE'VE GOT A VISITOR!
IT'S IN ZONE TWELVE, MOVING EAST... TOWARD ADVANCE STATION THREE-EIGHT.
AND IT'S METAL... DEFINITELY NOT ONE OF THOSE CREATURES. STATION THREE-EIGHT... THIS IS ECHO COMMAND. COME IN, STATION THREE-EIGHT!
THIS IS THREE-EIGHT, ECHO COMMAND! WE HAVE VISUAL CONTACT! IT LOOKS LIKE--
N-NO...!
AND THERE IS ONLY SILENCE FROM ADVANCE STATION THREE-EIGHT.

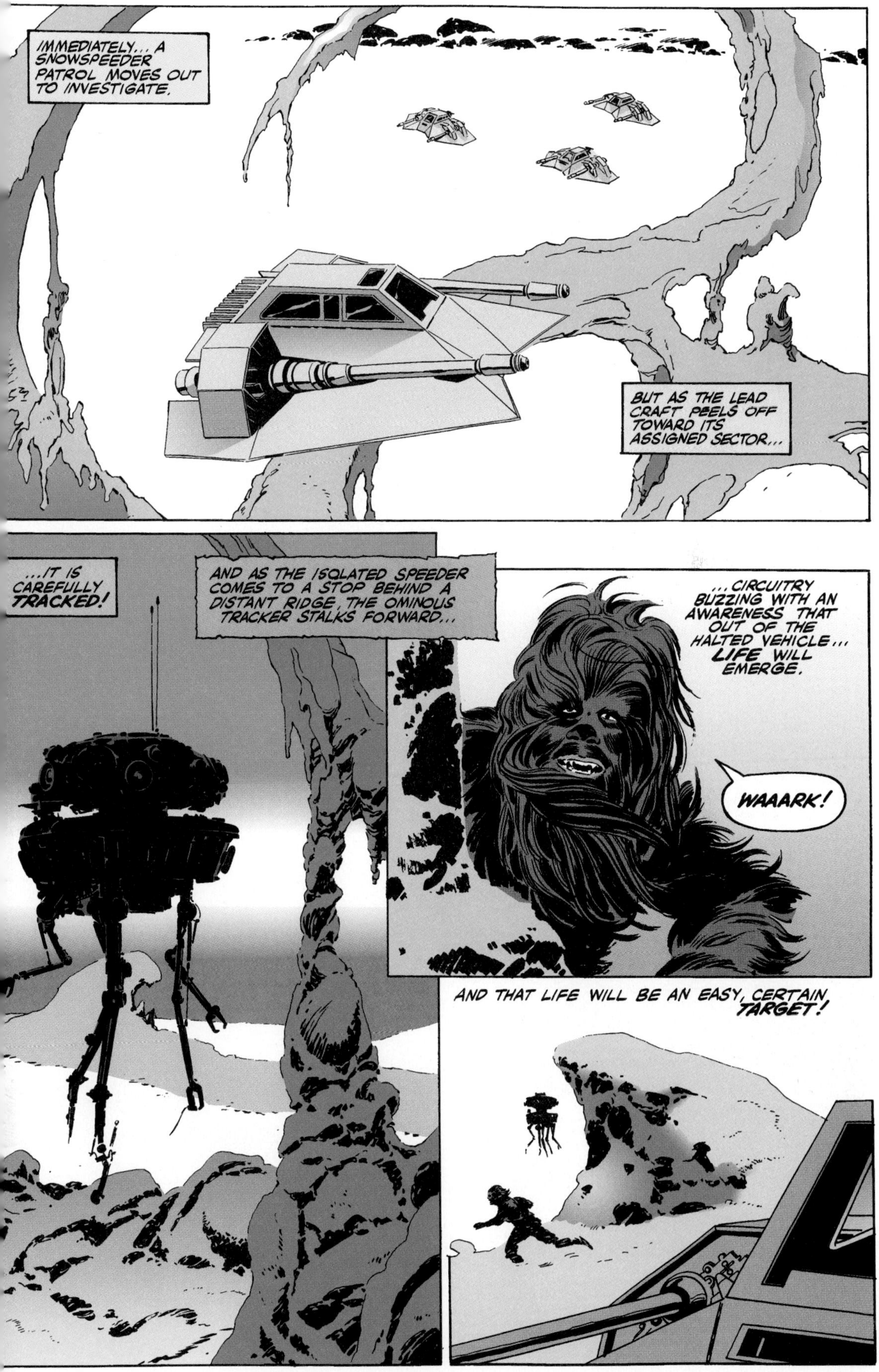
IMMEDIATELY... A SNOWSPEEDER PATROL MOVES OUT TO INVESTIGATE.
BUT AS THE LEAD CRAFT PEELS OFF TOWARD ITS ASSIGNED SECTOR...
...IT IS CAREFULLY TRACKED!
AND AS THE ISOLATED SPEEDER COMES TO A STOP BEHIND A DISTANT RIDGE, THE OMINOUS TRACKER STALKS FORWARD...
...CIRCUITRY BUZZING WITH AN AWARENESS THAT OUT OF THE HALTED VEHICLE... LIFE WILL EMERGE.
WAAARK!
AND THAT LIFE WILL BE AN EASY, CERTAIN TARGET!

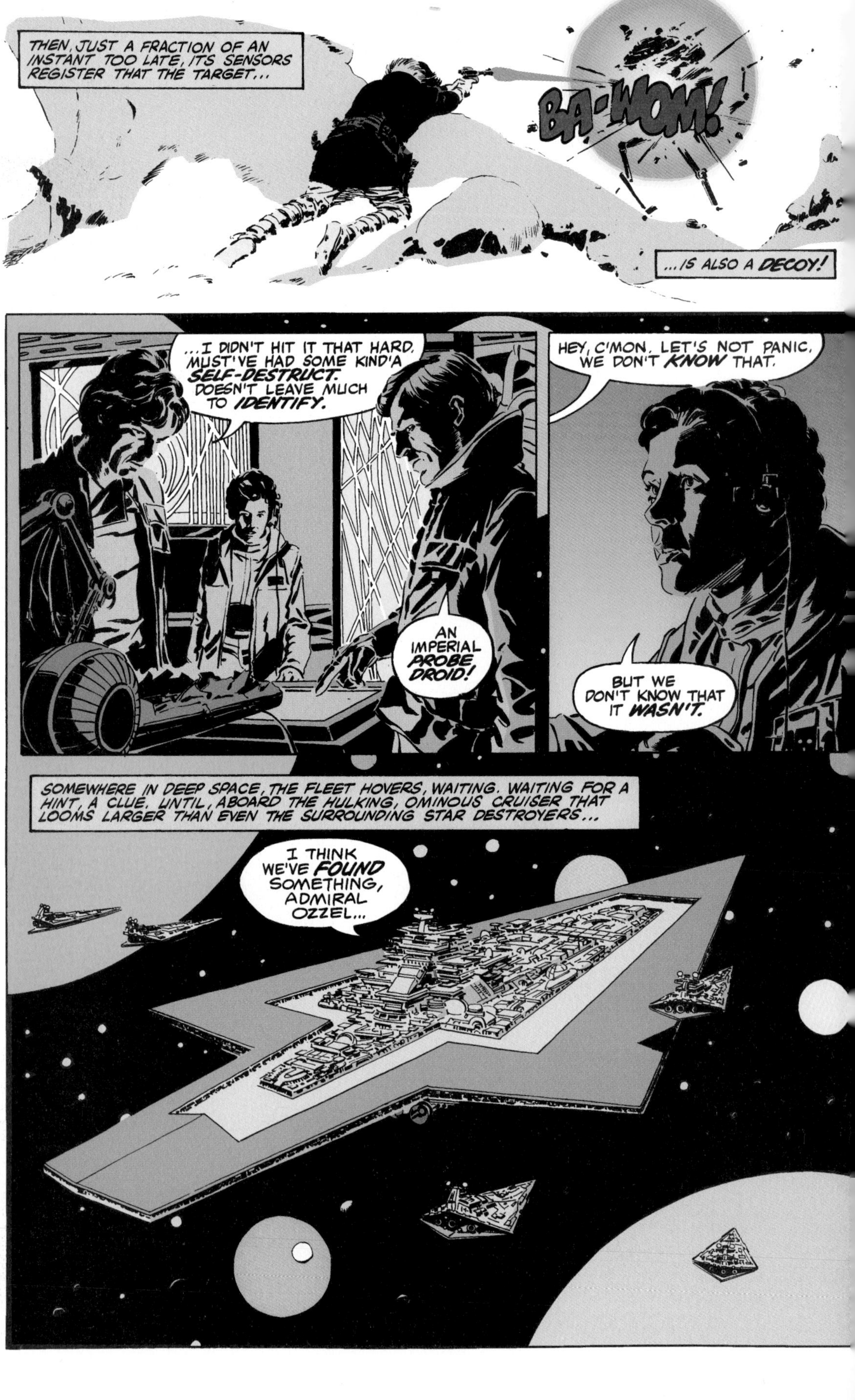
THEN, JUST A FRACTION OF AN INSTANT TOO LATE, ITS SENSORS REGISTER THAT THE TARGET...
BA-WOOM!
...IS ALSO A DECOY!
...I DIDN'T HIT IT THAT HARD. MUST'VE HAD SOME KIND'A SELF-DESTRUCT. DOESN'T LEAVE MUCH TO IDENTIFY.
AN IMPERIAL PROBE DROID!
HEY, C'MON, LET'S NOT PANIC. WE DON'T KNOW THAT.
BUT WE DON'T KNOW THAT IT WASN'T.
SOMEWHERE IN DEEP SPACE, THE FLEET HOVERS, WAITING. WAITING FOR A HINT, A CLUE. UNTIL, ABOARD THE HULKING, OMINOUS CRUISER THAT LOOMS LARGER THAN EVEN THE SURROUNDING STAR DESTROYERS...
I THINK WE'VE FOUND SOMETHING, ADMIRAL OZZEL...

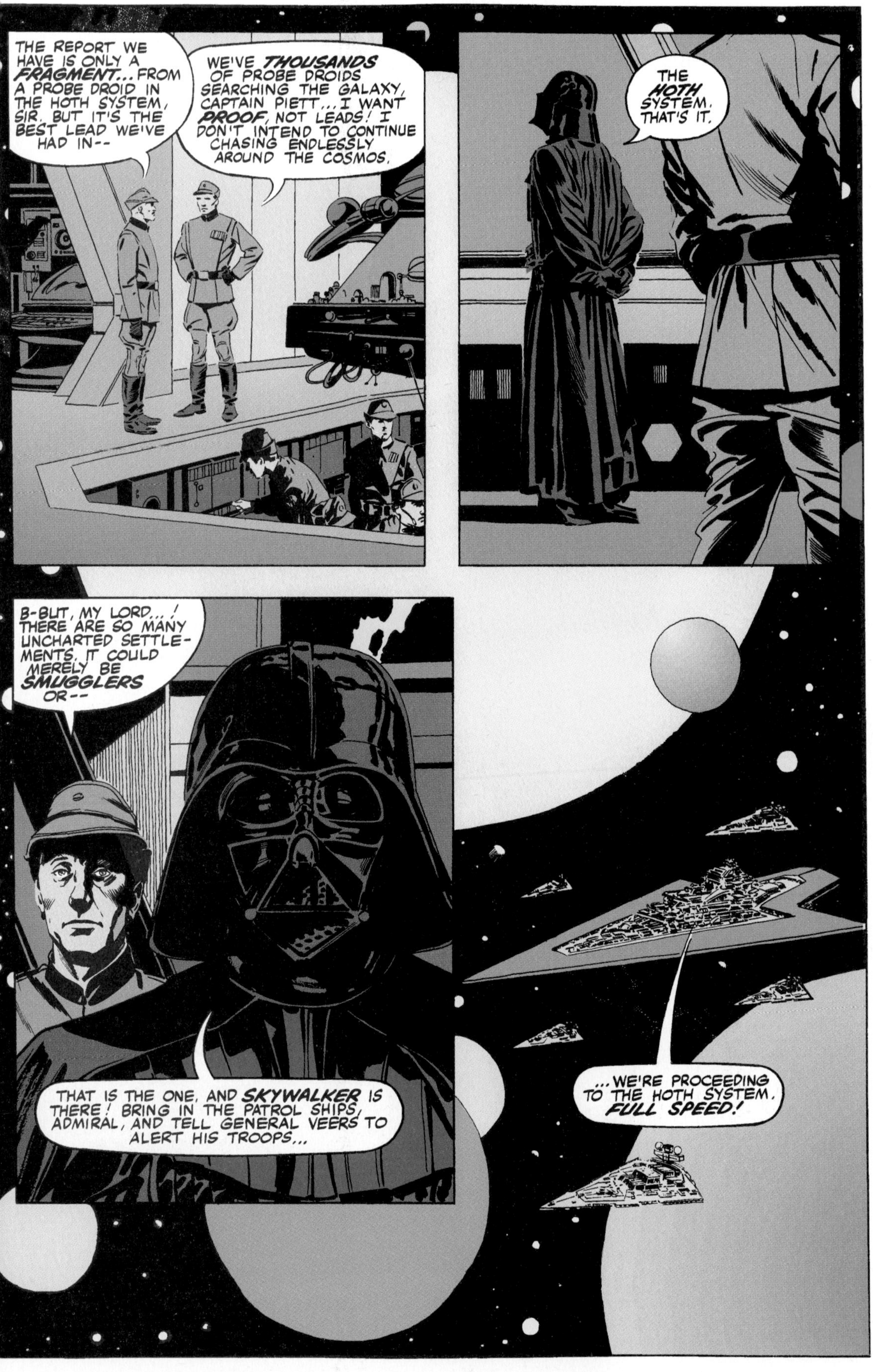
THE REPORT WE HAVE IS ONLY A FRAGMENT... FROM A PROBE DROID IN THE HOTH SYSTEM, SIR. BUT IT'S THE BEST LEAD WE'VE HAD IN--
WE'VE THOUSANDS OF PROBE DROIDS SEARCHING THE GALAXY, CAPTAIN PIETT... I WANT PROOF, NOT LEADS! I DON'T INTEND TO CONTINUE CHASING ENDLESSLY AROUND THE COSMOS.
THE HOTH SYSTEM. THAT'S IT.
B-BUT, MY LORD...! THERE ARE SO MANY UNCHARTED SETTLE-MENTS. IT COULD MERELY BE SMUGGLERS OR--
THAT IS THE ONE, AND SKYWALKER IS THERE! BRING IN THE PATROL SHIPS, ADMIRAL, AND TELL GENERAL VEERS TO ALERT HIS TROOPS...
...WE'RE PROCEEDING TO THE HOTH SYSTEM. FULL SPEED!

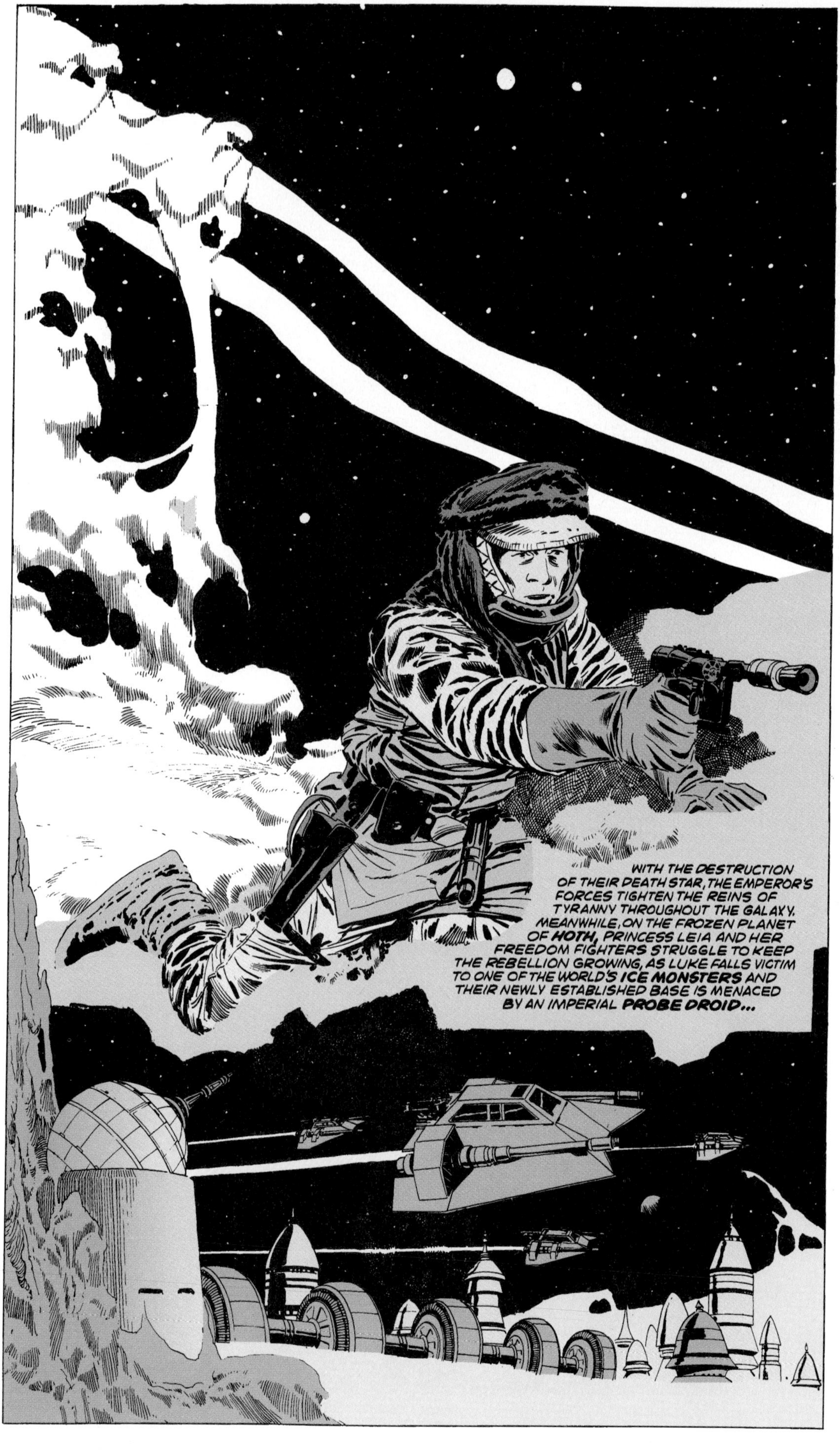
WITH THE DESTRUCTION OF THEIR DEATH STAR, THE EMPEROR'S FORCES TIGHTEN THE REINS OF TYRANNY THROUGHOUT THE GALAXY. MEANWHILE, ON THE FROZEN PLANET OF HOTH, PRINCESS LEIA AND HER FREEDOM FIGHTERS STRUGGLE TO KEEP THE REBELLION GROWING, AS LUKE FALLS VICTIM TO ONE OF THE WORLD'S ICE MONSTERS AND THEIR NEWLY ESTABLISHED BASE IS MENACED BY AN IMPERIAL PROBE DROID...

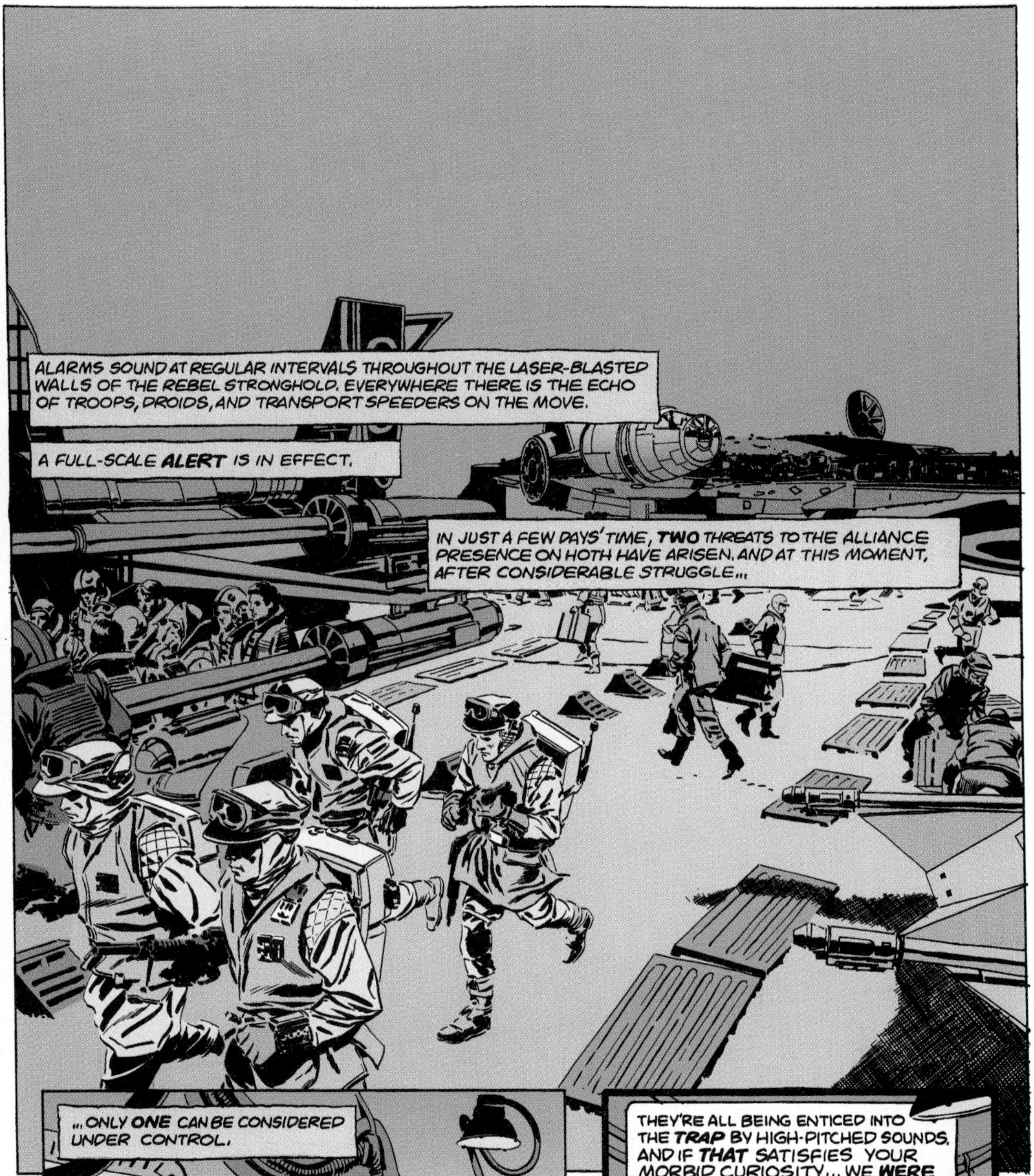
ALARMS SOUND AT REGULAR INTERVALS THROUGHOUT THE LASER-BLASTED WALLS OF THE REBEL STRONGHOLD. EVERYWHERE THERE IS THE ECHO OF TROOPS, DROIDS, AND TRANSPORT SPEEDERS ON THE MOVE.
A FULL-SCALE **ALERT** IS IN EFFECT.
IN JUST A FEW DAYS' TIME, **TWO** THREATS TO THE ALLIANCE PRESENCE ON HOTH HAVE ARISEN. AND AT THIS MOMENT, AFTER CONSIDERABLE STRUGGLE...

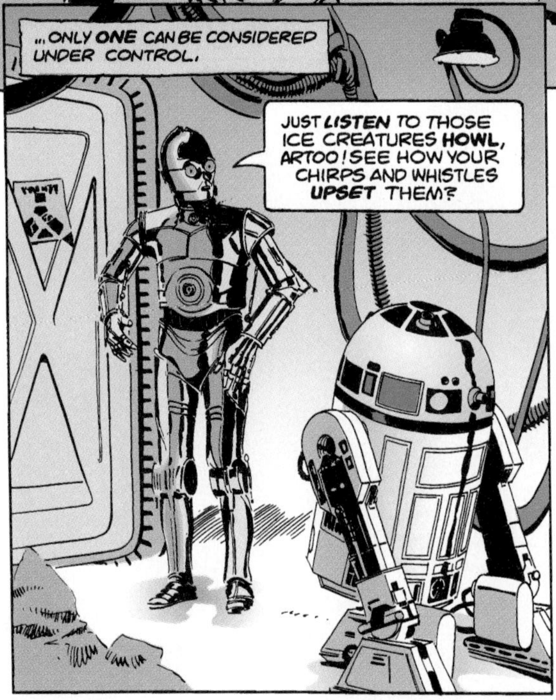
...ONLY **ONE** CAN BE CONSIDERED UNDER CONTROL.
JUST **LISTEN** TO THOSE ICE CREATURES **HOWL**, ARTOO! SEE HOW YOUR CHIRPS AND WHISTLES **UPSET** THEM?

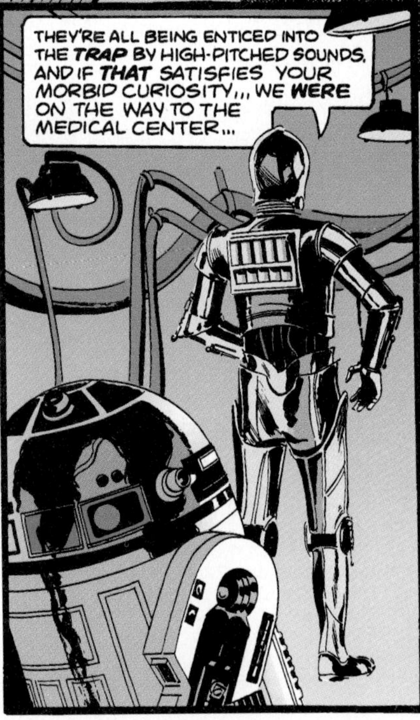
THEY'RE ALL BEING ENTICED INTO THE **TRAP** BY HIGH-PITCHED SOUNDS, AND IF **THAT** SATISFIES YOUR MORBID CURIOSITY... WE **WERE** ON THE WAY TO THE MEDICAL CENTER...

WHERE...

HOLD STILL FOR ONE MOMENT, COMMANDER SKYWALKER...

THERE, YES...

THE BACTA ARE GROWING WELL. THOSE SCARS SHOULD BE GONE IN A DAY OR SO.

THE SURGEON DROID TOO-ONEBEE, SLIDES BACK, AND LEIA ORGANA MOVES FORWARD WITH COMPASSION AND CONCERN. AND PERHAPS, SOMETHING MORE.

LUKE, DOES IT STILL *HURT* YOU?

I'M FINE, REALLY. BUT... Y'KNOW, LEIA... WHEN I WAS *LOST* OUT THERE IN THAT SNOW AND ICE AND IT LOOKED, LOOKED PRETTY *BAD*, WELL, I FELT...

I FELT AFRAID FOR YOU...

LEIA, I DON'T REALLY KNOW HOW TO *SAY* THIS. BUT YOU *MUST* KNOW THAT YOU... WELL... YOU'RE THE *ONLY* ONE I... I...

UNCERTAIN, BUT DRAWN BY THE MOMENT, THE PRINCESS LEANS CLOSE TO THE YOUNG REBEL HERO...

MASTER LUKE! IT'S SO GOOD TO SEE YOU *FUNCTIONAL* AGAIN!

VA-DOOT BIP!

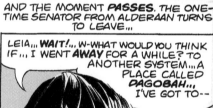

AND THE MOMENT *PASSES*. THE ONE-TIME SENATOR FROM ALDERAAN TURNS TO LEAVE...

LEIA... *WAIT!*... W-WHAT WOULD YOU THINK IF... I WENT *AWAY* FOR A WHILE? TO ANOTHER SYSTEM... A PLACE CALLED *DAGOBAH*... I'VE GOT TO--

WHAT? THAT'S JUST *FINE!* FIRST *HAN*... NOW *YOU!* I COULD GET MORE *LOYALTY* IF I RECRUITED SOME OF THOSE *ICE CREATURES* WE'VE TRAPPED!

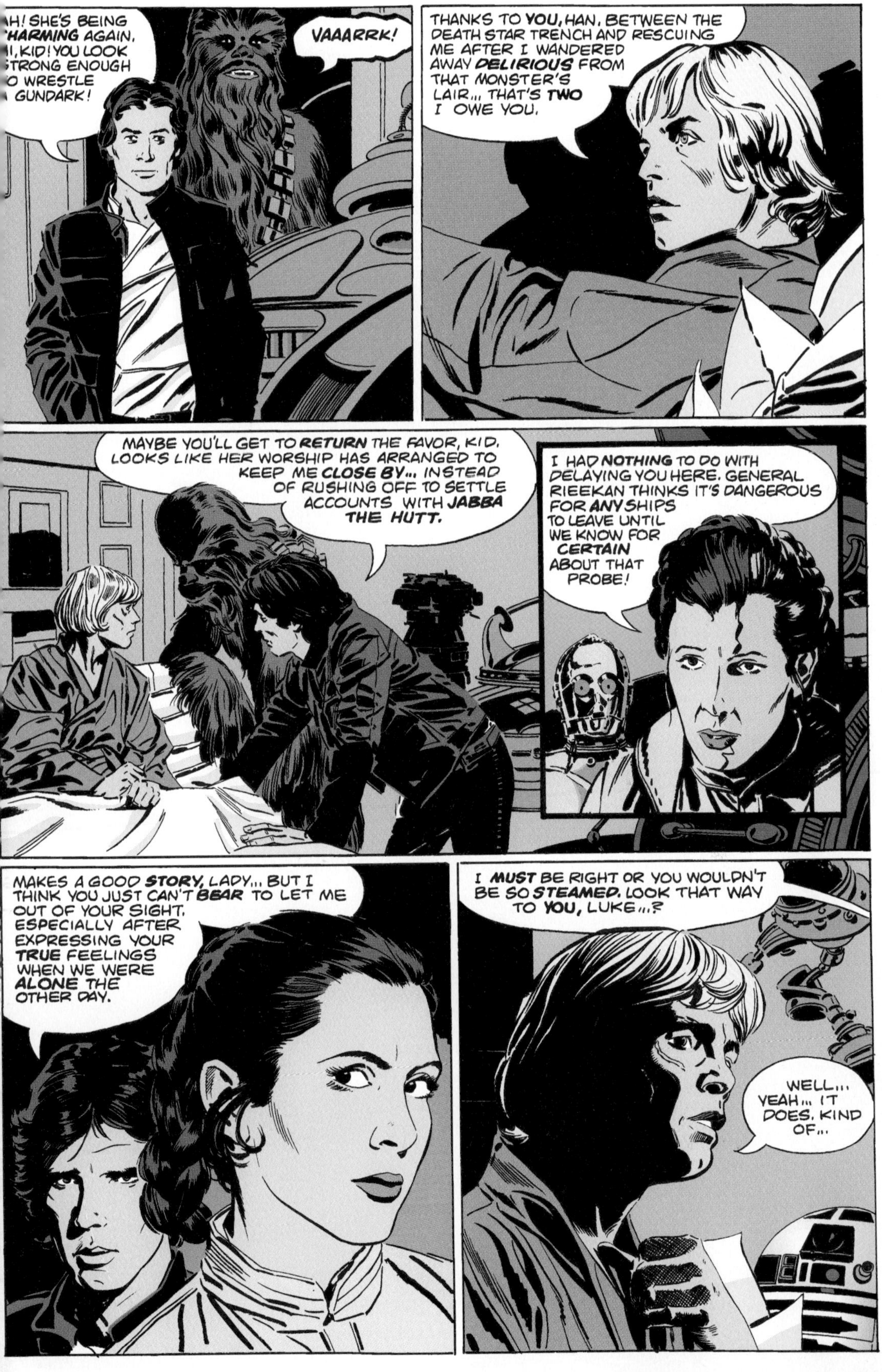
AH! SHE'S BEING CHARMING AGAIN. HI, KID! YOU LOOK STRONG ENOUGH TO WRESTLE A GUNDARK!
VAAARRK!
THANKS TO YOU, HAN. BETWEEN THE DEATH STAR TRENCH AND RESCUING ME AFTER I WANDERED AWAY DELIRIOUS FROM THAT MONSTER'S LAIR... THAT'S TWO I OWE YOU.
MAYBE YOU'LL GET TO RETURN THE FAVOR, KID. LOOKS LIKE HER WORSHIP HAS ARRANGED TO KEEP ME CLOSE BY... INSTEAD OF RUSHING OFF TO SETTLE ACCOUNTS WITH JABBA THE HUTT.
I HAD NOTHING TO DO WITH DELAYING YOU HERE. GENERAL RIEEKAN THINKS IT'S DANGEROUS FOR ANY SHIPS TO LEAVE UNTIL WE KNOW FOR CERTAIN ABOUT THAT PROBE!
MAKES A GOOD STORY, LADY... BUT I THINK YOU JUST CAN'T BEAR TO LET ME OUT OF YOUR SIGHT. ESPECIALLY AFTER EXPRESSING YOUR TRUE FEELINGS WHEN WE WERE ALONE THE OTHER DAY.
I MUST BE RIGHT OR YOU WOULDN'T BE SO STEAMED. LOOK THAT WAY TO YOU, LUKE...?
WELL... YEAH... IT DOES. KIND OF...

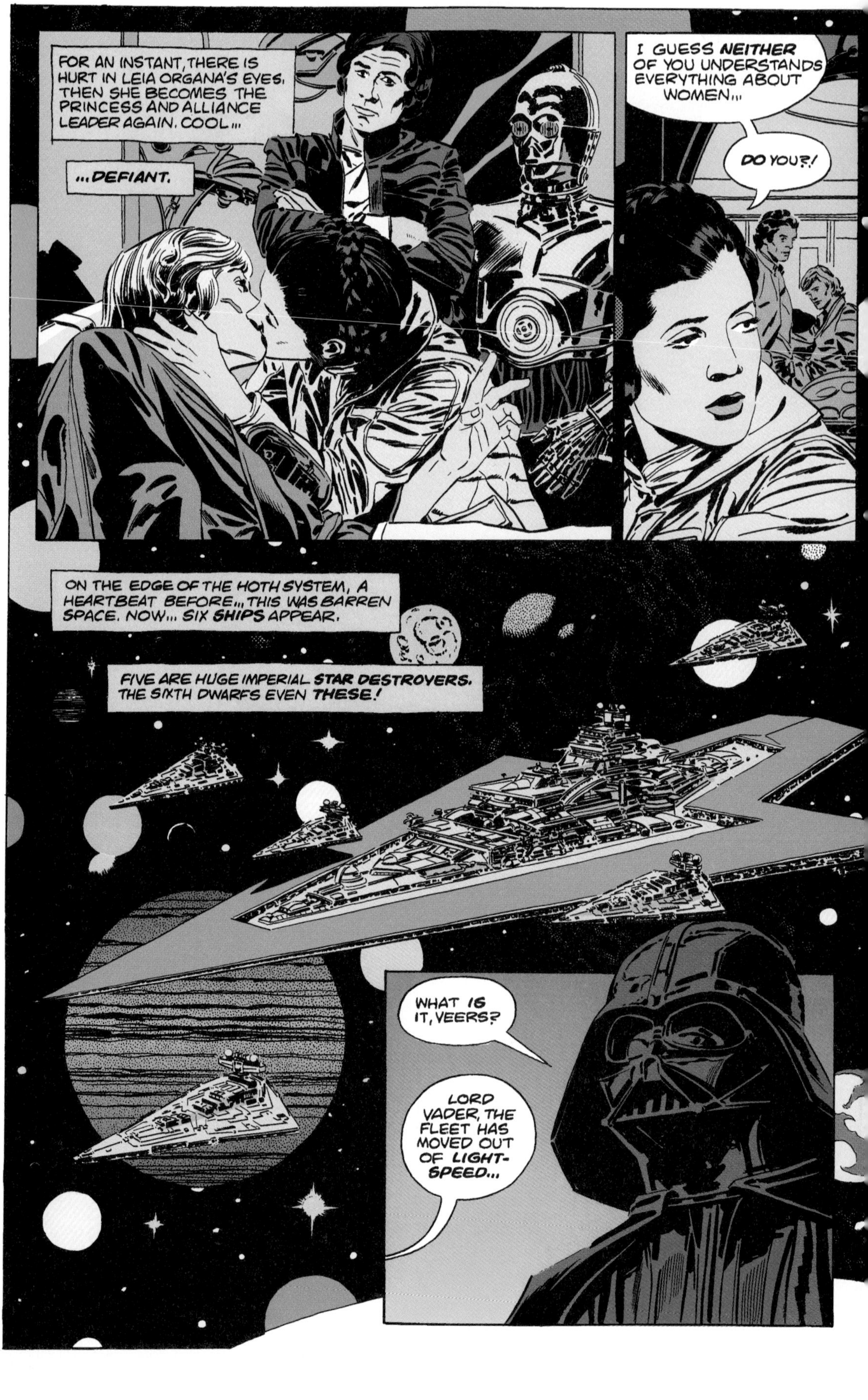

FOR AN INSTANT, THERE IS HURT IN LEIA ORGANA'S EYES. THEN SHE BECOMES THE PRINCESS AND ALLIANCE LEADER AGAIN. COOL...
...DEFIANT.
I GUESS NEITHER OF YOU UNDERSTANDS EVERYTHING ABOUT WOMEN...
DO YOU?!
ON THE EDGE OF THE HOTH SYSTEM, A HEARTBEAT BEFORE... THIS WAS BARREN SPACE. NOW... SIX SHIPS APPEAR.
FIVE ARE HUGE IMPERIAL STAR DESTROYERS. THE SIXTH DWARFS EVEN THESE!
WHAT IS IT, VEERS?
LORD VADER, THE FLEET HAS MOVED OUT OF LIGHT-SPEED...

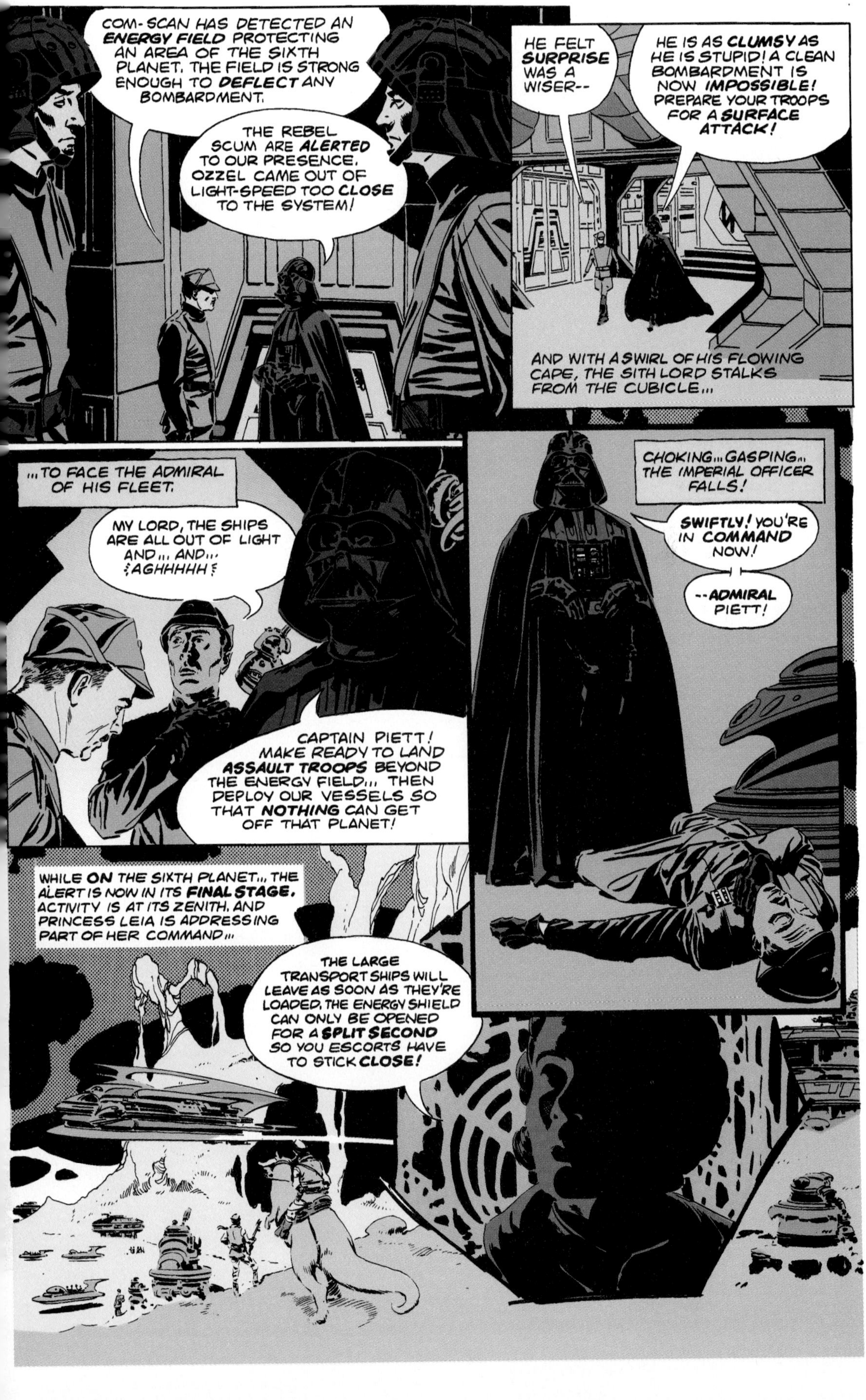

COM-SCAN HAS DETECTED AN ENERGY FIELD PROTECTING AN AREA OF THE SIXTH PLANET. THE FIELD IS STRONG ENOUGH TO DEFLECT ANY BOMBARDMENT.
THE REBEL SCUM ARE ALERTED TO OUR PRESENCE. OZZEL CAME OUT OF LIGHT-SPEED TOO CLOSE TO THE SYSTEM!
HE FELT SURPRISE WAS A WISER--
HE IS AS CLUMSY AS HE IS STUPID! A CLEAN BOMBARDMENT IS NOW IMPOSSIBLE! PREPARE YOUR TROOPS FOR A SURFACE ATTACK!
AND WITH A SWIRL OF HIS FLOWING CAPE, THE SITH LORD STALKS FROM THE CUBICLE...
...TO FACE THE ADMIRAL OF HIS FLEET.
MY LORD, THE SHIPS ARE ALL OUT OF LIGHT AND... AND... AGHHHHH
CAPTAIN PIETT! MAKE READY TO LAND ASSAULT TROOPS BEYOND THE ENERGY FIELD... THEN DEPLOY OUR VESSELS SO THAT NOTHING CAN GET OFF THAT PLANET!
CHOKING... GASPING... THE IMPERIAL OFFICER FALLS!
SWIFTLY! YOU'RE IN COMMAND NOW!
--ADMIRAL PIETT!
WHILE ON THE SIXTH PLANET... THE ALERT IS NOW IN ITS FINAL STAGE. ACTIVITY IS AT ITS ZENITH. AND PRINCESS LEIA IS ADDRESSING PART OF HER COMMAND...
THE LARGE TRANSPORT SHIPS WILL LEAVE AS SOON AS THEY'RE LOADED. THE ENERGY SHIELD CAN ONLY BE OPENED FOR A SPLIT SECOND SO YOU ESCORTS HAVE TO STICK CLOSE!

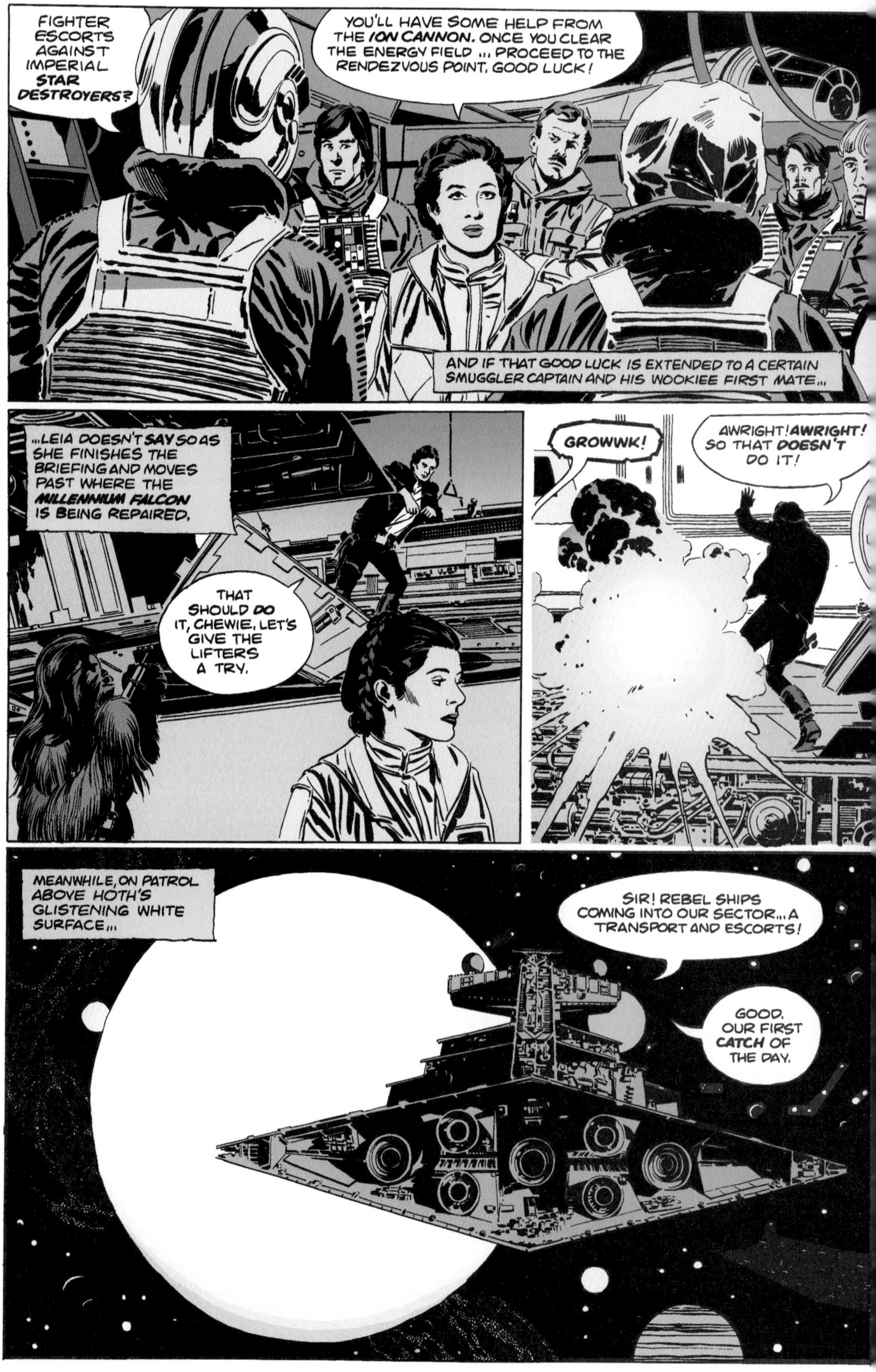
FIGHTER ESCORTS AGAINST IMPERIAL STAR DESTROYERS?
YOU'LL HAVE SOME HELP FROM THE ION CANNON. ONCE YOU CLEAR THE ENERGY FIELD ... PROCEED TO THE RENDEZVOUS POINT. GOOD LUCK!
AND IF THAT GOOD LUCK IS EXTENDED TO A CERTAIN SMUGGLER CAPTAIN AND HIS WOOKIEE FIRST MATE...
...LEIA DOESN'T SAY SO AS SHE FINISHES THE BRIEFING AND MOVES PAST WHERE THE MILLENNIUM FALCON IS BEING REPAIRED.
THAT SHOULD DO IT, CHEWIE. LET'S GIVE THE LIFTERS A TRY.
GROWWK!
AWRIGHT! AWRIGHT! SO THAT DOESN'T DO IT!
MEANWHILE, ON PATROL ABOVE HOTH'S GLISTENING WHITE SURFACE...
SIR! REBEL SHIPS COMING INTO OUR SECTOR... A TRANSPORT AND ESCORTS!
GOOD. OUR FIRST CATCH OF THE DAY.

ECHO C-130 IS APPROACHING THE SHIELD, GENERAL RIEEKAN.

STAND BY TO *OPEN* IT, AND SIGNAL *ION CONTROL*--

"...TO START FIRING THE *INSTANT* IT DOES!"

AND FROM THE GIANT WEAPON, CRIMSON ENERGY BOLTS BLAST SPACEWARD...

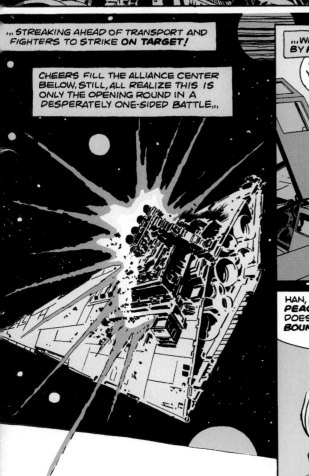

...STREAKING AHEAD OF TRANSPORT AND FIGHTERS TO STRIKE *ON TARGET!*

CHEERS FILL THE ALLIANCE CENTER BELOW, STILL, ALL REALIZE THIS IS ONLY THE OPENING ROUND IN A DESPERATELY ONE-SIDED BATTLE...

...WHERE VICTORY CAN ONLY BE MEASURED BY *HOW LONG* THEY HOLD OFF THE ENEMY.

CHEWIE, TAKE CARE OF YOURSELF,...AND WATCH OUT FOR THIS GUY, WILL YOU?

WAAARRK!

HAN, I HOPE YOU MAKE YOUR *PEACE* WITH JABBA...EVEN IF IT DOES THROW HALF THE GALAXY'S *BOUNTY HUNTERS* OUT OF WORK.

GIVE 'EM HELL, KID!

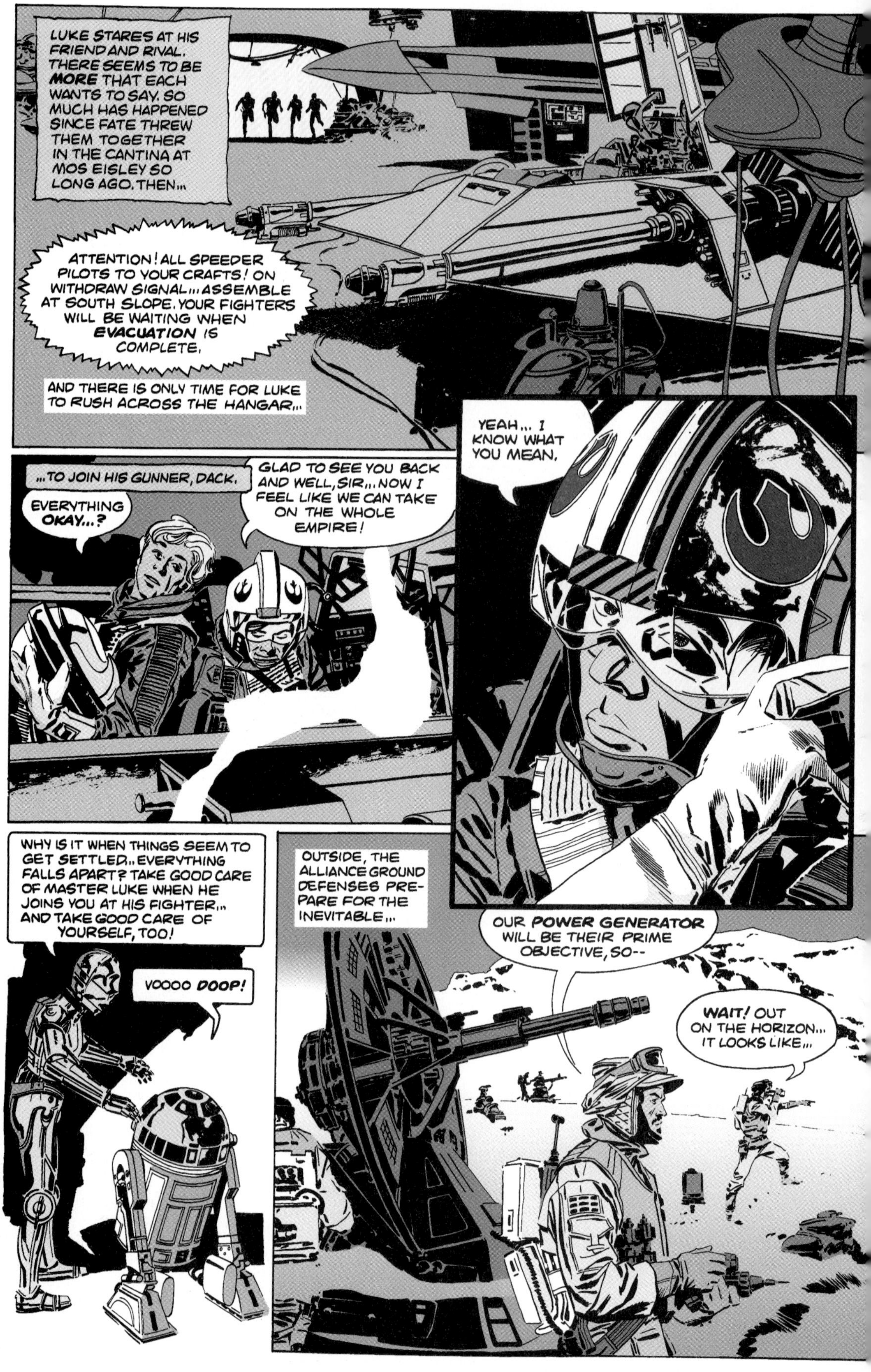

LUKE STARES AT HIS FRIEND AND RIVAL. THERE SEEMS TO BE MORE THAT EACH WANTS TO SAY. SO MUCH HAS HAPPENED SINCE FATE THREW THEM TOGETHER IN THE CANTINA AT MOS EISLEY SO LONG AGO. THEN...
ATTENTION! ALL SPEEDER PILOTS TO YOUR CRAFTS! ON WITHDRAW SIGNAL... ASSEMBLE AT SOUTH SLOPE. YOUR FIGHTERS WILL BE WAITING WHEN EVACUATION IS COMPLETE.
AND THERE IS ONLY TIME FOR LUKE TO RUSH ACROSS THE HANGAR...
...TO JOIN HIS GUNNER, DACK.
EVERYTHING OKAY...?
GLAD TO SEE YOU BACK AND WELL, SIR... NOW I FEEL LIKE WE CAN TAKE ON THE WHOLE EMPIRE!
YEAH... I KNOW WHAT YOU MEAN.
WHY IS IT WHEN THINGS SEEM TO GET SETTLED.. EVERYTHING FALLS APART? TAKE GOOD CARE OF MASTER LUKE WHEN HE JOINS YOU AT HIS FIGHTER... AND TAKE GOOD CARE OF YOURSELF, TOO!
VOOOO DOOP!
OUTSIDE, THE ALLIANCE GROUND DEFENSES PREPARE FOR THE INEVITABLE...
OUR POWER GENERATOR WILL BE THEIR PRIME OBJECTIVE, SO--
WAIT! OUT ON THE HORIZON... IT LOOKS LIKE...

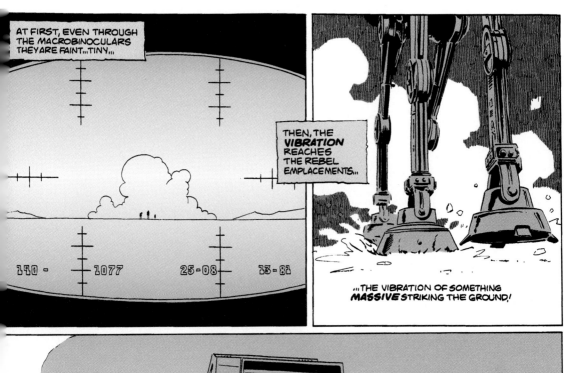

AT FIRST, EVEN THROUGH THE MACROBINOCULARS THEY ARE FAINT...TINY...

140 - 1077 25-08 13-81

THEN, THE **VIBRATION** REACHES THE REBEL EMPLACEMENTS...

...THE VIBRATION OF SOMETHING **MASSIVE** STRIKING THE GROUND!

POINT RIDER FIVE TO ECHO DEFENSE! ENEMY CONTACT! **ENEMY CONTACT!**

IMPERIAL **WALKERS** ADVANCING ON YOUR POSITION!

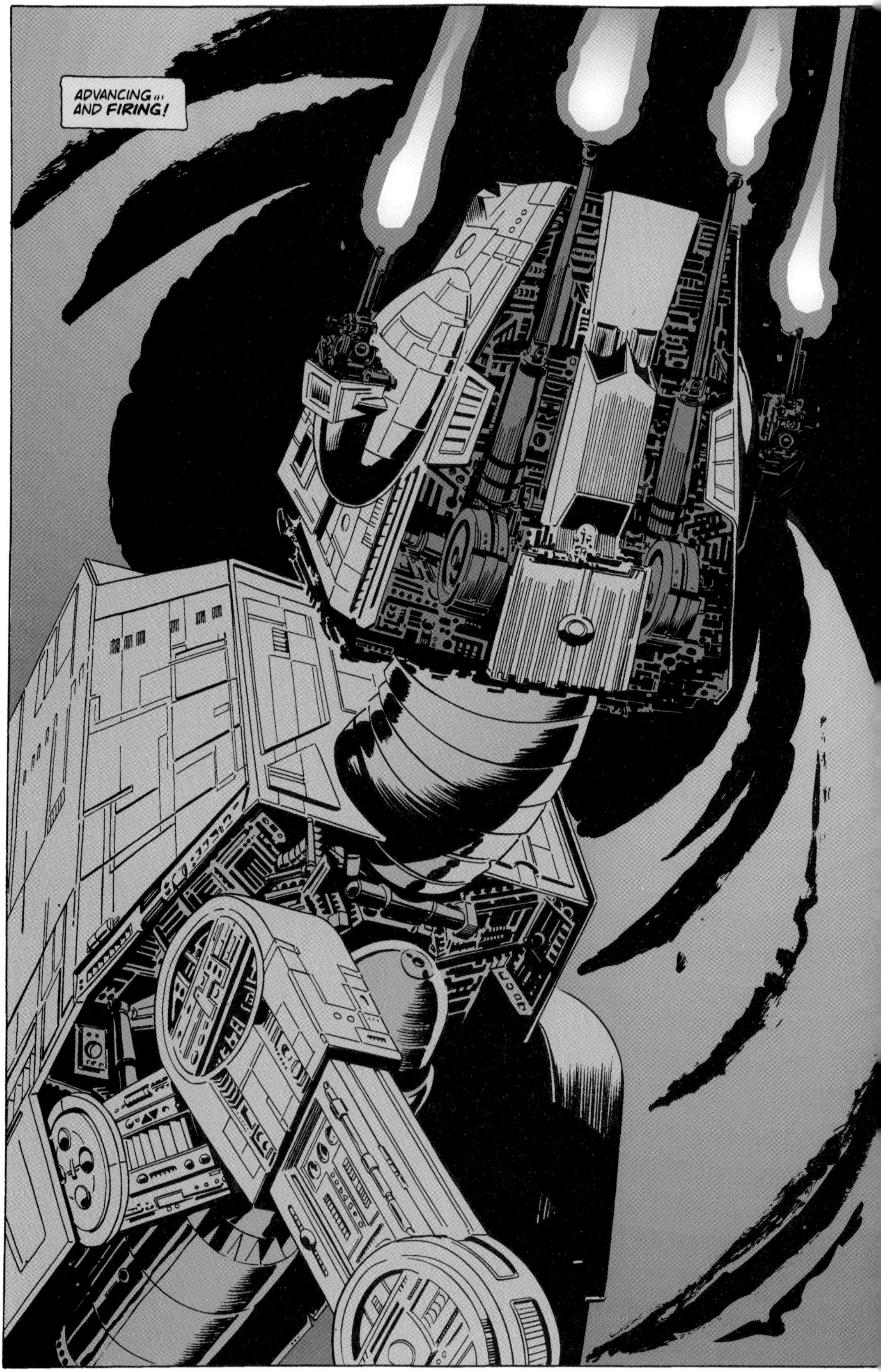
ADVANCING... AND FIRING!

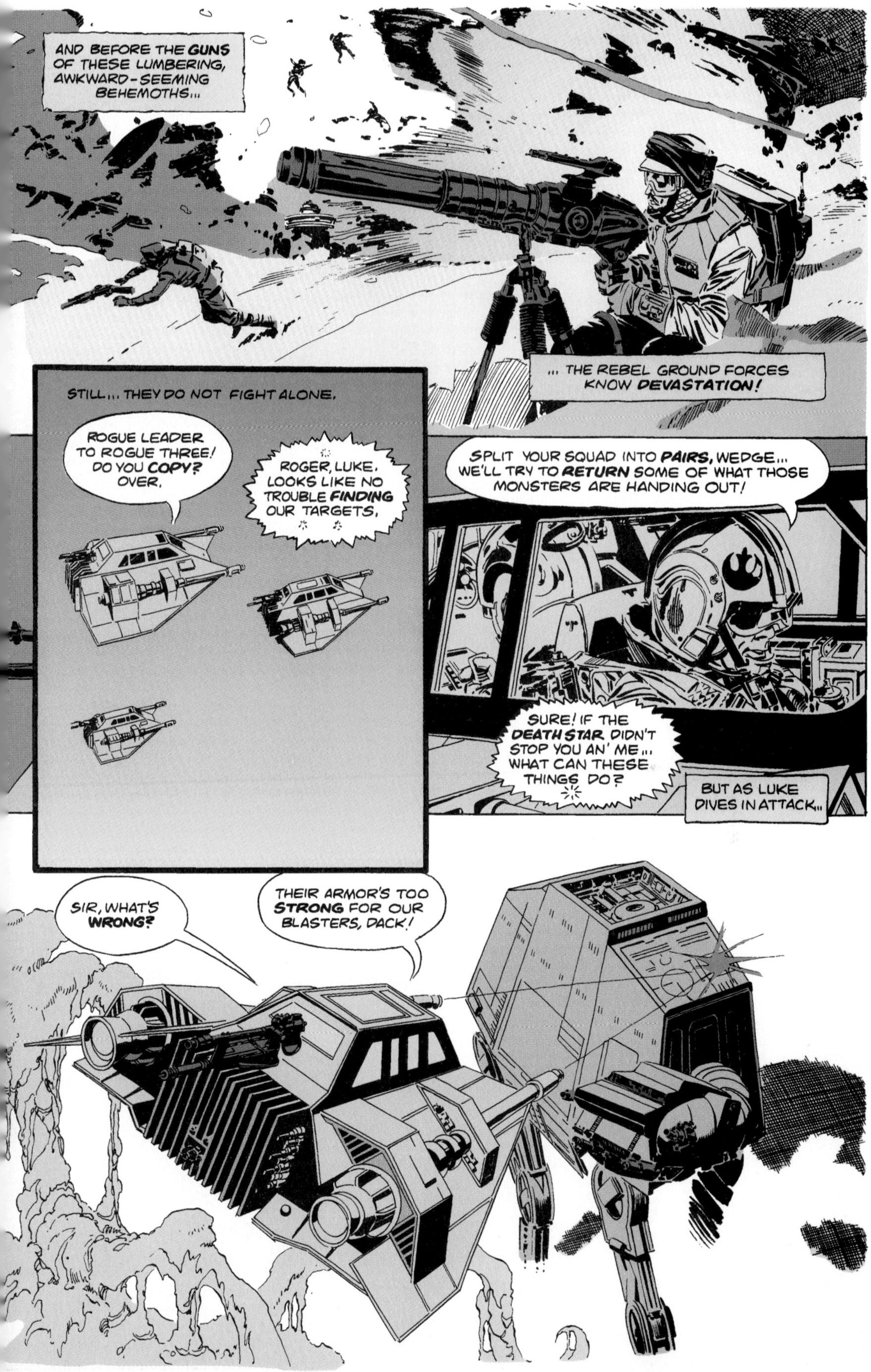

AND BEFORE THE GUNS OF THESE LUMBERING, AWKWARD-SEEMING BEHEMOTHS...
... THE REBEL GROUND FORCES KNOW DEVASTATION!
STILL... THEY DO NOT FIGHT ALONE.
ROGUE LEADER TO ROGUE THREE! DO YOU COPY? OVER.
ROGER, LUKE. LOOKS LIKE NO TROUBLE FINDING OUR TARGETS.
SPLIT YOUR SQUAD INTO PAIRS, WEDGE... WE'LL TRY TO RETURN SOME OF WHAT THOSE MONSTERS ARE HANDING OUT!
SURE! IF THE DEATH STAR DIDN'T STOP YOU AN' ME... WHAT CAN THESE THINGS DO?
BUT AS LUKE DIVES IN ATTACK...
SIR, WHAT'S WRONG?
THEIR ARMOR'S TOO STRONG FOR OUR BLASTERS, DACK!

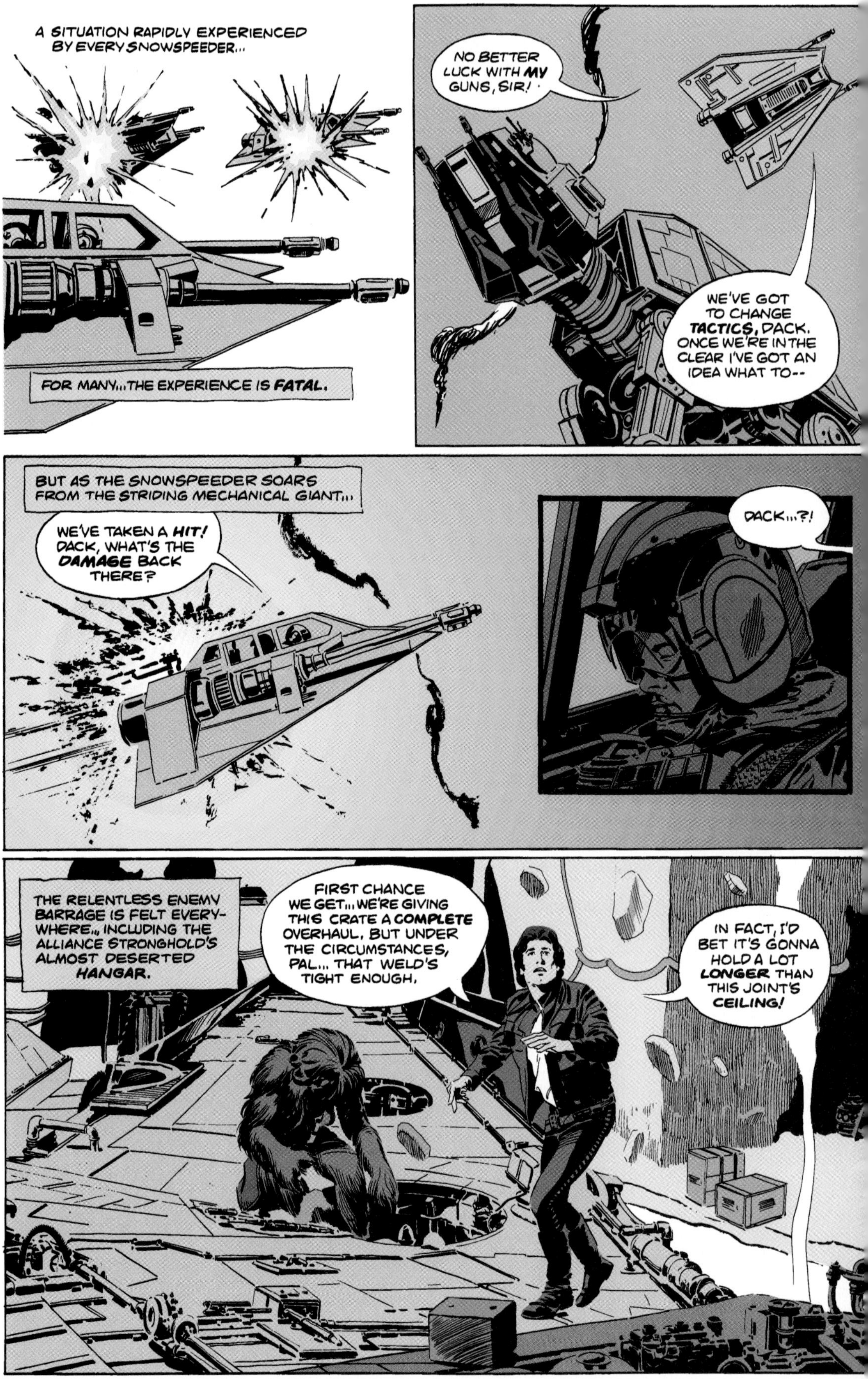

A SITUATION RAPIDLY EXPERIENCED BY EVERY SNOWSPEEDER...
FOR MANY... THE EXPERIENCE IS FATAL.
NO BETTER LUCK WITH MY GUNS, SIR!
WE'VE GOT TO CHANGE TACTICS, DACK. ONCE WE'RE IN THE CLEAR I'VE GOT AN IDEA WHAT TO--
BUT AS THE SNOWSPEEDER SOARS FROM THE STRIDING MECHANICAL GIANT...
WE'VE TAKEN A HIT! DACK, WHAT'S THE DAMAGE BACK THERE?
DACK...?!
THE RELENTLESS ENEMY BARRAGE IS FELT EVERY-WHERE... INCLUDING THE ALLIANCE STRONGHOLD'S ALMOST DESERTED HANGAR.
FIRST CHANCE WE GET... WE'RE GIVING THIS CRATE A COMPLETE OVERHAUL. BUT UNDER THE CIRCUMSTANCES, PAL... THAT WELD'S TIGHT ENOUGH.
IN FACT, I'D BET IT'S GONNA HOLD A LOT LONGER THAN THIS JOINT'S CEILING!

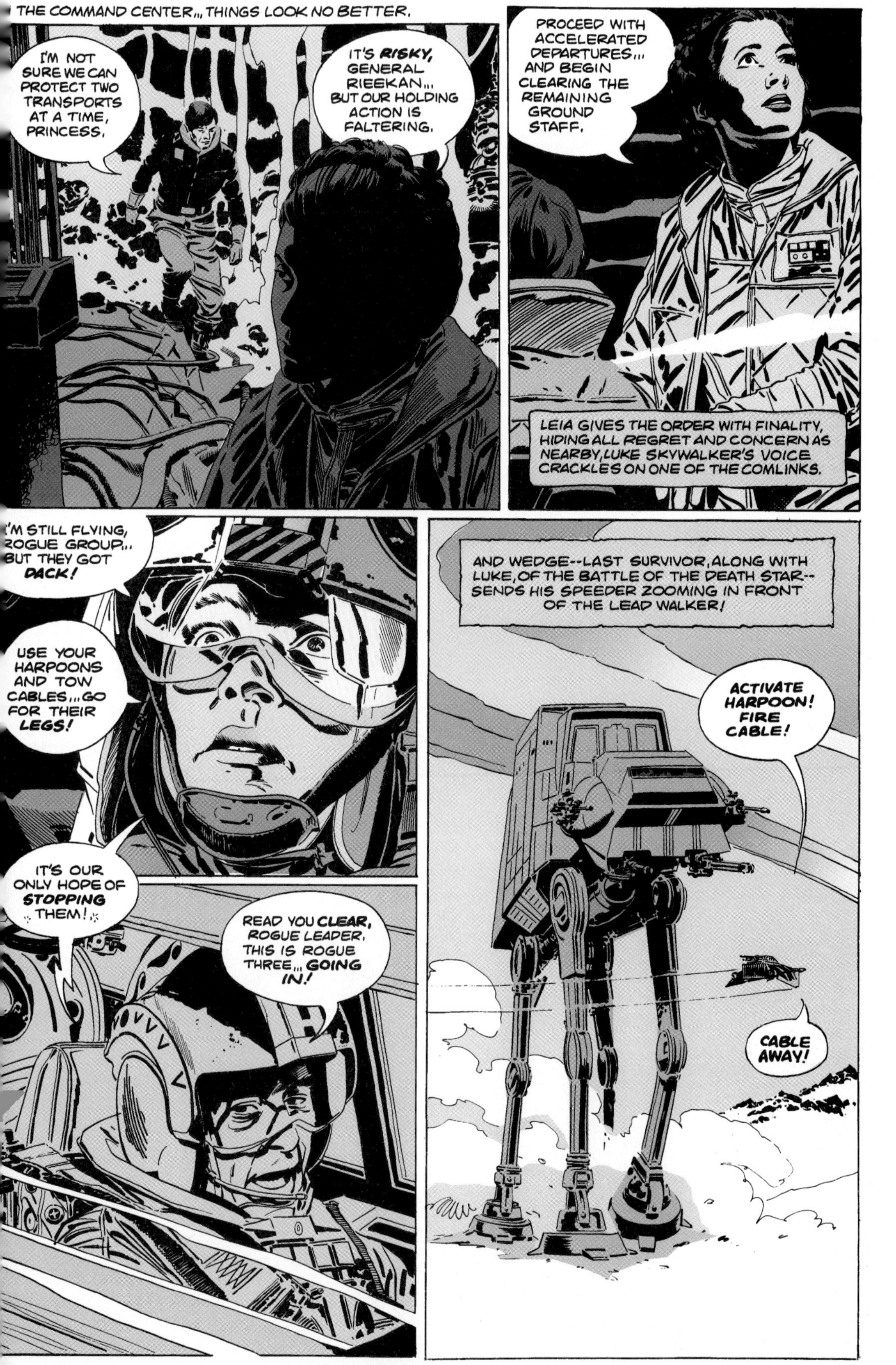
THE COMMAND CENTER... THINGS LOOK NO BETTER.
I'M NOT SURE WE CAN PROTECT TWO TRANSPORTS AT A TIME, PRINCESS.
IT'S RISKY, GENERAL RIEEKAN... BUT OUR HOLDING ACTION IS FALTERING.
PROCEED WITH ACCELERATED DEPARTURES... AND BEGIN CLEARING THE REMAINING GROUND STAFF.
LEIA GIVES THE ORDER WITH FINALITY, HIDING ALL REGRET AND CONCERN AS NEARBY, LUKE SKYWALKER'S VOICE CRACKLES ON ONE OF THE COMLINKS.
'M STILL FLYING, ROGUE GROUP... BUT THEY GOT DACK!
USE YOUR HARPOONS AND TOW CABLES... GO FOR THEIR LEGS!
IT'S OUR ONLY HOPE OF STOPPING THEM!
READ YOU CLEAR, ROGUE LEADER. THIS IS ROGUE THREE... GOING IN!
AND WEDGE--LAST SURVIVOR, ALONG WITH LUKE, OF THE BATTLE OF THE DEATH STAR--SENDS HIS SPEEDER ZOOMING IN FRONT OF THE LEAD WALKER!
ACTIVATE HARPOON! FIRE CABLE!
CABLE AWAY!

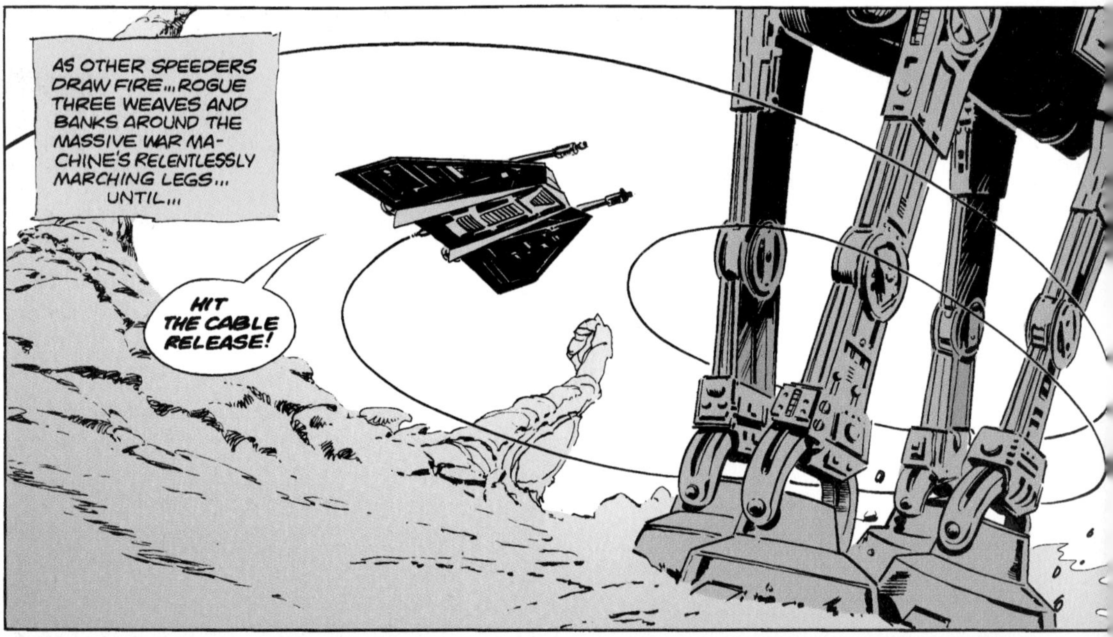
AS OTHER SPEEDERS DRAW FIRE... ROGUE THREE WEAVES AND BANKS AROUND THE MASSIVE WAR MACHINE'S RELENTLESSLY MARCHING LEGS... UNTIL...
HIT THE CABLE RELEASE!

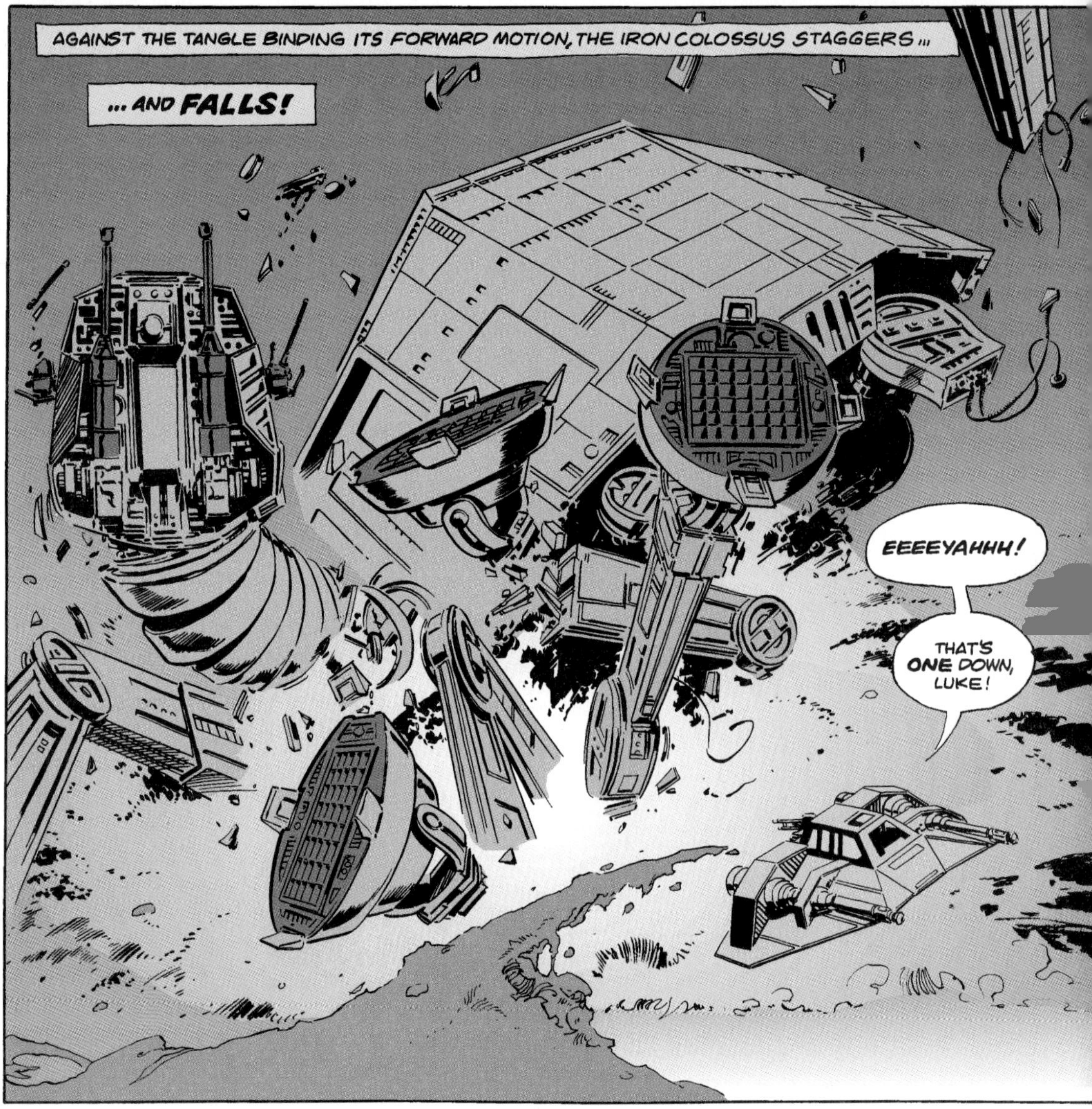
AGAINST THE TANGLE BINDING ITS FORWARD MOTION, THE IRON COLOSSUS STAGGERS...
... AND FALLS!
EEEEYAHHH!
THAT'S ONE DOWN, LUKE!

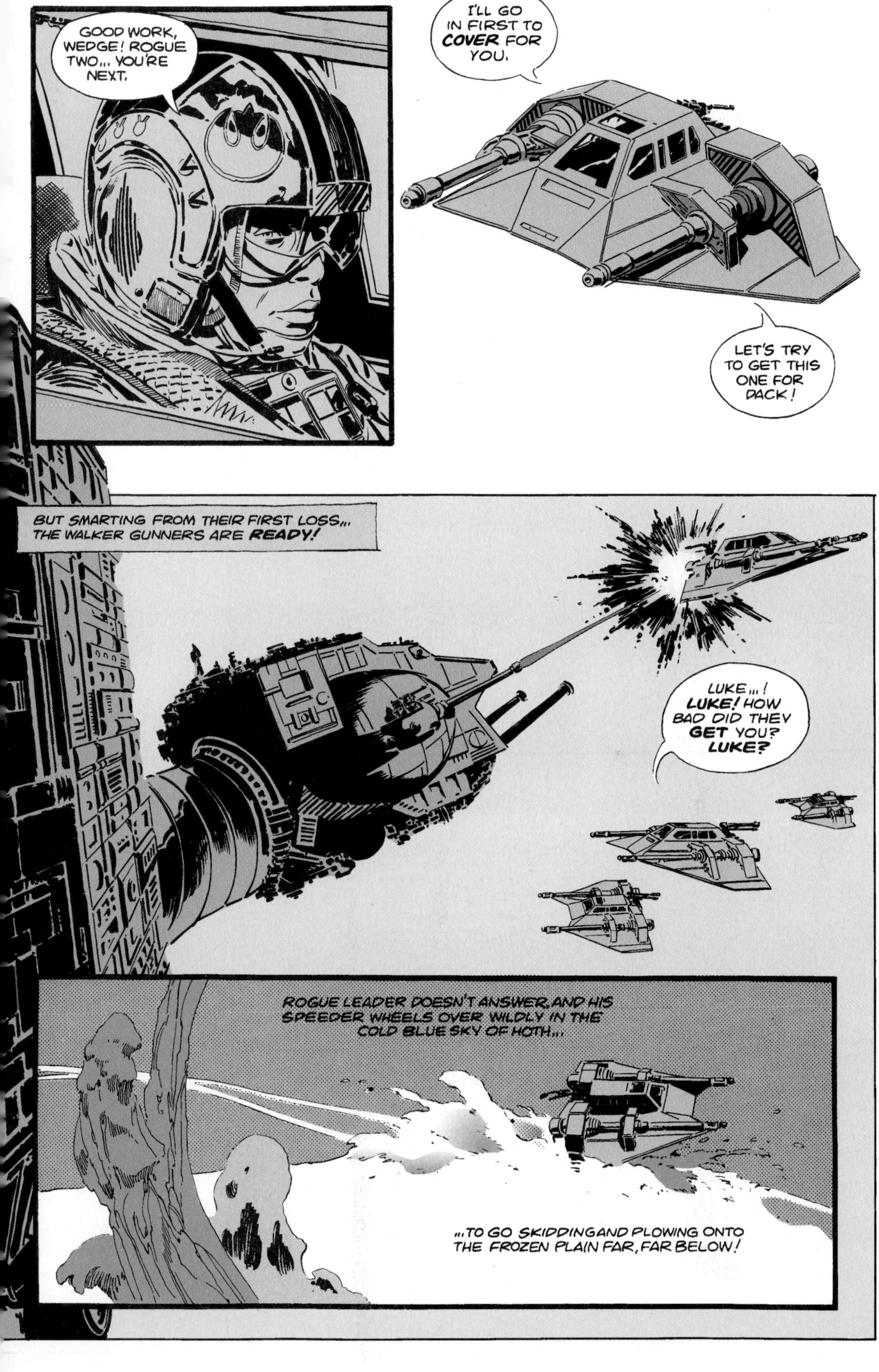
GOOD WORK, WEDGE! ROGUE TWO... YOU'RE NEXT.
I'LL GO IN FIRST TO COVER FOR YOU.
LET'S TRY TO GET THIS ONE FOR DACK!
BUT SMARTING FROM THEIR FIRST LOSS... THE WALKER GUNNERS ARE READY!
LUKE...! LUKE! HOW BAD DID THEY GET YOU? LUKE?
ROGUE LEADER DOESN'T ANSWER, AND HIS SPEEDER WHEELS OVER WILDLY IN THE COLD BLUE SKY OF HOTH...
...TO GO SKIDDING AND PLOWING ONTO THE FROZEN PLAIN FAR, FAR BELOW!

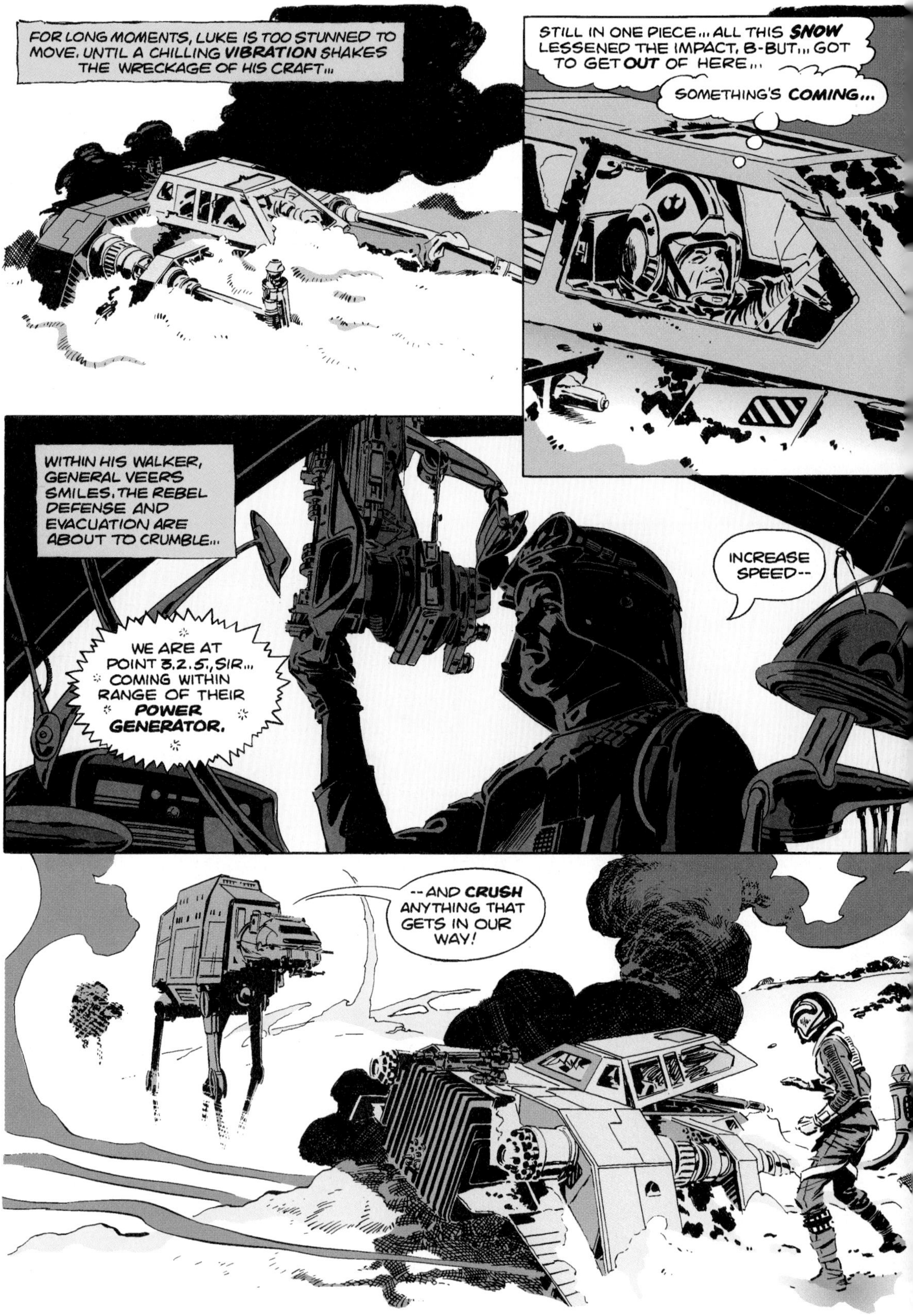
FOR LONG MOMENTS, LUKE IS TOO STUNNED TO MOVE, UNTIL A CHILLING VIBRATION SHAKES THE WRECKAGE OF HIS CRAFT...
STILL IN ONE PIECE... ALL THIS SNOW LESSENED THE IMPACT, B-BUT... GOT TO GET OUT OF HERE...
SOMETHING'S COMING...
WITHIN HIS WALKER, GENERAL VEERS SMILES. THE REBEL DEFENSE AND EVACUATION ARE ABOUT TO CRUMBLE...
INCREASE SPEED--
WE ARE AT POINT 3.2.5., SIR... COMING WITHIN RANGE OF THEIR POWER GENERATOR.
--AND CRUSH ANYTHING THAT GETS IN OUR WAY!

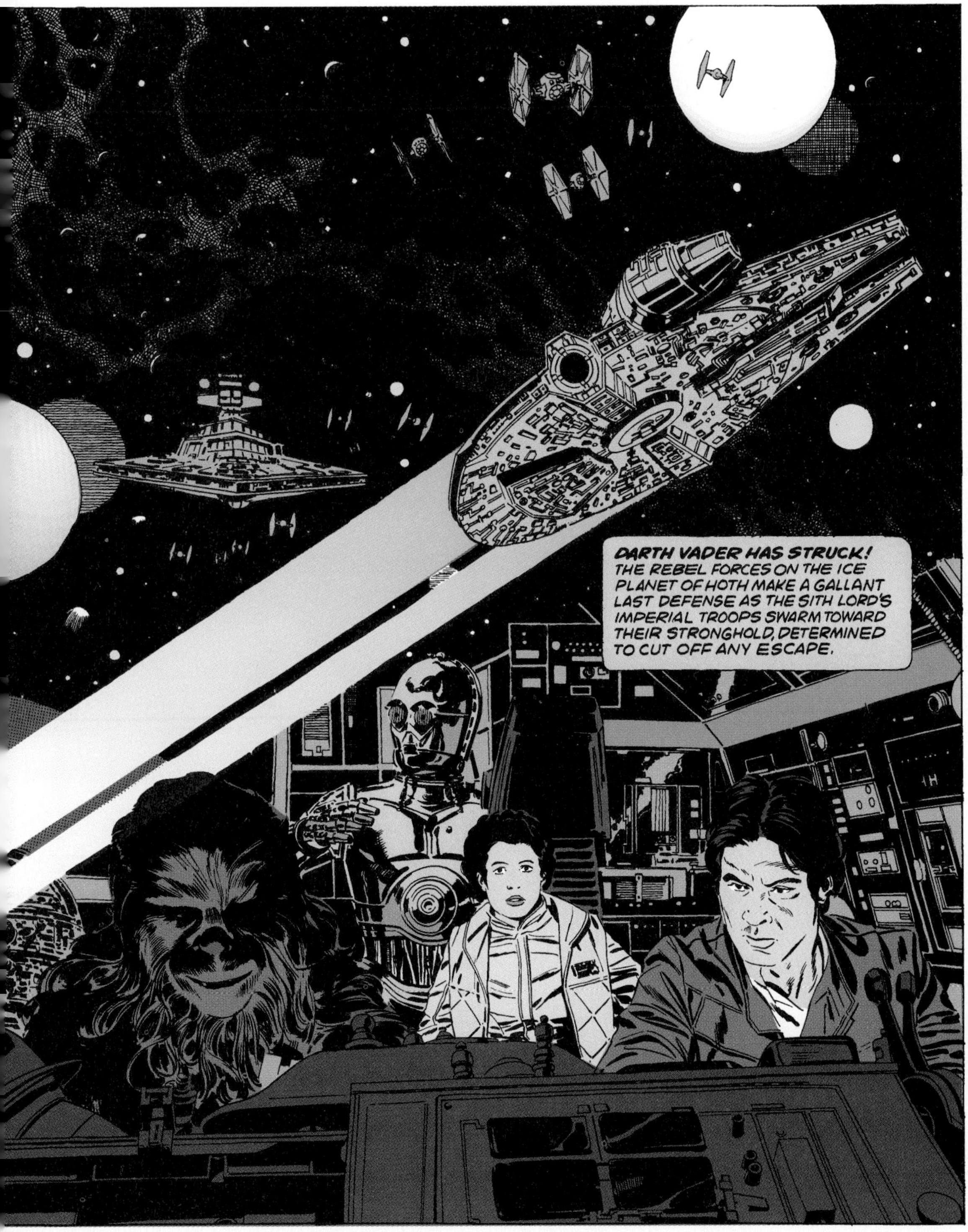
DARTH VADER HAS STRUCK! THE REBEL FORCES ON THE ICE PLANET OF HOTH MAKE A GALLANT LAST DEFENSE AS THE SITH LORD'S IMPERIAL TROOPS SWARM TOWARD THEIR STRONGHOLD, DETERMINED TO CUT OFF ANY ESCAPE.

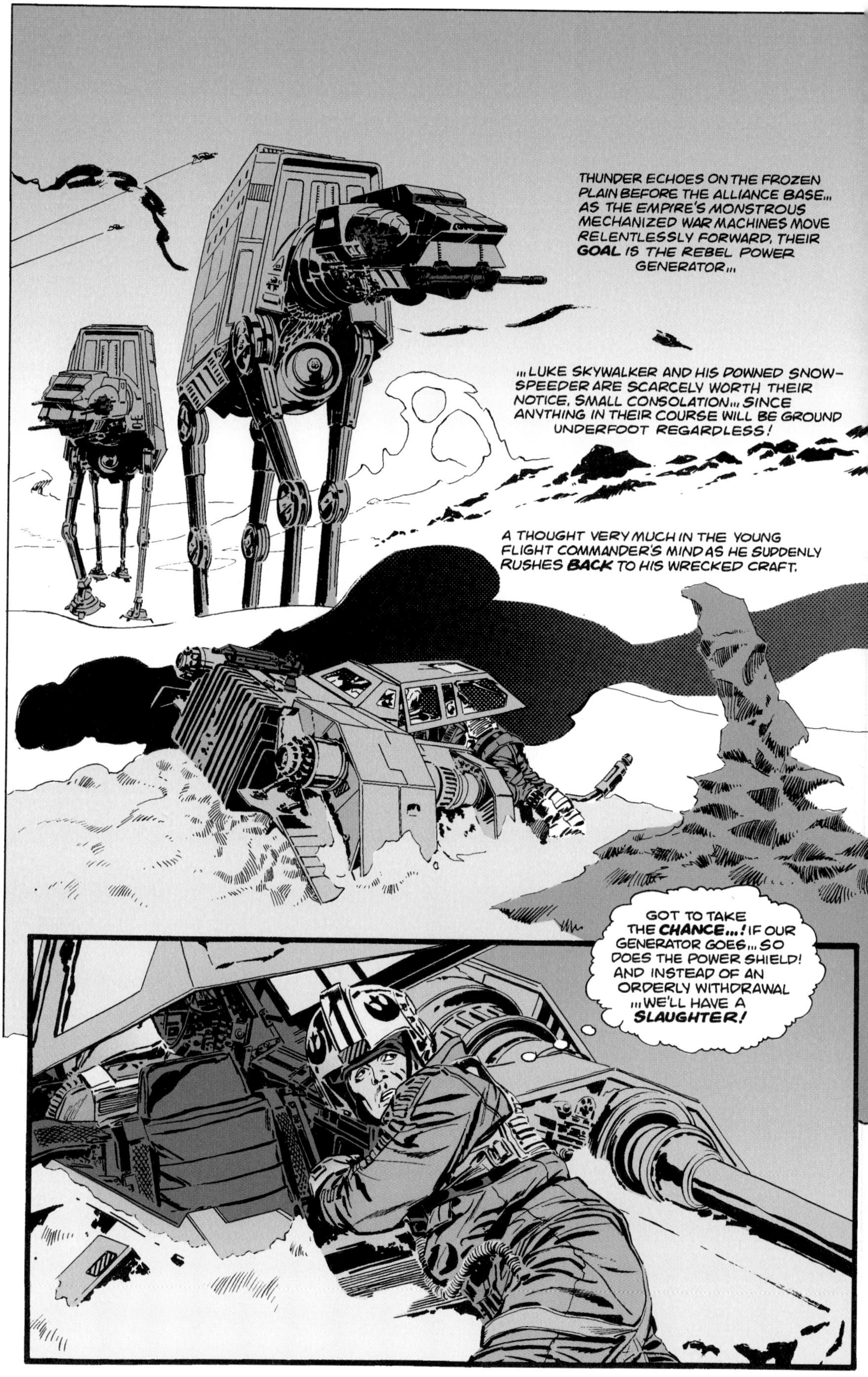
THUNDER ECHOES ON THE FROZEN PLAIN BEFORE THE ALLIANCE BASE... AS THE EMPIRE'S MONSTROUS MECHANIZED WAR MACHINES MOVE RELENTLESSLY FORWARD. THEIR GOAL IS THE REBEL POWER GENERATOR...
...LUKE SKYWALKER AND HIS DOWNED SNOW-SPEEDER ARE SCARCELY WORTH THEIR NOTICE. SMALL CONSOLATION... SINCE ANYTHING IN THEIR COURSE WILL BE GROUND UNDERFOOT REGARDLESS!
A THOUGHT VERY MUCH IN THE YOUNG FLIGHT COMMANDER'S MIND AS HE SUDDENLY RUSHES BACK TO HIS WRECKED CRAFT.
GOT TO TAKE THE CHANCE...! IF OUR GENERATOR GOES... SO DOES THE POWER SHIELD! AND INSTEAD OF AN ORDERLY WITHDRAWAL ...WE'LL HAVE A SLAUGHTER!

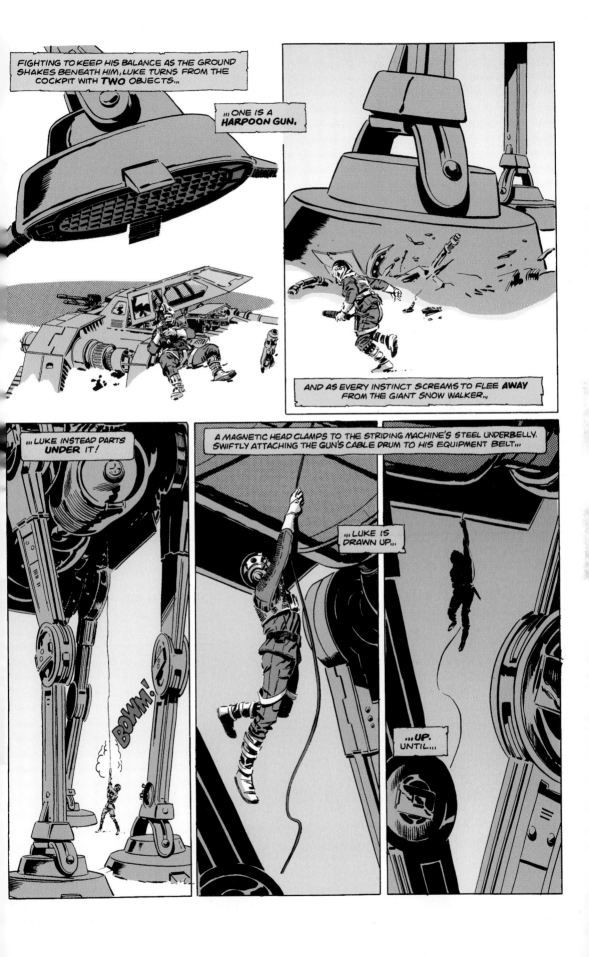

FIGHTING TO KEEP HIS BALANCE AS THE GROUND SHAKES BENEATH HIM, LUKE TURNS FROM THE COCKPIT WITH **TWO** OBJECTS...

...ONE IS A **HARPOON GUN.**

AND AS EVERY INSTINCT SCREAMS TO FLEE **AWAY** FROM THE GIANT SNOW WALKER...

...LUKE INSTEAD DARTS **UNDER** IT!

A MAGNETIC HEAD CLAMPS TO THE STRIDING MACHINE'S STEEL UNDERBELLY, SWIFTLY ATTACHING THE GUN'S CABLE DRUM TO HIS EQUIPMENT BELT...

...LUKE IS DRAWN UP...

BOWM!

...UP. UNTIL...

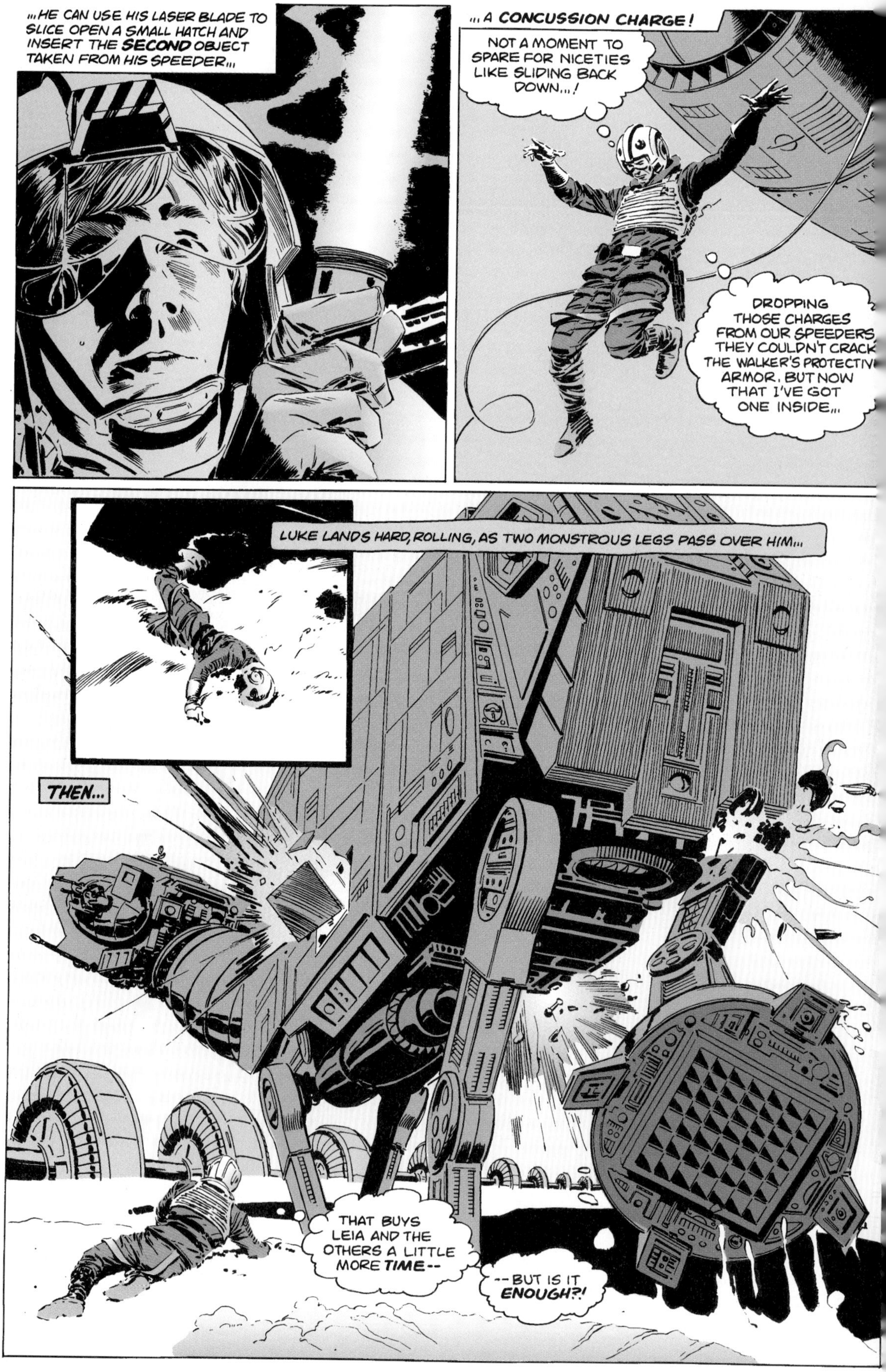
...HE CAN USE HIS LASER BLADE TO SLICE OPEN A SMALL HATCH AND INSERT THE SECOND OBJECT TAKEN FROM HIS SPEEDER...
...A CONCUSSION CHARGE!
NOT A MOMENT TO SPARE FOR NICETIES LIKE SLIDING BACK DOWN...!
DROPPING THOSE CHARGES FROM OUR SPEEDERS THEY COULDN'T CRACK THE WALKER'S PROTECTIVE ARMOR. BUT NOW THAT I'VE GOT ONE INSIDE...
LUKE LANDS HARD, ROLLING, AS TWO MONSTROUS LEGS PASS OVER HIM...
THEN...
THAT BUYS LEIA AND THE OTHERS A LITTLE MORE TIME--
--BUT IS IT ENOUGH?!

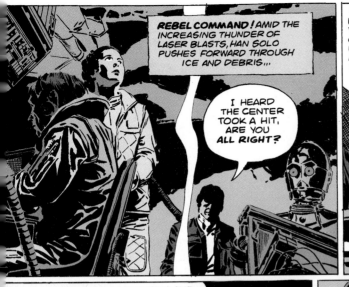

REBEL COMMAND! AMID THE INCREASING THUNDER OF LASER BLASTS, HAN SOLO PUSHES FORWARD THROUGH ICE AND DEBRIS...

I HEARD THE CENTER TOOK A HIT, ARE YOU ALL RIGHT?

SO FAR, I...I DIDN'T EXPECT YOU'D BE CONCERNED. WITH REPAIRS TO THE FALCON TO WORRY ABOUT AND--

COME ON! A LITTLE MORE POUNDING AND THE WHOLE PLACE WILL GO TO PIECES. YOU'VE GOT TO GET TO YOUR SHIP.

W-WAIT!

GIVE THE EVACUATION CODE SIGNAL... AND GET TO THE TRANSPORT!

YES, YOUR HIGHNESS! ALL UNITS... ALL UNITS! DISENGAGE... DISENGAGE! BEGIN RETREAT ACTION!

THAT MEANS YOU TOO, BRONZE BRITCHES! LET'S HIT THE CORRIDORS!

PERHAPS YOU'RE RIGHT, SIR... THINGS ARE DEFINITELY FALLING APART HERE!

BUT ONCE IN THE CORRIDORS...

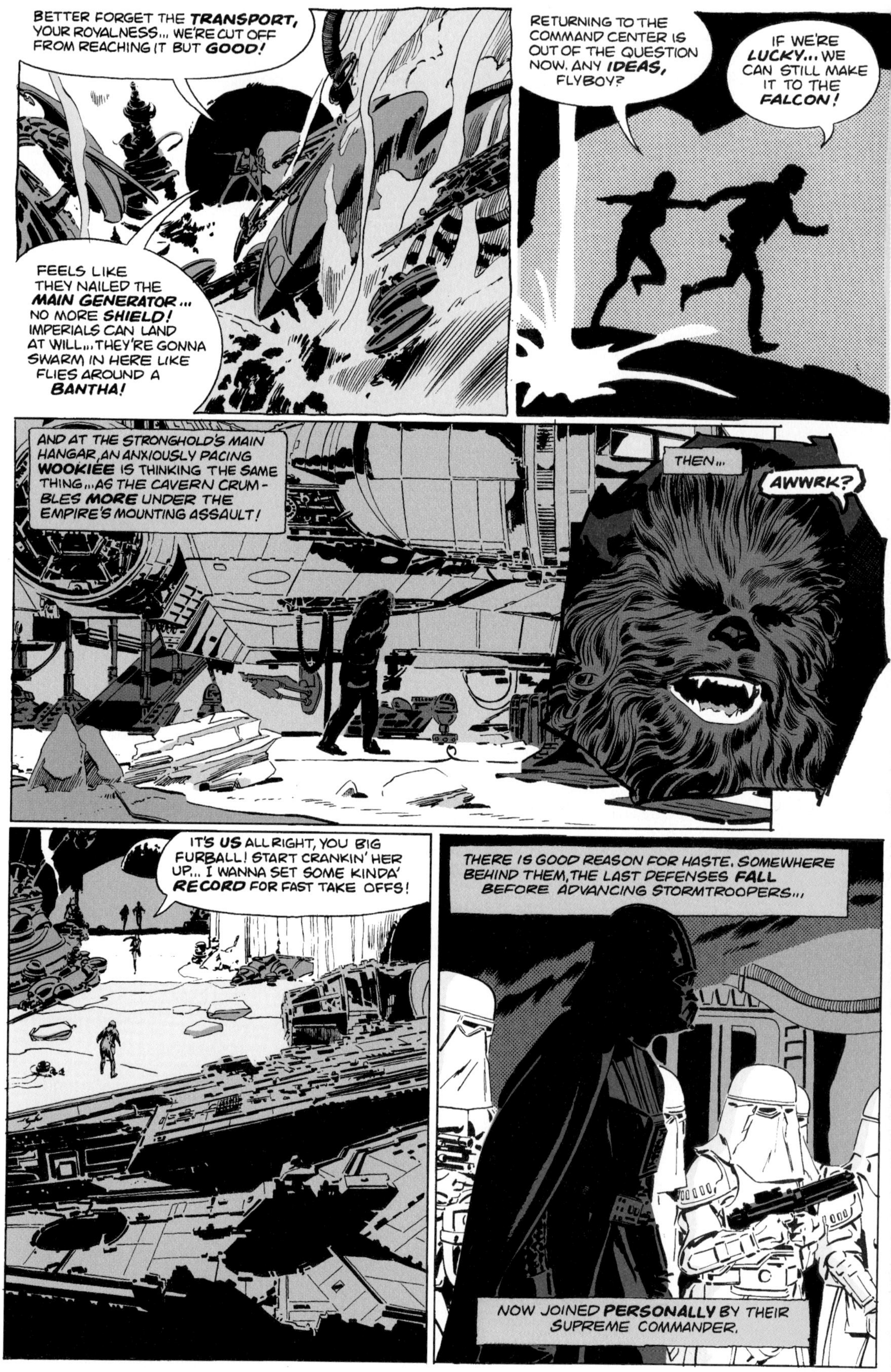
BETTER FORGET THE TRANSPORT, YOUR ROYALNESS... WE'RE CUT OFF FROM REACHING IT BUT GOOD!
FEELS LIKE THEY NAILED THE MAIN GENERATOR... NO MORE SHIELD! IMPERIALS CAN LAND AT WILL... THEY'RE GONNA SWARM IN HERE LIKE FLIES AROUND A BANTHA!
RETURNING TO THE COMMAND CENTER IS OUT OF THE QUESTION NOW. ANY IDEAS, FLYBOY?
IF WE'RE LUCKY... WE CAN STILL MAKE IT TO THE FALCON!
AND AT THE STRONGHOLD'S MAIN HANGAR, AN ANXIOUSLY PACING WOOKIEE IS THINKING THE SAME THING... AS THE CAVERN CRUMBLES MORE UNDER THE EMPIRE'S MOUNTING ASSAULT!
THEN...
AWWRK?
IT'S US ALL RIGHT, YOU BIG FURBALL! START CRANKIN' HER UP... I WANNA SET SOME KINDA' RECORD FOR FAST TAKE OFFS!
THERE IS GOOD REASON FOR HASTE. SOMEWHERE BEHIND THEM, THE LAST DEFENSES FALL BEFORE ADVANCING STORMTROOPERS...
NOW JOINED PERSONALLY BY THEIR SUPREME COMMANDER.

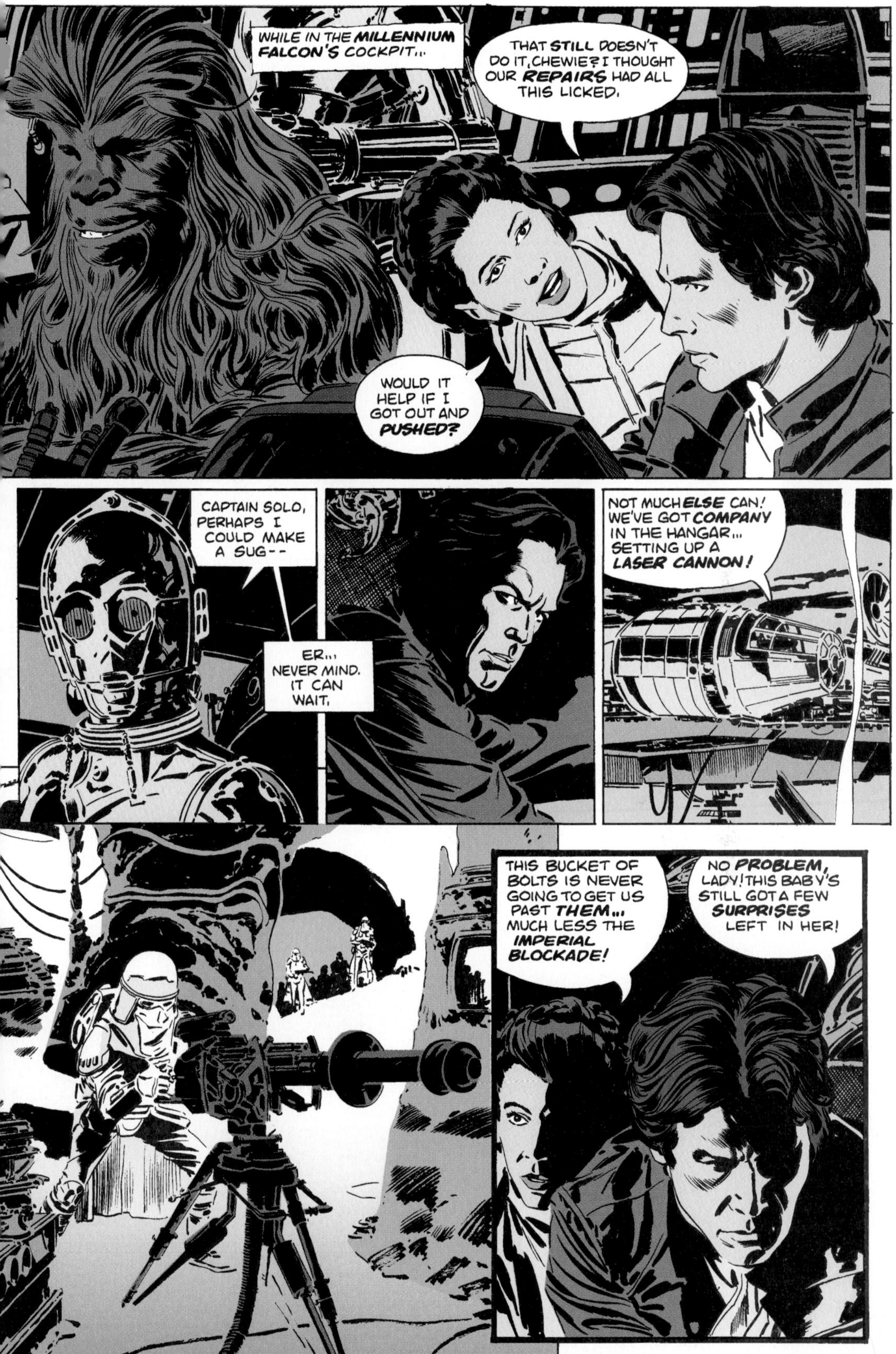
WHILE IN THE MILLENNIUM FALCON'S COCKPIT...
THAT STILL DOESN'T DO IT, CHEWIE? I THOUGHT OUR REPAIRS HAD ALL THIS LICKED.
WOULD IT HELP IF I GOT OUT AND PUSHED?
CAPTAIN SOLO, PERHAPS I COULD MAKE A SUG--
ER... NEVER MIND. IT CAN WAIT.
NOT MUCH ELSE CAN! WE'VE GOT COMPANY IN THE HANGAR... SETTING UP A LASER CANNON!
THIS BUCKET OF BOLTS IS NEVER GOING TO GET US PAST THEM... MUCH LESS THE IMPERIAL BLOCKADE!
NO PROBLEM, LADY! THIS BABY'S STILL GOT A FEW SURPRISES LEFT IN HER!

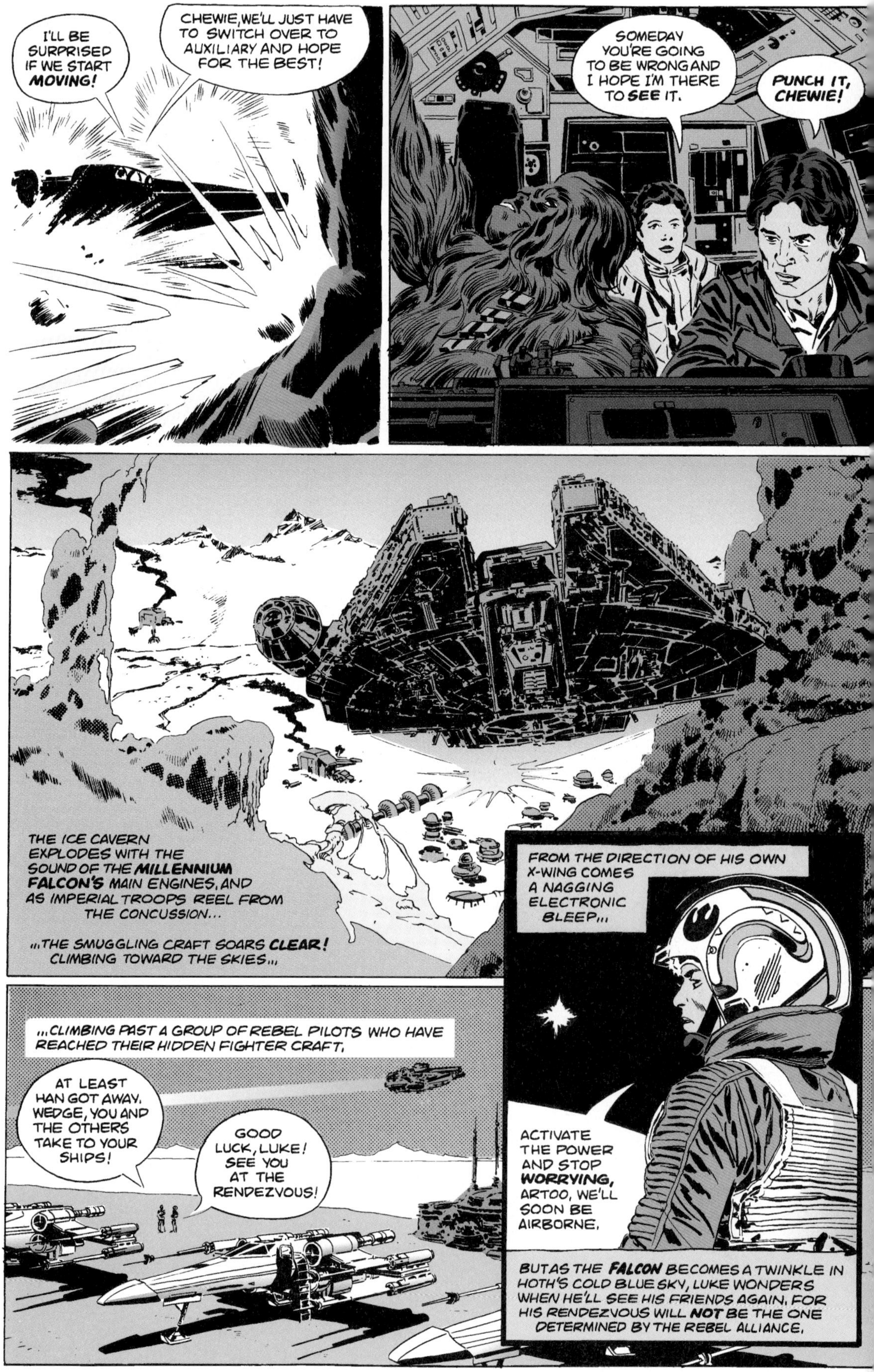
I'LL BE SURPRISED IF WE START MOVING!
CHEWIE, WE'LL JUST HAVE TO SWITCH OVER TO AUXILIARY AND HOPE FOR THE BEST!
SOMEDAY YOU'RE GOING TO BE WRONG AND I HOPE I'M THERE TO SEE IT.
PUNCH IT, CHEWIE!
THE ICE CAVERN EXPLODES WITH THE SOUND OF THE MILLENNIUM FALCON'S MAIN ENGINES, AND AS IMPERIAL TROOPS REEL FROM THE CONCUSSION...
...THE SMUGGLING CRAFT SOARS CLEAR! CLIMBING TOWARD THE SKIES...
...CLIMBING PAST A GROUP OF REBEL PILOTS WHO HAVE REACHED THEIR HIDDEN FIGHTER CRAFT.
AT LEAST HAN GOT AWAY. WEDGE, YOU AND THE OTHERS TAKE TO YOUR SHIPS!
GOOD LUCK, LUKE! SEE YOU AT THE RENDEZVOUS!
FROM THE DIRECTION OF HIS OWN X-WING COMES A NAGGING ELECTRONIC BLEEP...
ACTIVATE THE POWER AND STOP WORRYING, ARTOO, WE'LL SOON BE AIRBORNE.
BUT AS THE FALCON BECOMES A TWINKLE IN HOTH'S COLD BLUE SKY, LUKE WONDERS WHEN HE'LL SEE HIS FRIENDS AGAIN. FOR HIS RENDEZVOUS WILL NOT BE THE ONE DETERMINED BY THE REBEL ALLIANCE.

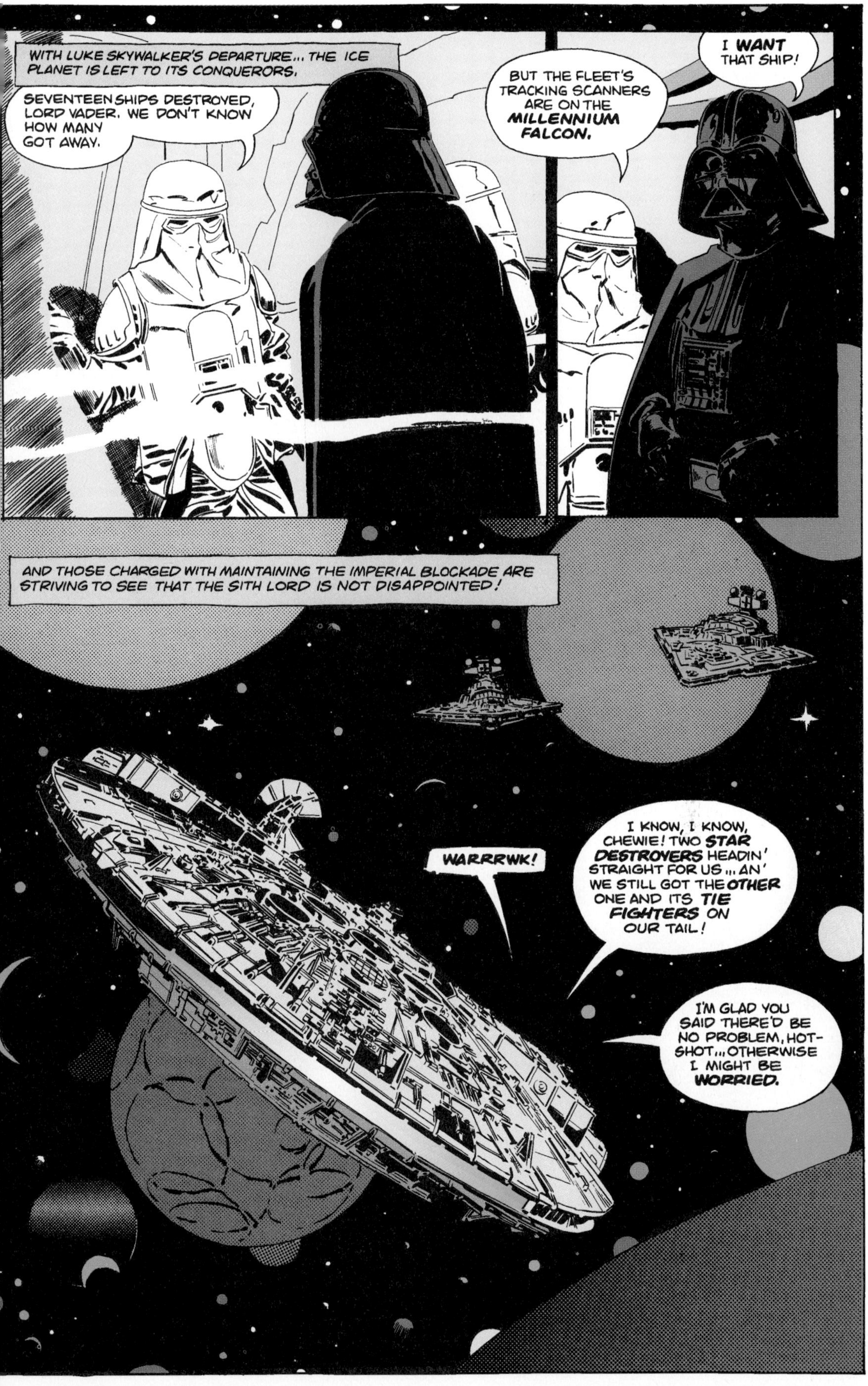
WITH LUKE SKYWALKER'S DEPARTURE... THE ICE PLANET IS LEFT TO ITS CONQUERORS.
SEVENTEEN SHIPS DESTROYED, LORD VADER. WE DON'T KNOW HOW MANY GOT AWAY.
BUT THE FLEET'S TRACKING SCANNERS ARE ON THE MILLENNIUM FALCON.
I WANT THAT SHIP!
AND THOSE CHARGED WITH MAINTAINING THE IMPERIAL BLOCKADE ARE STRIVING TO SEE THAT THE SITH LORD IS NOT DISAPPOINTED!
WARRRWK!
I KNOW, I KNOW, CHEWIE! TWO STAR DESTROYERS HEADIN' STRAIGHT FOR US... AN' WE STILL GOT THE OTHER ONE AND ITS TIE FIGHTERS ON OUR TAIL!
I'M GLAD YOU SAID THERE'D BE NO PROBLEM, HOT-SHOT... OTHERWISE I MIGHT BE WORRIED.

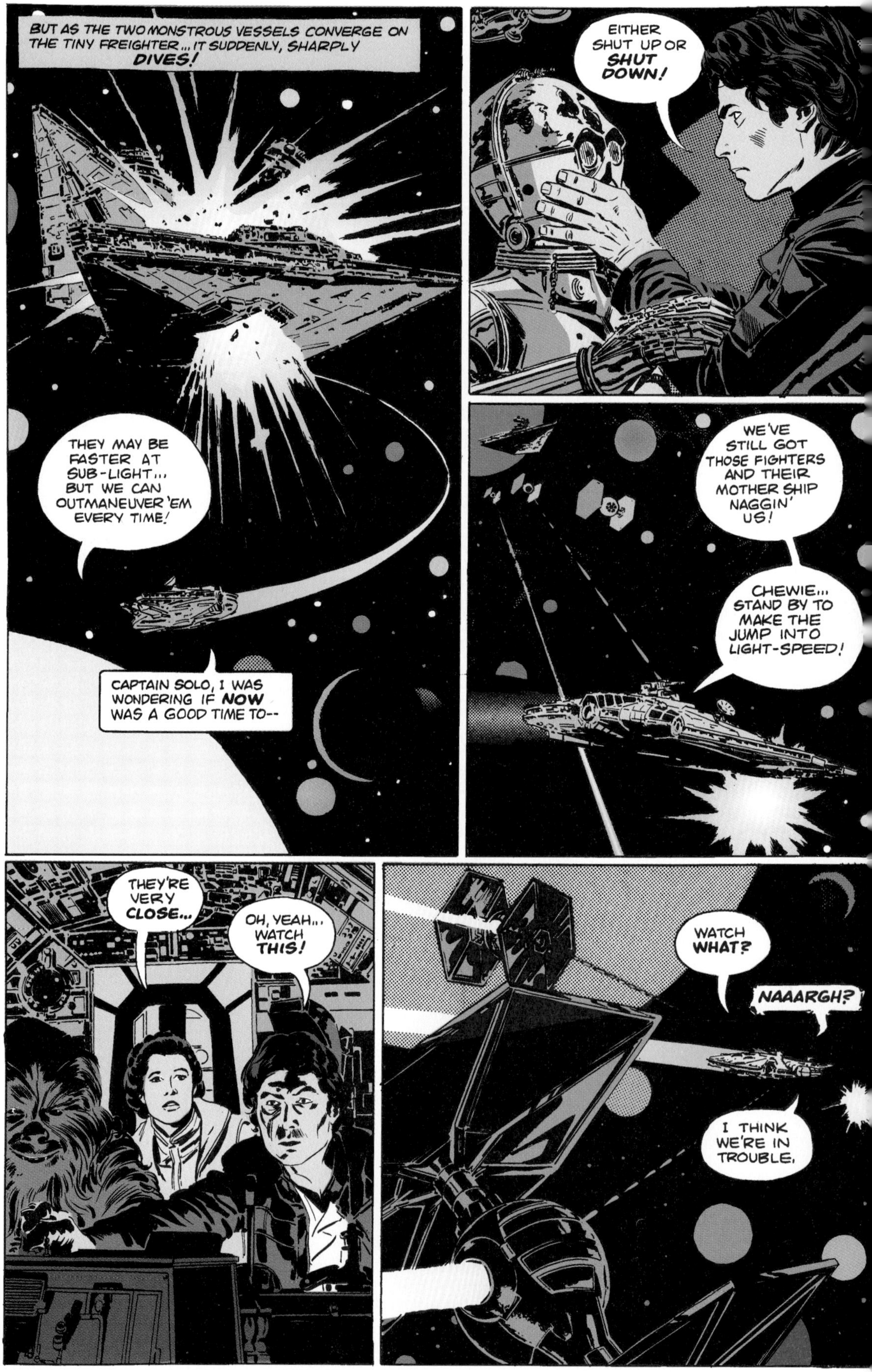
BUT AS THE TWO MONSTROUS VESSELS CONVERGE ON THE TINY FREIGHTER... IT SUDDENLY, SHARPLY DIVES!
THEY MAY BE FASTER AT SUB-LIGHT... BUT WE CAN OUTMANEUVER 'EM EVERY TIME!
CAPTAIN SOLO, I WAS WONDERING IF NOW WAS A GOOD TIME TO--
EITHER SHUT UP OR SHUT DOWN!
WE'VE STILL GOT THOSE FIGHTERS AND THEIR MOTHER SHIP NAGGIN' US!
CHEWIE... STAND BY TO MAKE THE JUMP INTO LIGHT-SPEED!
THEY'RE VERY CLOSE...
OH, YEAH... WATCH THIS!
WATCH WHAT?
NAAARGH?
I THINK WE'RE IN TROUBLE.

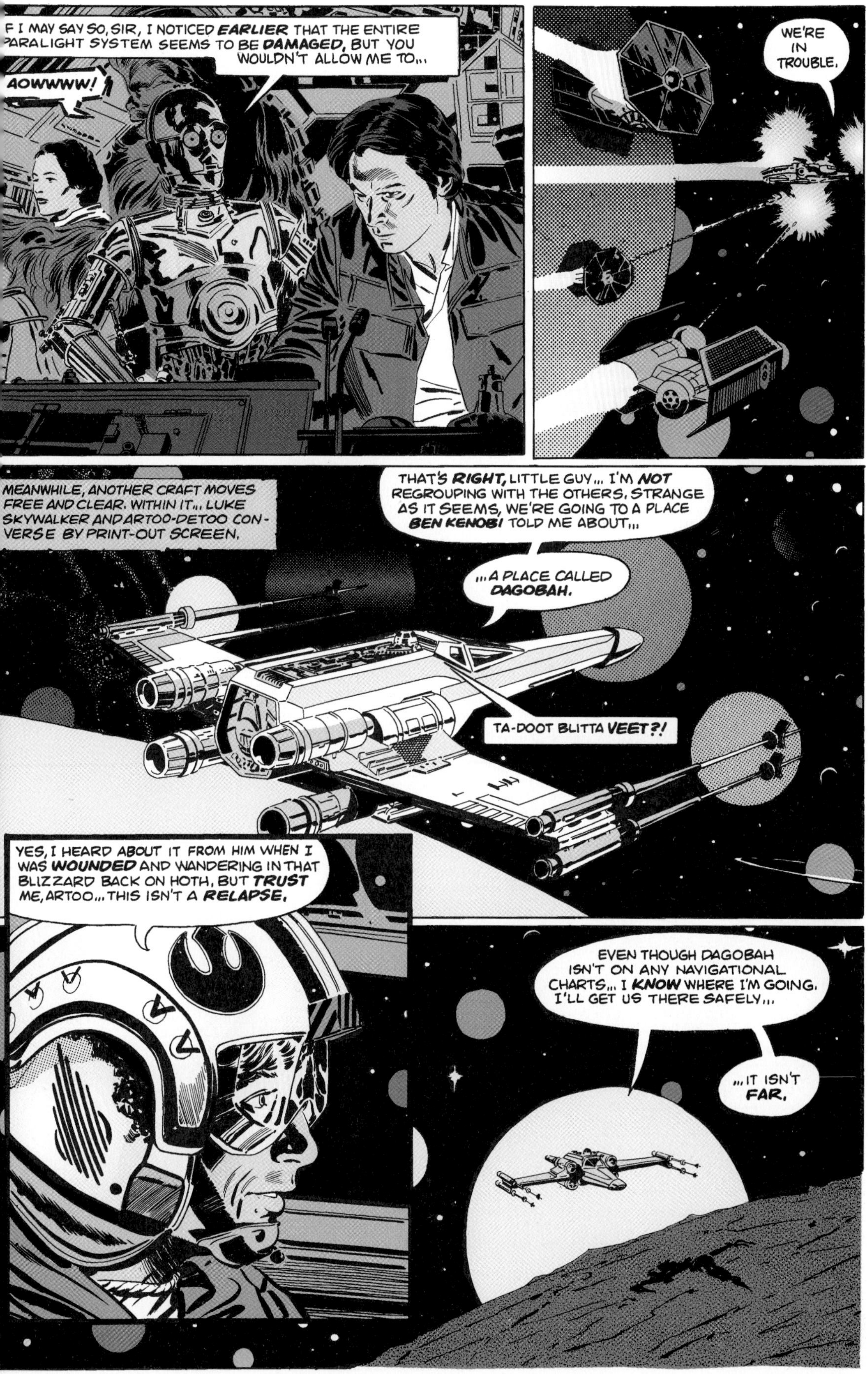

F I MAY SAY SO, SIR, I NOTICED EARLIER THAT THE ENTIRE PARALIGHT SYSTEM SEEMS TO BE DAMAGED, BUT YOU WOULDN'T ALLOW ME TO...
AOWWWW!
WE'RE IN TROUBLE.
MEANWHILE, ANOTHER CRAFT MOVES FREE AND CLEAR. WITHIN IT... LUKE SKYWALKER AND ARTOO-DETOO CONVERSE BY PRINT-OUT SCREEN.
THAT'S RIGHT, LITTLE GUY... I'M NOT REGROUPING WITH THE OTHERS. STRANGE AS IT SEEMS, WE'RE GOING TO A PLACE BEN KENOBI TOLD ME ABOUT...
...A PLACE CALLED DAGOBAH.
TA-DOOT BLITTA VEET?!
YES, I HEARD ABOUT IT FROM HIM WHEN I WAS WOUNDED AND WANDERING IN THAT BLIZZARD BACK ON HOTH, BUT TRUST ME, ARTOO... THIS ISN'T A RELAPSE.
EVEN THOUGH DAGOBAH ISN'T ON ANY NAVIGATIONAL CHARTS... I KNOW WHERE I'M GOING. I'LL GET US THERE SAFELY...
...IT ISN'T FAR.

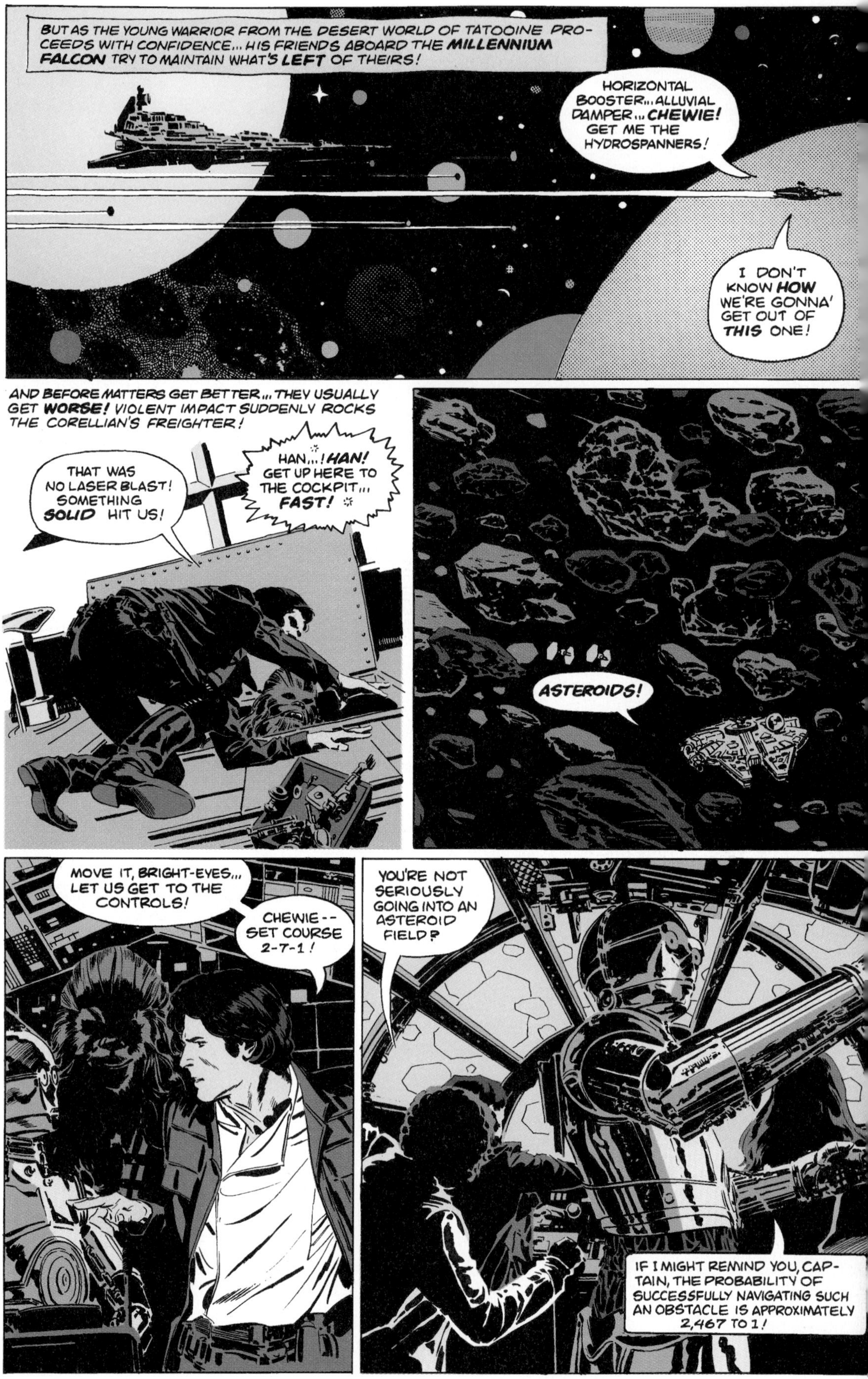
BUT AS THE YOUNG WARRIOR FROM THE DESERT WORLD OF TATOOINE PROCEEDS WITH CONFIDENCE... HIS FRIENDS ABOARD THE MILLENNIUM FALCON TRY TO MAINTAIN WHAT'S LEFT OF THEIRS!
HORIZONTAL BOOSTER... ALLUVIAL DAMPER... CHEWIE! GET ME THE HYDROSPANNERS!
I DON'T KNOW HOW WE'RE GONNA' GET OUT OF THIS ONE!
AND BEFORE MATTERS GET BETTER... THEY USUALLY GET WORSE! VIOLENT IMPACT SUDDENLY ROCKS THE CORELLIAN'S FREIGHTER!
THAT WAS NO LASER BLAST! SOMETHING SOLID HIT US!
HAN...! HAN! GET UP HERE TO THE COCKPIT... FAST!
ASTEROIDS!
MOVE IT, BRIGHT-EYES... LET US GET TO THE CONTROLS!
CHEWIE -- SET COURSE 2-7-1!
YOU'RE NOT SERIOUSLY GOING INTO AN ASTEROID FIELD?
IF I MIGHT REMIND YOU, CAPTAIN, THE PROBABILITY OF SUCCESSFULLY NAVIGATING SUCH AN OBSTACLE IS APPROXIMATELY 2,467 TO 1!

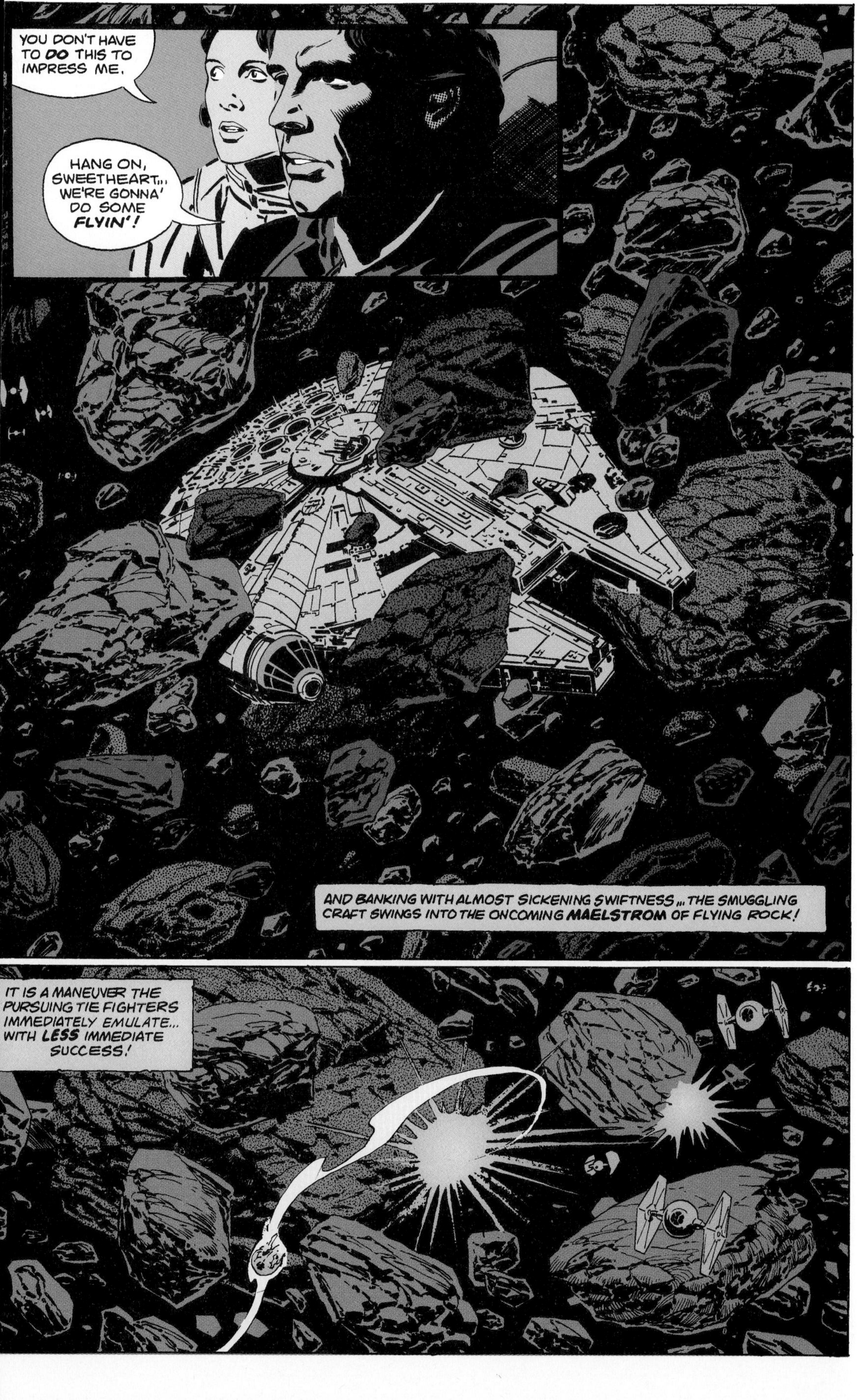
YOU DON'T HAVE TO DO THIS TO IMPRESS ME.
HANG ON, SWEETHEART... WE'RE GONNA' DO SOME FLYIN'!
AND BANKING WITH ALMOST SICKENING SWIFTNESS... THE SMUGGLING CRAFT SWINGS INTO THE ONCOMING MAELSTROM OF FLYING ROCK!
IT IS A MANEUVER THE PURSUING TIE FIGHTERS IMMEDIATELY EMULATE... WITH LESS IMMEDIATE SUCCESS!

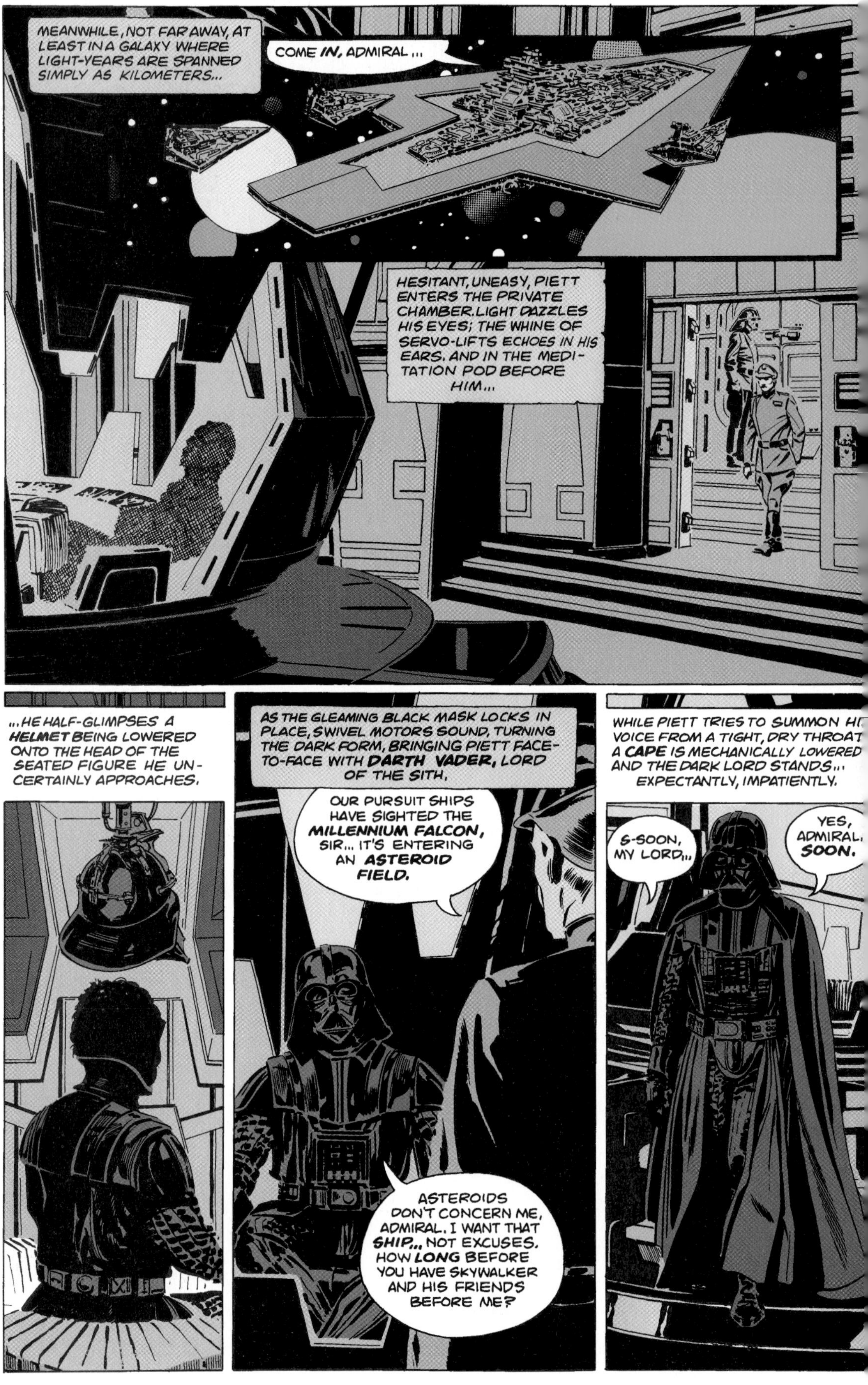

MEANWHILE, NOT FAR AWAY, AT LEAST IN A GALAXY WHERE LIGHT-YEARS ARE SPANNED SIMPLY AS KILOMETERS...
COME IN, ADMIRAL...
HESITANT, UNEASY, PIETT ENTERS THE PRIVATE CHAMBER. LIGHT DAZZLES HIS EYES; THE WHINE OF SERVO-LIFTS ECHOES IN HIS EARS. AND IN THE MEDITATION POD BEFORE HIM...
...HE HALF-GLIMPSES A HELMET BEING LOWERED ONTO THE HEAD OF THE SEATED FIGURE HE UNCERTAINLY APPROACHES.
AS THE GLEAMING BLACK MASK LOCKS IN PLACE, SWIVEL MOTORS SOUND, TURNING THE DARK FORM, BRINGING PIETT FACE-TO-FACE WITH DARTH VADER, LORD OF THE SITH.
OUR PURSUIT SHIPS HAVE SIGHTED THE MILLENNIUM FALCON, SIR... IT'S ENTERING AN ASTEROID FIELD.
ASTEROIDS DON'T CONCERN ME, ADMIRAL. I WANT THAT SHIP... NOT EXCUSES. HOW LONG BEFORE YOU HAVE SKYWALKER AND HIS FRIENDS BEFORE ME?
WHILE PIETT TRIES TO SUMMON HI VOICE FROM A TIGHT, DRY THROAT A CAPE IS MECHANICALLY LOWERED AND THE DARK LORD STANDS... EXPECTANTLY, IMPATIENTLY.
S-SOON, MY LORD...
YES, ADMIRAL. SOON.

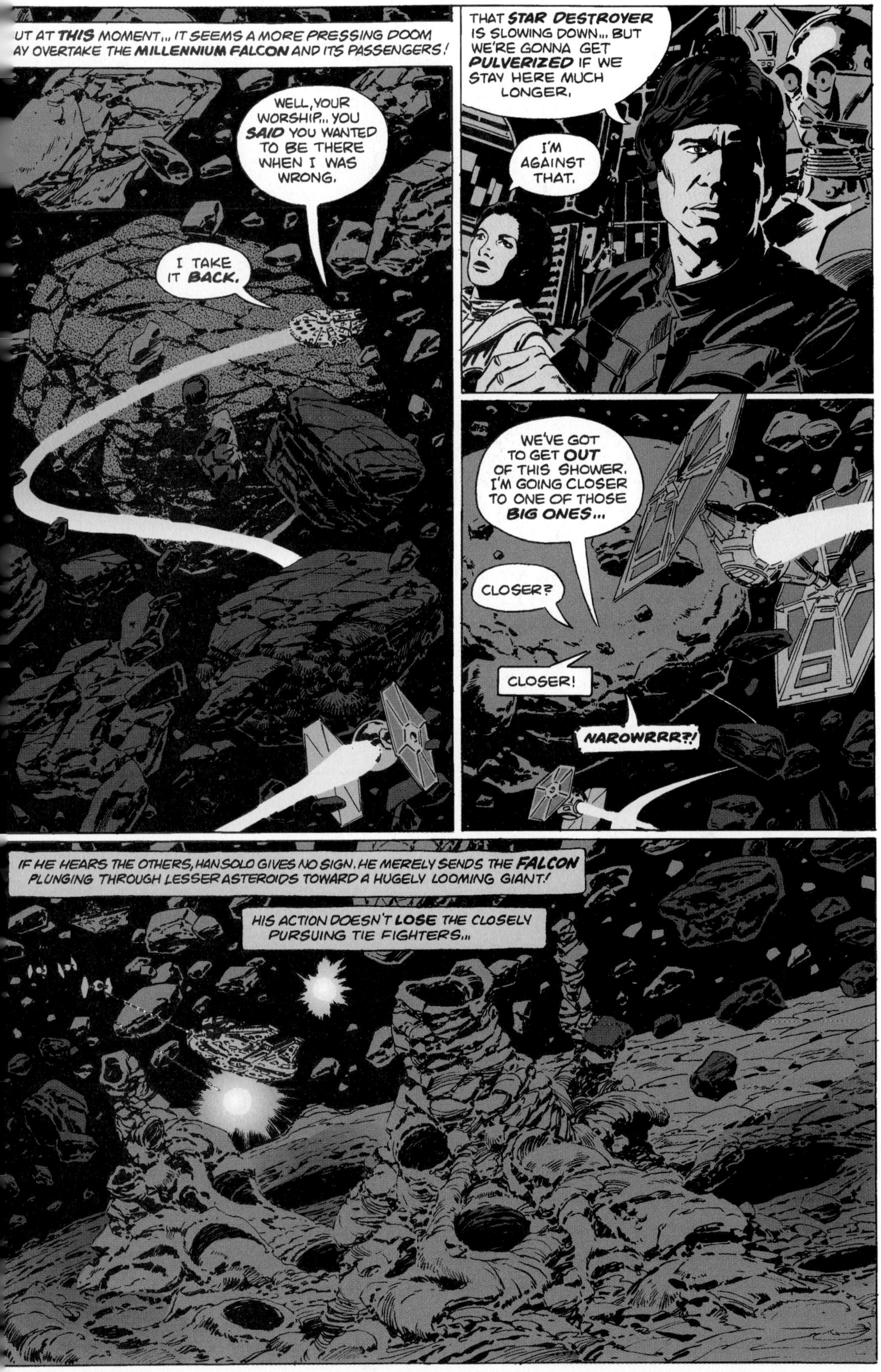
UT AT THIS MOMENT... IT SEEMS A MORE PRESSING DOOM
AY OVERTAKE THE MILLENNIUM FALCON AND ITS PASSENGERS!
WELL, YOUR WORSHIP... YOU SAID YOU WANTED TO BE THERE WHEN I WAS WRONG.
I TAKE IT BACK.
THAT STAR DESTROYER IS SLOWING DOWN... BUT WE'RE GONNA GET PULVERIZED IF WE STAY HERE MUCH LONGER.
I'M AGAINST THAT.
WE'VE GOT TO GET OUT OF THIS SHOWER. I'M GOING CLOSER TO ONE OF THOSE BIG ONES...
CLOSER?
CLOSER!
NAROWRRR?!
IF HE HEARS THE OTHERS, HAN SOLO GIVES NO SIGN. HE MERELY SENDS THE FALCON PLUNGING THROUGH LESSER ASTEROIDS TOWARD A HUGELY LOOMING GIANT!
HIS ACTION DOESN'T LOSE THE CLOSELY PURSUING TIE FIGHTERS...

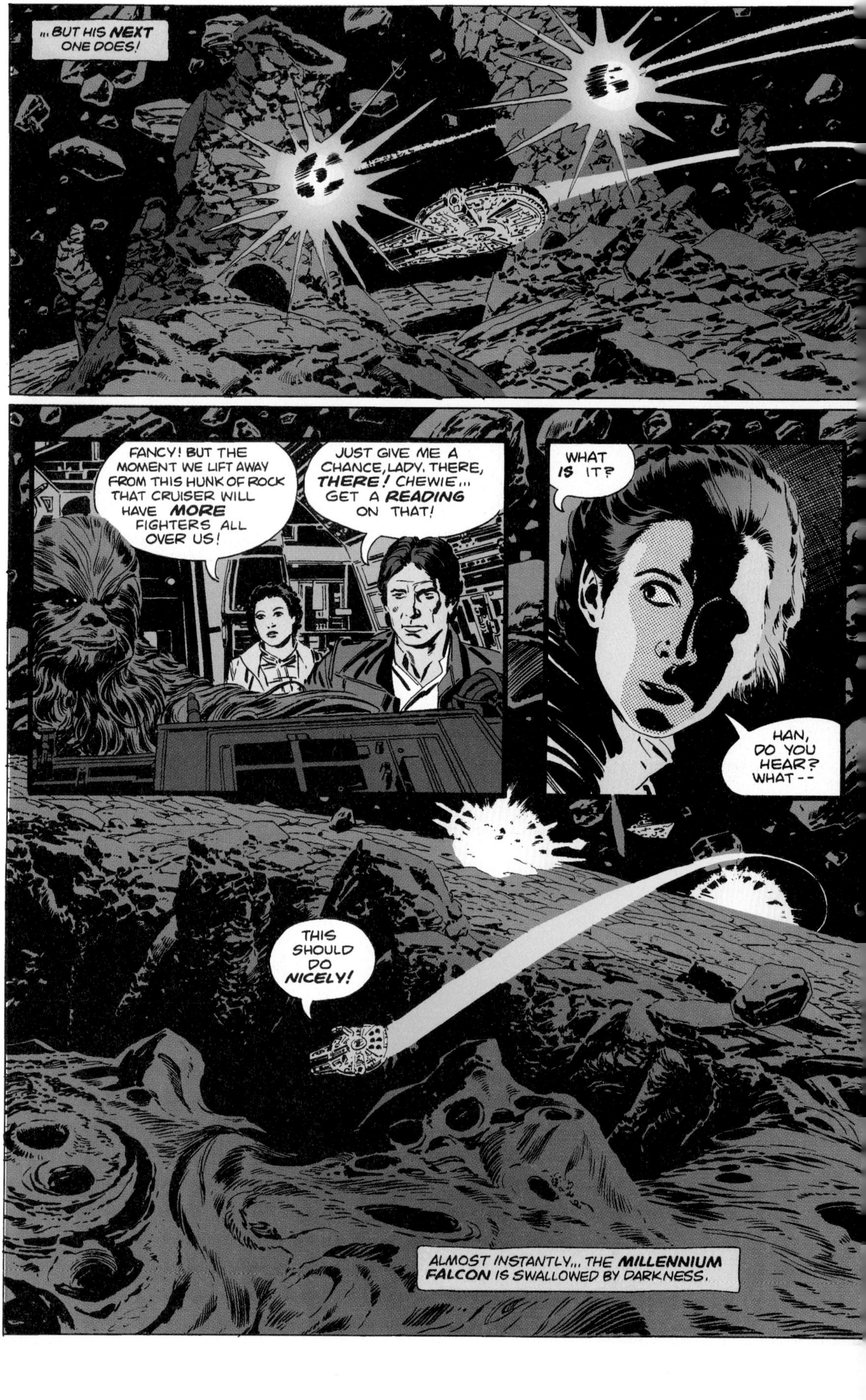
...BUT HIS NEXT ONE DOES!
FANCY! BUT THE MOMENT WE LIFT AWAY FROM THIS HUNK OF ROCK THAT CRUISER WILL HAVE MORE FIGHTERS ALL OVER US!
JUST GIVE ME A CHANCE, LADY. THERE, THERE! CHEWIE... GET A READING ON THAT!
WHAT IS IT?
HAN, DO YOU HEAR? WHAT --
THIS SHOULD DO NICELY!
ALMOST INSTANTLY... THE MILLENNIUM FALCON IS SWALLOWED BY DARKNESS.

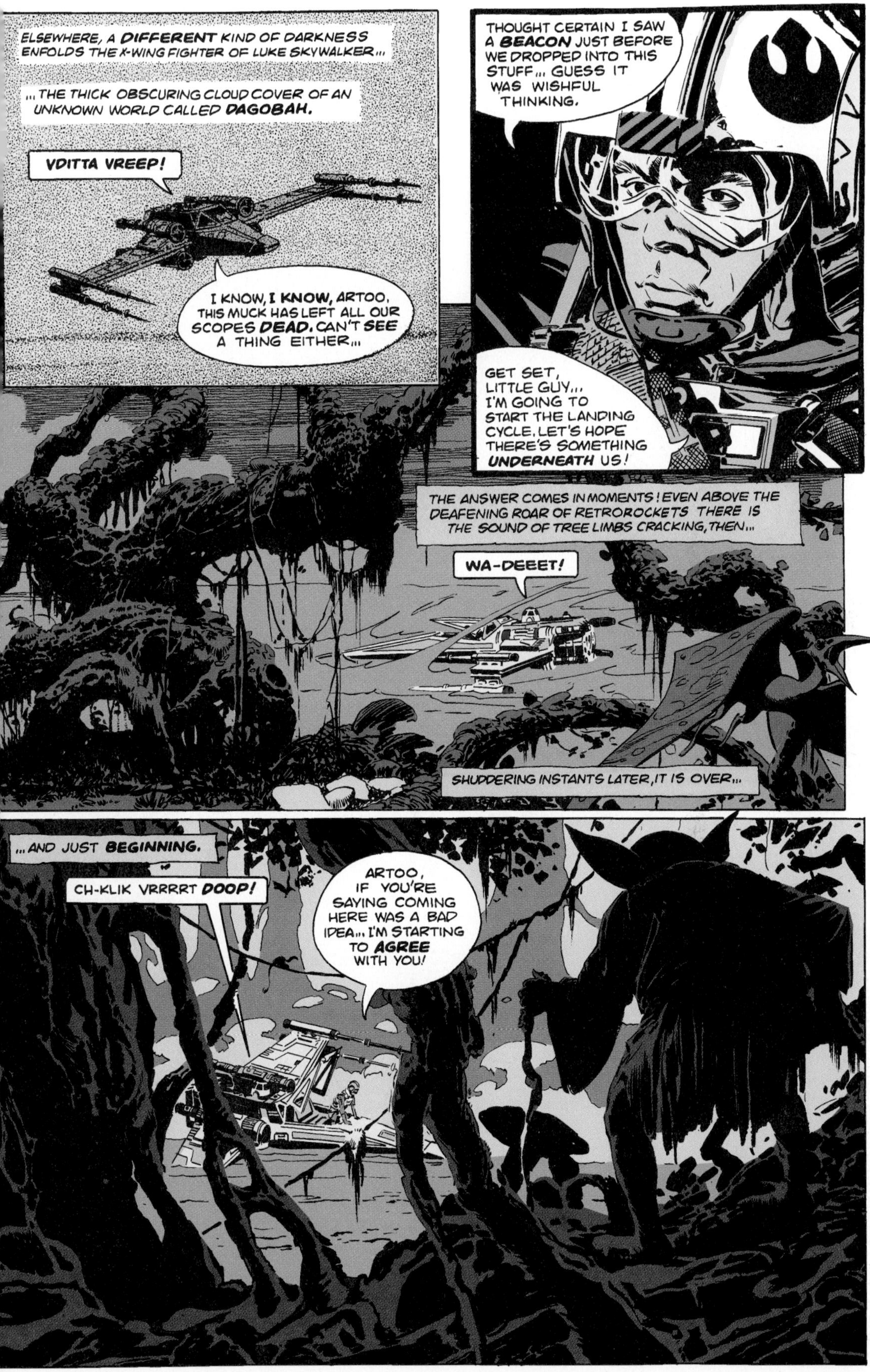
ELSEWHERE, A DIFFERENT KIND OF DARKNESS ENFOLDS THE X-WING FIGHTER OF LUKE SKYWALKER...
...THE THICK OBSCURING CLOUD COVER OF AN UNKNOWN WORLD CALLED DAGOBAH.
VDITTA VREEP!
I KNOW, I KNOW, ARTOO, THIS MUCK HAS LEFT ALL OUR SCOPES DEAD. CAN'T SEE A THING EITHER...
THOUGHT CERTAIN I SAW A BEACON JUST BEFORE WE DROPPED INTO THIS STUFF... GUESS IT WAS WISHFUL THINKING.
GET SET, LITTLE GUY... I'M GOING TO START THE LANDING CYCLE. LET'S HOPE THERE'S SOMETHING UNDERNEATH US!
THE ANSWER COMES IN MOMENTS! EVEN ABOVE THE DEAFENING ROAR OF RETROROCKETS THERE IS THE SOUND OF TREE LIMBS CRACKING, THEN...
WA-DEEET!
SHUDDERING INSTANTS LATER, IT IS OVER...
...AND JUST BEGINNING.
CH-KLIK VRRRRT DOOP!
ARTOO, IF YOU'RE SAYING COMING HERE WAS A BAD IDEA... I'M STARTING TO AGREE WITH YOU!

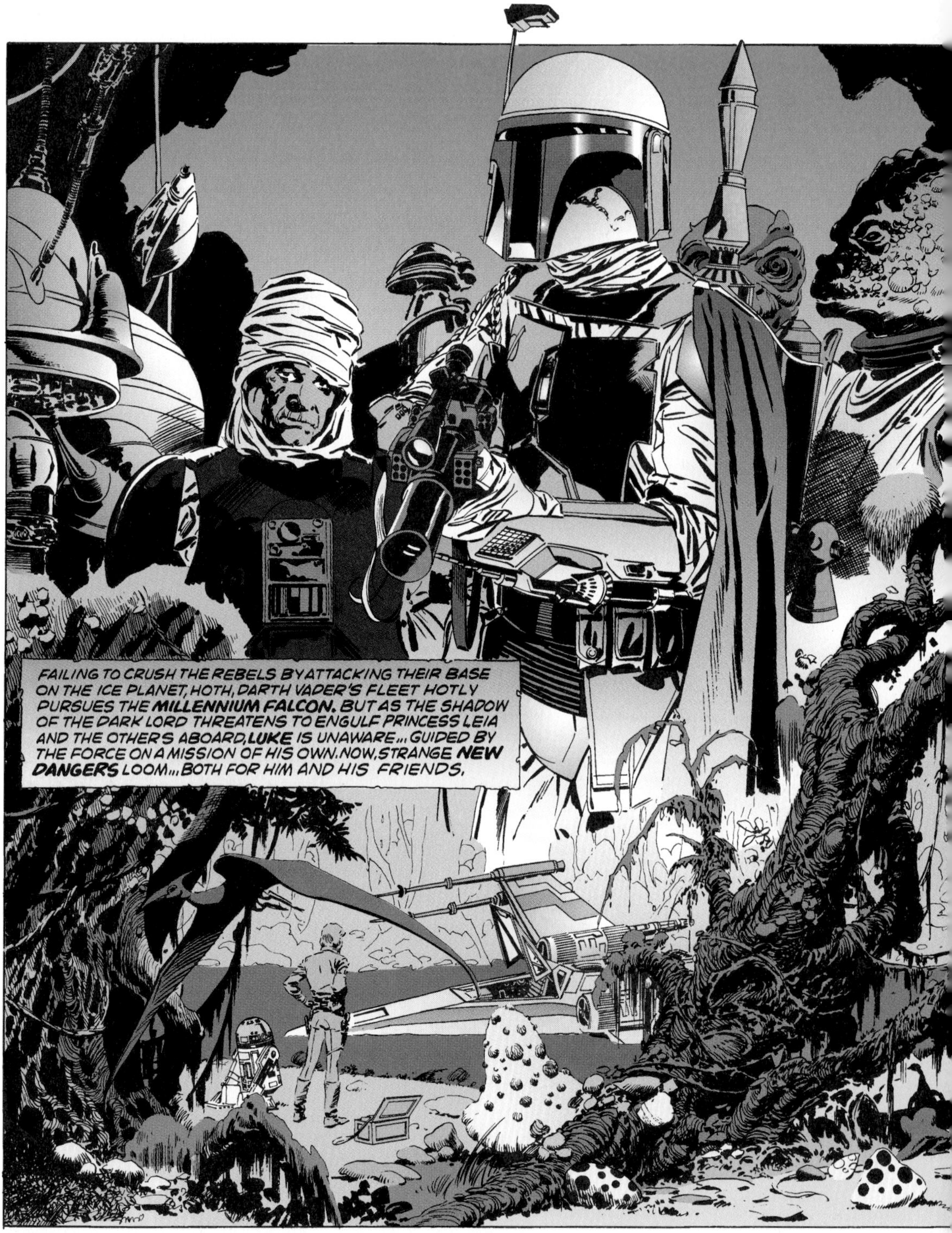
FAILING TO CRUSH THE REBELS BY ATTACKING THEIR BASE ON THE ICE PLANET, HOTH, DARTH VADER'S FLEET HOTLY PURSUES THE MILLENNIUM FALCON. BUT AS THE SHADOW OF THE DARK LORD THREATENS TO ENGULF PRINCESS LEIA AND THE OTHERS ABOARD, LUKE IS UNAWARE... GUIDED BY THE FORCE ON A MISSION OF HIS OWN. NOW, STRANGE NEW DANGERS LOOM... BOTH FOR HIM AND HIS FRIENDS.

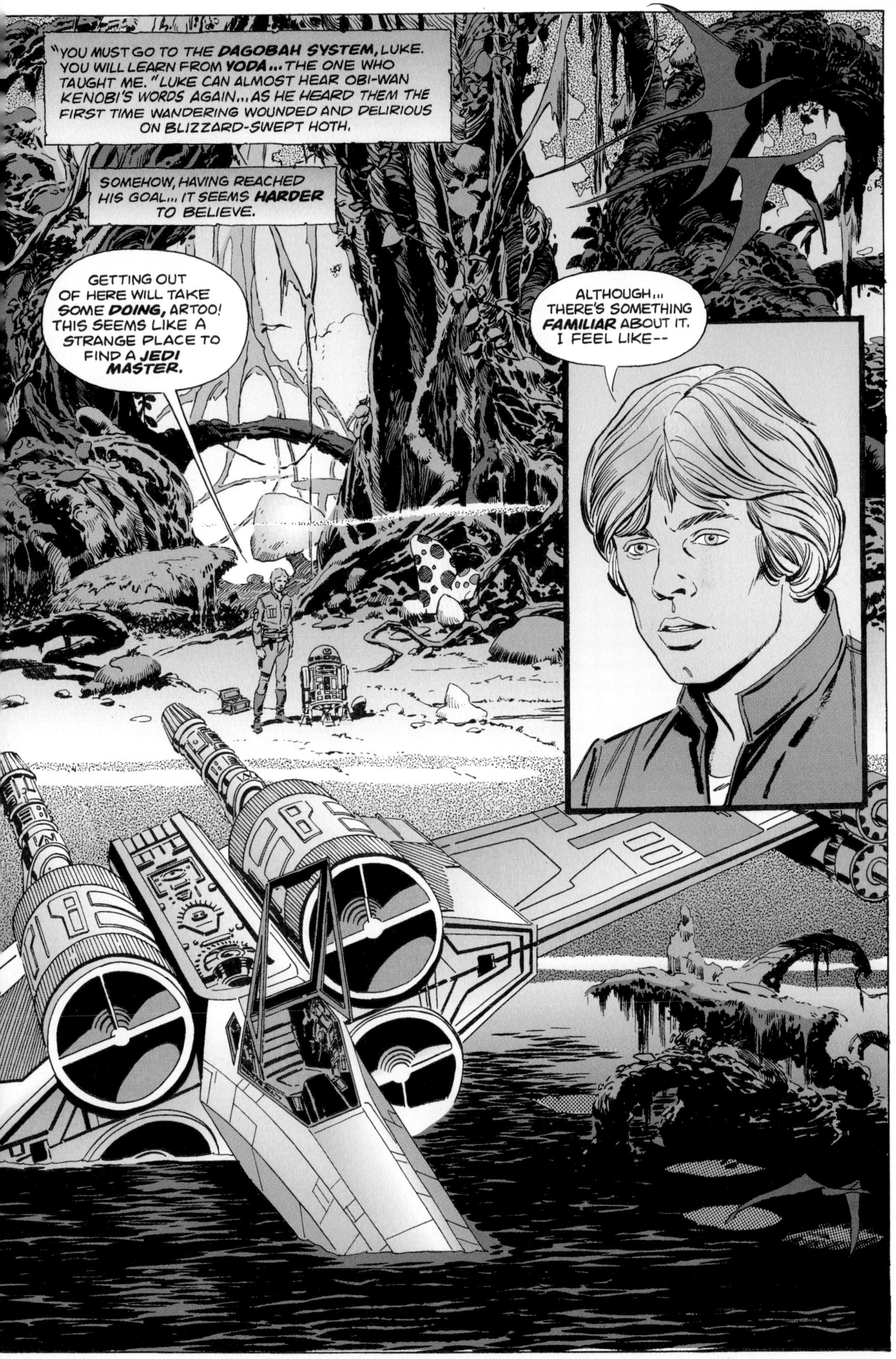
"YOU MUST GO TO THE DAGOBAH SYSTEM, LUKE. YOU WILL LEARN FROM YODA... THE ONE WHO TAUGHT ME." LUKE CAN ALMOST HEAR OBI-WAN KENOBI'S WORDS AGAIN... AS HE HEARD THEM THE FIRST TIME WANDERING WOUNDED AND DELIRIOUS ON BLIZZARD-SWEPT HOTH.
SOMEHOW, HAVING REACHED HIS GOAL... IT SEEMS HARDER TO BELIEVE.
GETTING OUT OF HERE WILL TAKE SOME DOING, ARTOO! THIS SEEMS LIKE A STRANGE PLACE TO FIND A JEDI MASTER.
ALTHOUGH... THERE'S SOMETHING FAMILIAR ABOUT IT. I FEEL LIKE--

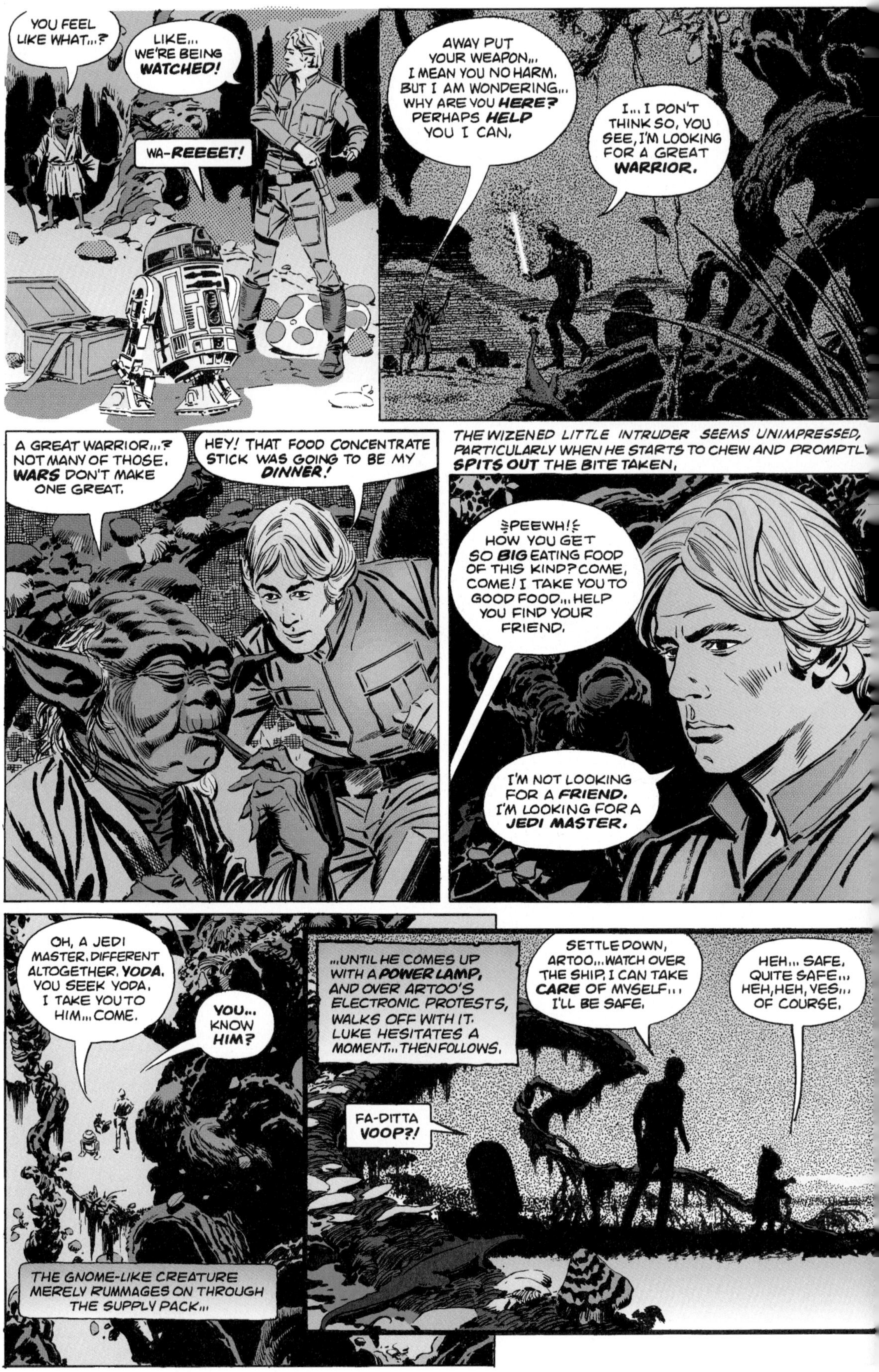
YOU FEEL LIKE WHAT...?
LIKE... WE'RE BEING WATCHED!
WA-REEEET!
AWAY PUT YOUR WEAPON... I MEAN YOU NO HARM. BUT I AM WONDERING... WHY ARE YOU HERE? PERHAPS HELP YOU I CAN.
I... I DON'T THINK SO, YOU SEE, I'M LOOKING FOR A GREAT WARRIOR.
A GREAT WARRIOR...? NOT MANY OF THOSE. WARS DON'T MAKE ONE GREAT.
HEY! THAT FOOD CONCENTRATE STICK WAS GOING TO BE MY DINNER!
THE WIZENED LITTLE INTRUDER SEEMS UNIMPRESSED, PARTICULARLY WHEN HE STARTS TO CHEW AND PROMPTLY SPITS OUT THE BITE TAKEN.
PEEWH! HOW YOU GET SO BIG EATING FOOD OF THIS KIND? COME, COME! I TAKE YOU TO GOOD FOOD... HELP YOU FIND YOUR FRIEND.
I'M NOT LOOKING FOR A FRIEND. I'M LOOKING FOR A JEDI MASTER.
OH, A JEDI MASTER. DIFFERENT ALTOGETHER. YODA. YOU SEEK YODA. I TAKE YOU TO HIM... COME.
YOU... KNOW HIM?
THE GNOME-LIKE CREATURE MERELY RUMMAGES ON THROUGH THE SUPPLY PACK...
...UNTIL HE COMES UP WITH A POWER LAMP, AND OVER ARTOO'S ELECTRONIC PROTESTS, WALKS OFF WITH IT. LUKE HESITATES A MOMENT... THEN FOLLOWS.
FA-DITTA VOOP?!
SETTLE DOWN, ARTOO... WATCH OVER THE SHIP. I CAN TAKE CARE OF MYSELF... I'LL BE SAFE.
HEH... SAFE. QUITE SAFE... HEH, HEH, YES... OF COURSE.

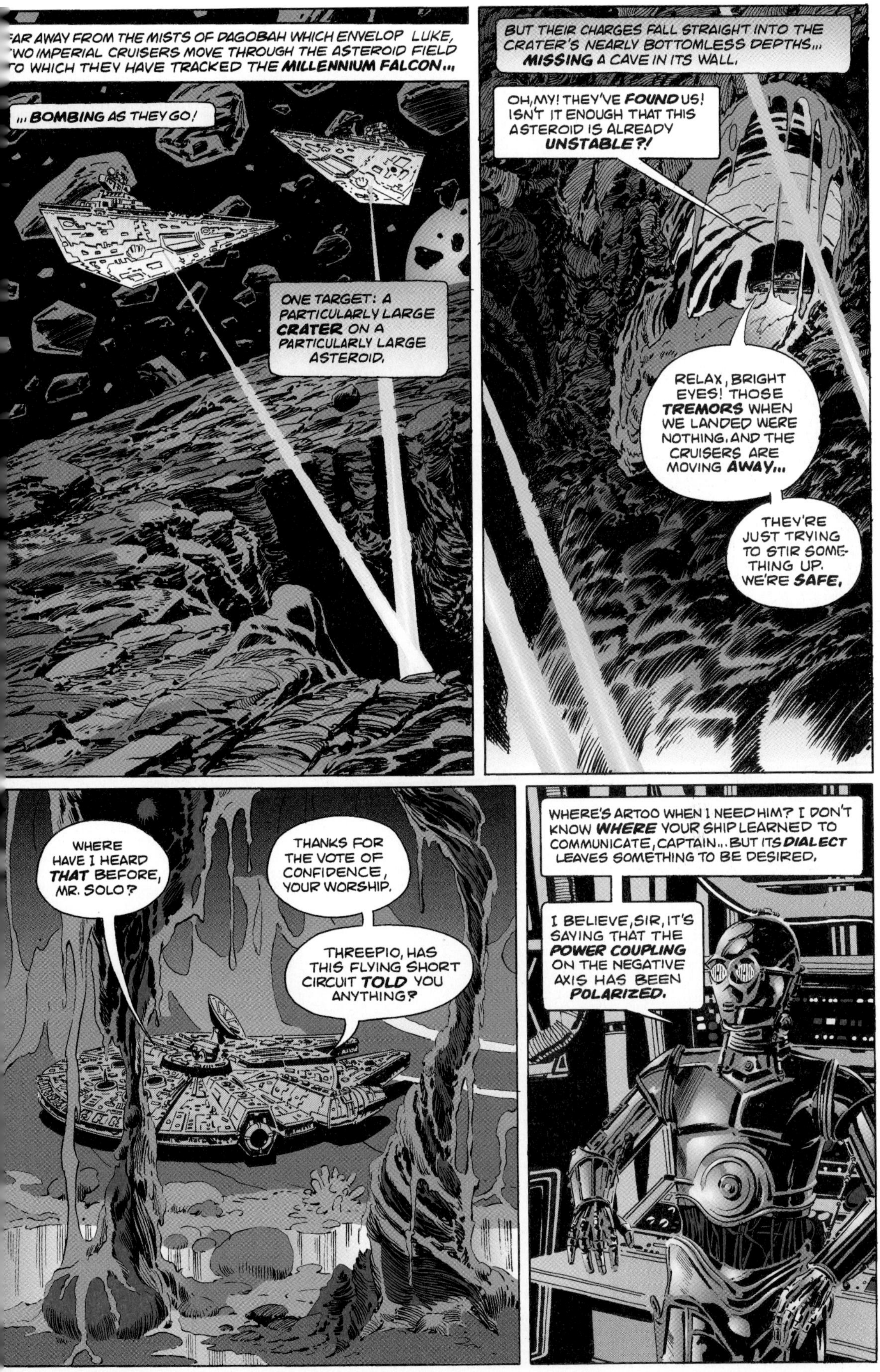
FAR AWAY FROM THE MISTS OF DAGOBAH WHICH ENVELOP LUKE, TWO IMPERIAL CRUISERS MOVE THROUGH THE ASTEROID FIELD TO WHICH THEY HAVE TRACKED THE MILLENNIUM FALCON...
...BOMBING AS THEY GO!
ONE TARGET: A PARTICULARLY LARGE CRATER ON A PARTICULARLY LARGE ASTEROID.
BUT THEIR CHARGES FALL STRAIGHT INTO THE CRATER'S NEARLY BOTTOMLESS DEPTHS... MISSING A CAVE IN ITS WALL.
OH, MY! THEY'VE FOUND US! ISN'T IT ENOUGH THAT THIS ASTEROID IS ALREADY UNSTABLE?!
RELAX, BRIGHT EYES! THOSE TREMORS WHEN WE LANDED WERE NOTHING. AND THE CRUISERS ARE MOVING AWAY...
THEY'RE JUST TRYING TO STIR SOME-THING UP. WE'RE SAFE.
WHERE HAVE I HEARD THAT BEFORE, MR. SOLO?
THANKS FOR THE VOTE OF CONFIDENCE, YOUR WORSHIP.
THREEPIO, HAS THIS FLYING SHORT CIRCUIT TOLD YOU ANYTHING?
WHERE'S ARTOO WHEN I NEED HIM? I DON'T KNOW WHERE YOUR SHIP LEARNED TO COMMUNICATE, CAPTAIN... BUT ITS DIALECT LEAVES SOMETHING TO BE DESIRED.
I BELIEVE, SIR, IT'S SAYING THAT THE POWER COUPLING ON THE NEGATIVE AXIS HAS BEEN POLARIZED.

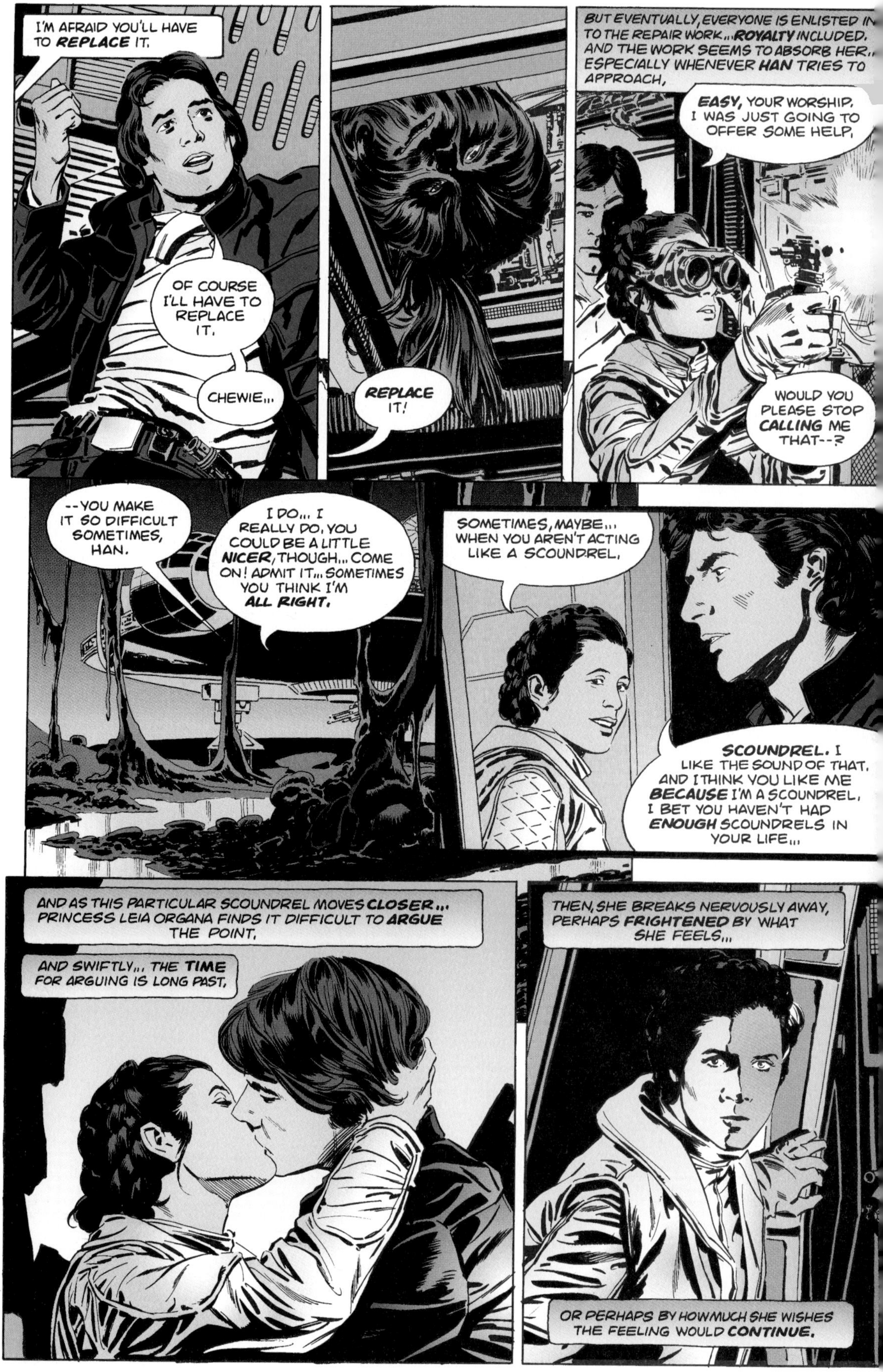
I'M AFRAID YOU'LL HAVE TO **REPLACE** IT.
OF COURSE I'LL HAVE TO REPLACE IT.
CHEWIE...
REPLACE IT!
BUT EVENTUALLY, EVERYONE IS ENLISTED INTO THE REPAIR WORK... **ROYALTY** INCLUDED. AND THE WORK SEEMS TO ABSORB HER... ESPECIALLY WHENEVER **HAN** TRIES TO APPROACH.
EASY, YOUR WORSHIP. I WAS JUST GOING TO OFFER SOME HELP.
WOULD YOU PLEASE STOP **CALLING** ME THAT--?
--YOU MAKE IT SO DIFFICULT SOMETIMES, HAN.
I DO... I REALLY DO. YOU COULD BE A LITTLE **NICER**, THOUGH... COME ON! ADMIT IT... SOMETIMES YOU THINK I'M **ALL RIGHT.**
SOMETIMES, MAYBE... WHEN YOU AREN'T ACTING LIKE A SCOUNDREL.
SCOUNDREL. I LIKE THE SOUND OF THAT. AND I THINK YOU LIKE ME **BECAUSE** I'M A SCOUNDREL. I BET YOU HAVEN'T HAD **ENOUGH** SCOUNDRELS IN YOUR LIFE...
AND AS THIS PARTICULAR SCOUNDREL MOVES **CLOSER**... PRINCESS LEIA ORGANA FINDS IT DIFFICULT TO **ARGUE** THE POINT.
AND SWIFTLY... THE **TIME** FOR ARGUING IS LONG PAST.
THEN, SHE BREAKS NERVOUSLY AWAY, PERHAPS **FRIGHTENED** BY WHAT SHE FEELS...
OR PERHAPS BY HOW MUCH SHE WISHES THE FEELING WOULD **CONTINUE.**

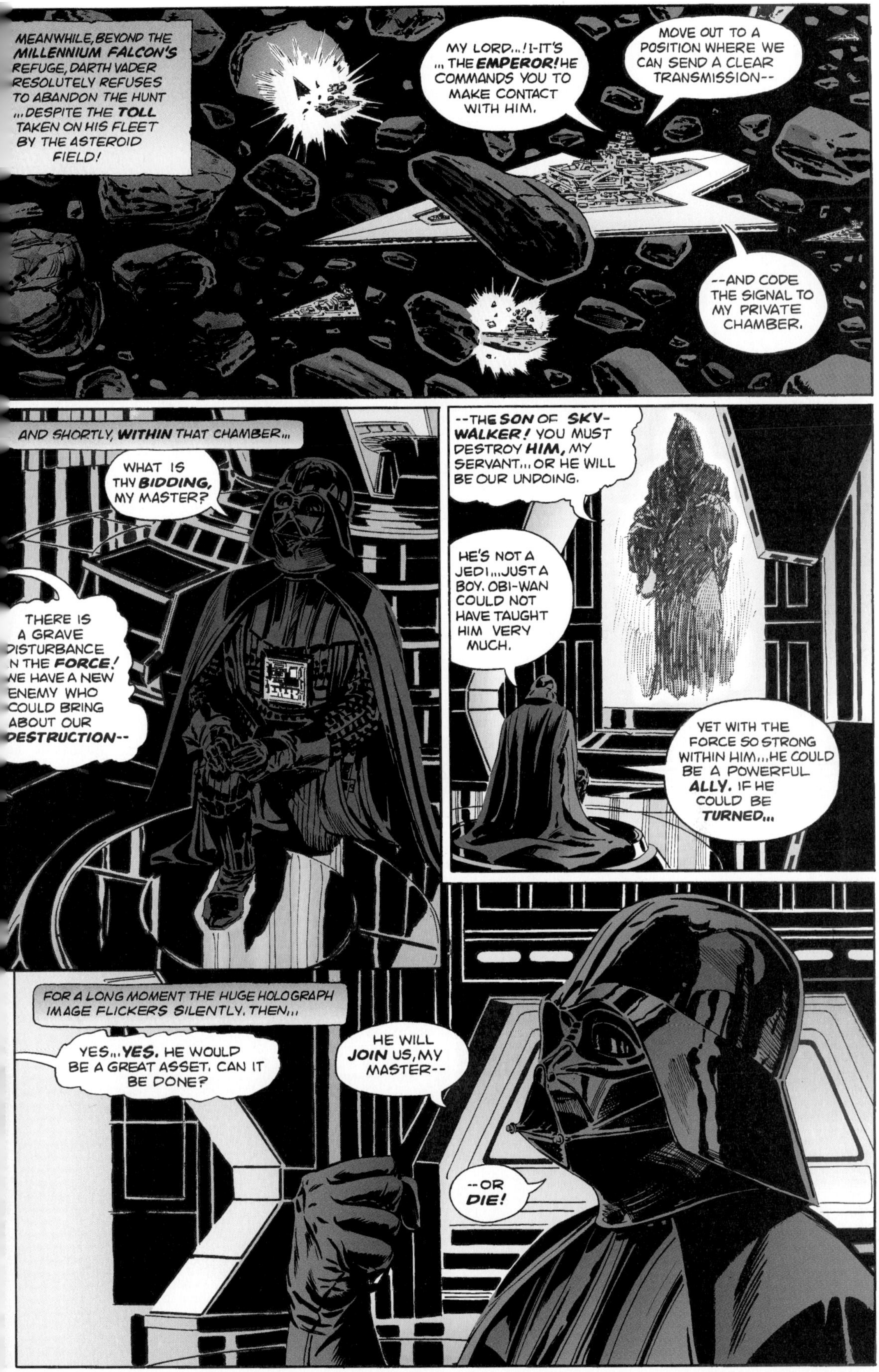
MEANWHILE, BEYOND THE MILLENNIUM FALCON'S REFUGE, DARTH VADER RESOLUTELY REFUSES TO ABANDON THE HUNT ...DESPITE THE TOLL TAKEN ON HIS FLEET BY THE ASTEROID FIELD!
MY LORD...! I-IT'S ... THE EMPEROR! HE COMMANDS YOU TO MAKE CONTACT WITH HIM.
MOVE OUT TO A POSITION WHERE WE CAN SEND A CLEAR TRANSMISSION--
--AND CODE THE SIGNAL TO MY PRIVATE CHAMBER.
AND SHORTLY, WITHIN THAT CHAMBER...
WHAT IS THY BIDDING, MY MASTER?
THERE IS A GRAVE DISTURBANCE IN THE FORCE! WE HAVE A NEW ENEMY WHO COULD BRING ABOUT OUR DESTRUCTION--
--THE SON OF SKYWALKER! YOU MUST DESTROY HIM, MY SERVANT... OR HE WILL BE OUR UNDOING.
HE'S NOT A JEDI... JUST A BOY. OBI-WAN COULD NOT HAVE TAUGHT HIM VERY MUCH.
YET WITH THE FORCE SO STRONG WITHIN HIM... HE COULD BE A POWERFUL ALLY. IF HE COULD BE TURNED...
FOR A LONG MOMENT THE HUGE HOLOGRAPH IMAGE FLICKERS SILENTLY. THEN...
YES... YES. HE WOULD BE A GREAT ASSET. CAN IT BE DONE?
HE WILL JOIN US, MY MASTER--
--OR DIE!

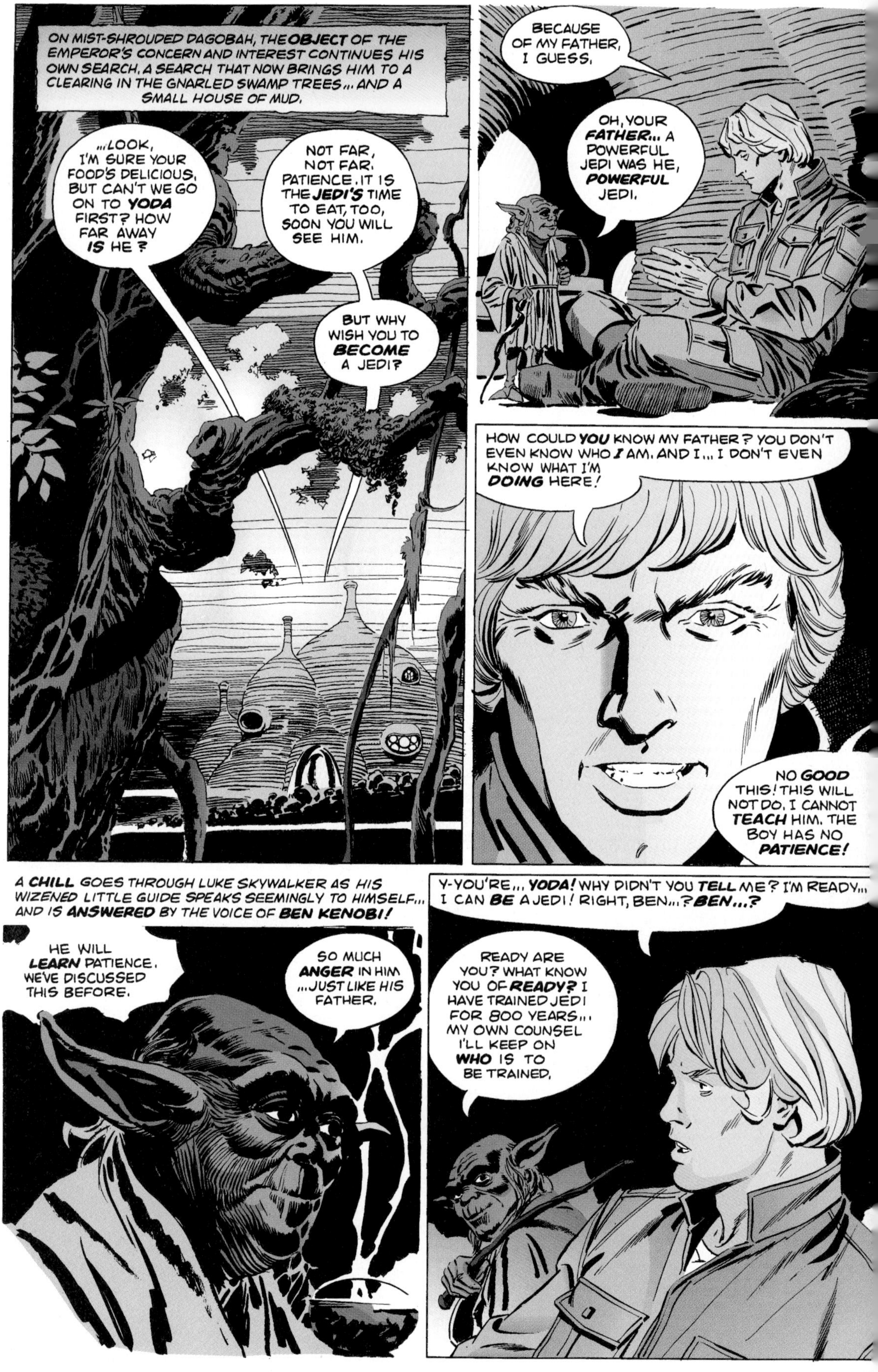
ON MIST-SHROUDED DAGOBAH, THE OBJECT OF THE EMPEROR'S CONCERN AND INTEREST CONTINUES HIS OWN SEARCH, A SEARCH THAT NOW BRINGS HIM TO A CLEARING IN THE GNARLED SWAMP TREES... AND A SMALL HOUSE OF MUD.
...LOOK, I'M SURE YOUR FOOD'S DELICIOUS, BUT CAN'T WE GO ON TO YODA FIRST? HOW FAR AWAY IS HE?
NOT FAR, NOT FAR. PATIENCE. IT IS THE JEDI'S TIME TO EAT, TOO. SOON YOU WILL SEE HIM.
BUT WHY WISH YOU TO BECOME A JEDI?
BECAUSE OF MY FATHER, I GUESS.
OH, YOUR FATHER... A POWERFUL JEDI WAS HE, POWERFUL JEDI.
HOW COULD YOU KNOW MY FATHER? YOU DON'T EVEN KNOW WHO I AM. AND I... I DON'T EVEN KNOW WHAT I'M DOING HERE!
NO GOOD THIS! THIS WILL NOT DO. I CANNOT TEACH HIM. THE BOY HAS NO PATIENCE!
A CHILL GOES THROUGH LUKE SKYWALKER AS HIS WIZENED LITTLE GUIDE SPEAKS SEEMINGLY TO HIMSELF... AND IS ANSWERED BY THE VOICE OF BEN KENOBI!
HE WILL LEARN PATIENCE. WE'VE DISCUSSED THIS BEFORE.
SO MUCH ANGER IN HIM ...JUST LIKE HIS FATHER.
Y-YOU'RE... YODA! WHY DIDN'T YOU TELL ME? I'M READY... I CAN BE A JEDI! RIGHT, BEN...? BEN...?
READY ARE YOU? WHAT KNOW YOU OF READY? I HAVE TRAINED JEDI FOR 800 YEARS... MY OWN COUNSEL I'LL KEEP ON WHO IS TO BE TRAINED.

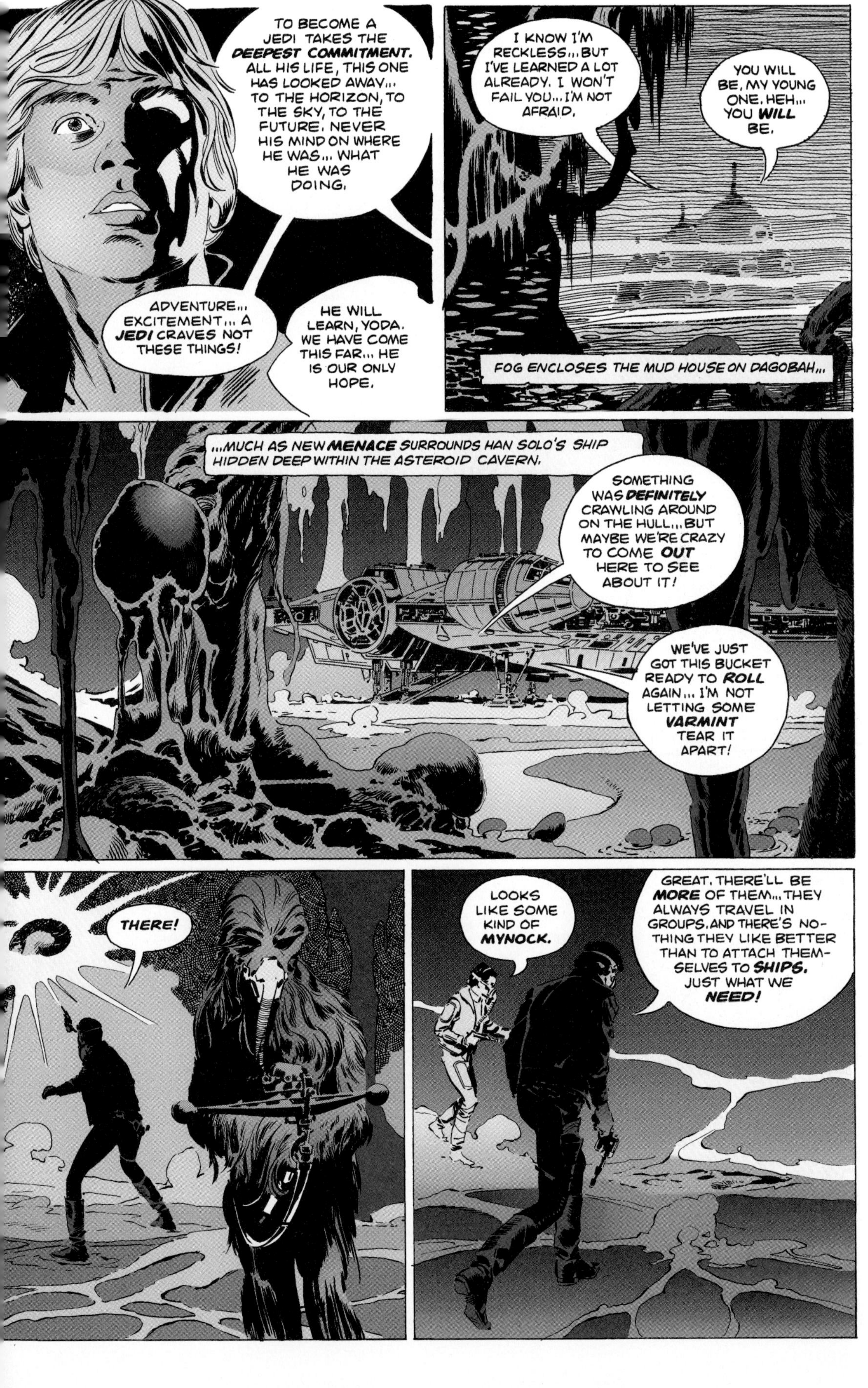

TO BECOME A JEDI TAKES THE DEEPEST COMMITMENT. ALL HIS LIFE, THIS ONE HAS LOOKED AWAY... TO THE HORIZON, TO THE SKY, TO THE FUTURE. NEVER HIS MIND ON WHERE HE WAS... WHAT HE WAS DOING.
ADVENTURE... EXCITEMENT... A JEDI CRAVES NOT THESE THINGS!
HE WILL LEARN, YODA. WE HAVE COME THIS FAR... HE IS OUR ONLY HOPE.
I KNOW I'M RECKLESS... BUT I'VE LEARNED A LOT ALREADY. I WON'T FAIL YOU... I'M NOT AFRAID.
YOU WILL BE, MY YOUNG ONE. HEH... YOU WILL BE.
FOG ENCLOSES THE MUD HOUSE ON DAGOBAH...
...MUCH AS NEW MENACE SURROUNDS HAN SOLO'S SHIP HIDDEN DEEP WITHIN THE ASTEROID CAVERN.
SOMETHING WAS DEFINITELY CRAWLING AROUND ON THE HULL... BUT MAYBE WE'RE CRAZY TO COME OUT HERE TO SEE ABOUT IT!
WE'VE JUST GOT THIS BUCKET READY TO ROLL AGAIN... I'M NOT LETTING SOME VARMINT TEAR IT APART!
THERE!
LOOKS LIKE SOME KIND OF MYNOCK.
GREAT. THERE'LL BE MORE OF THEM... THEY ALWAYS TRAVEL IN GROUPS. AND THERE'S NOTHING THEY LIKE BETTER THAN TO ATTACH THEMSELVES TO SHIPS. JUST WHAT WE NEED!

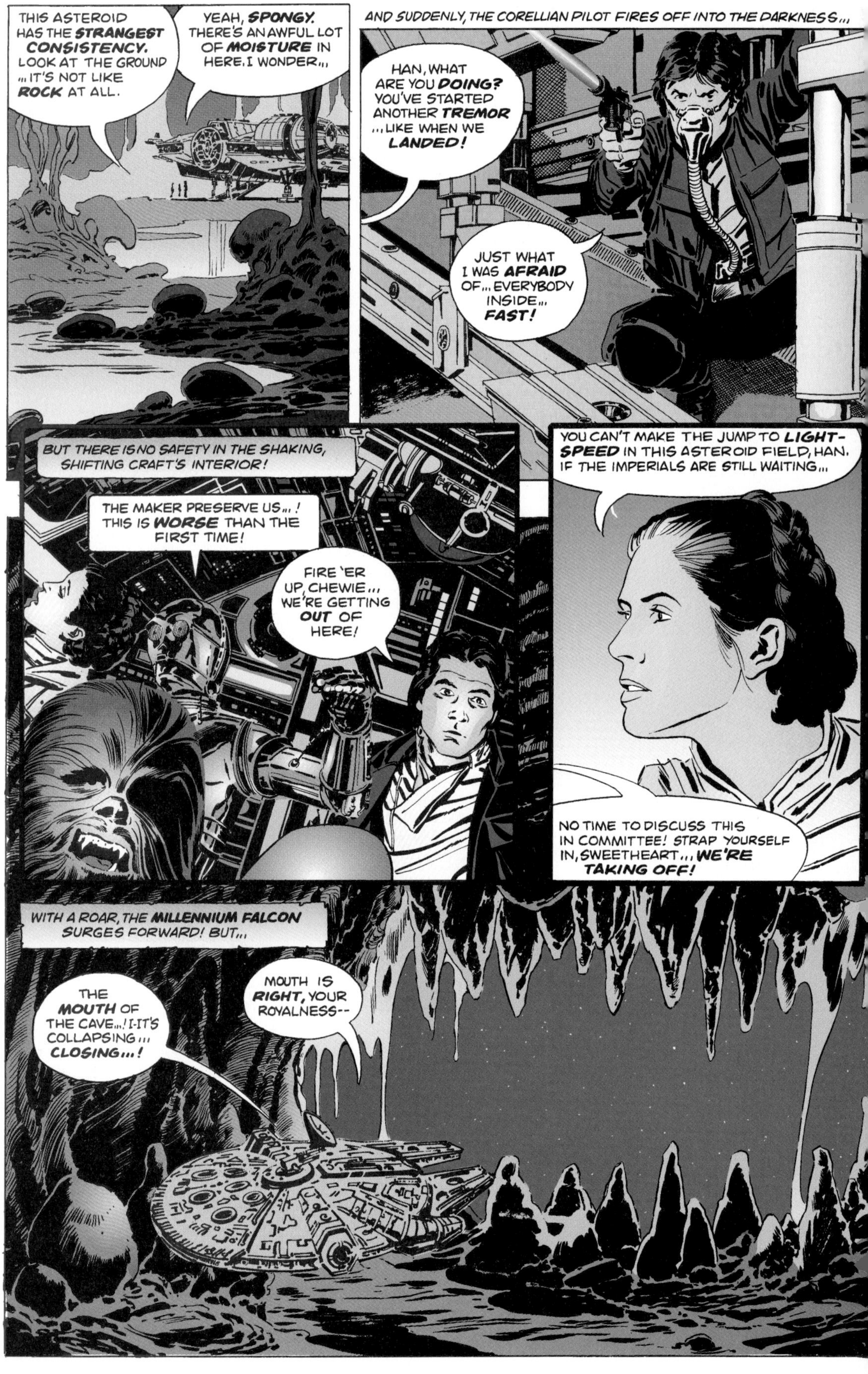
THIS ASTEROID HAS THE STRANGEST CONSISTENCY. LOOK AT THE GROUND ...IT'S NOT LIKE ROCK AT ALL.
YEAH, SPONGY. THERE'S AN AWFUL LOT OF MOISTURE IN HERE. I WONDER...
AND SUDDENLY, THE CORELLIAN PILOT FIRES OFF INTO THE DARKNESS...
HAN, WHAT ARE YOU DOING? YOU'VE STARTED ANOTHER TREMOR ...LIKE WHEN WE LANDED!
JUST WHAT I WAS AFRAID OF... EVERYBODY INSIDE... FAST!
BUT THERE IS NO SAFETY IN THE SHAKING, SHIFTING CRAFT'S INTERIOR!
THE MAKER PRESERVE US...! THIS IS WORSE THAN THE FIRST TIME!
FIRE 'ER UP, CHEWIE... WE'RE GETTING OUT OF HERE!
YOU CAN'T MAKE THE JUMP TO LIGHT-SPEED IN THIS ASTEROID FIELD, HAN. IF THE IMPERIALS ARE STILL WAITING...
NO TIME TO DISCUSS THIS IN COMMITTEE! STRAP YOURSELF IN, SWEETHEART... WE'RE TAKING OFF!
WITH A ROAR, THE MILLENNIUM FALCON SURGES FORWARD! BUT...
THE MOUTH OF THE CAVE...! I-IT'S COLLAPSING... CLOSING...!
MOUTH IS RIGHT, YOUR ROYALNESS--

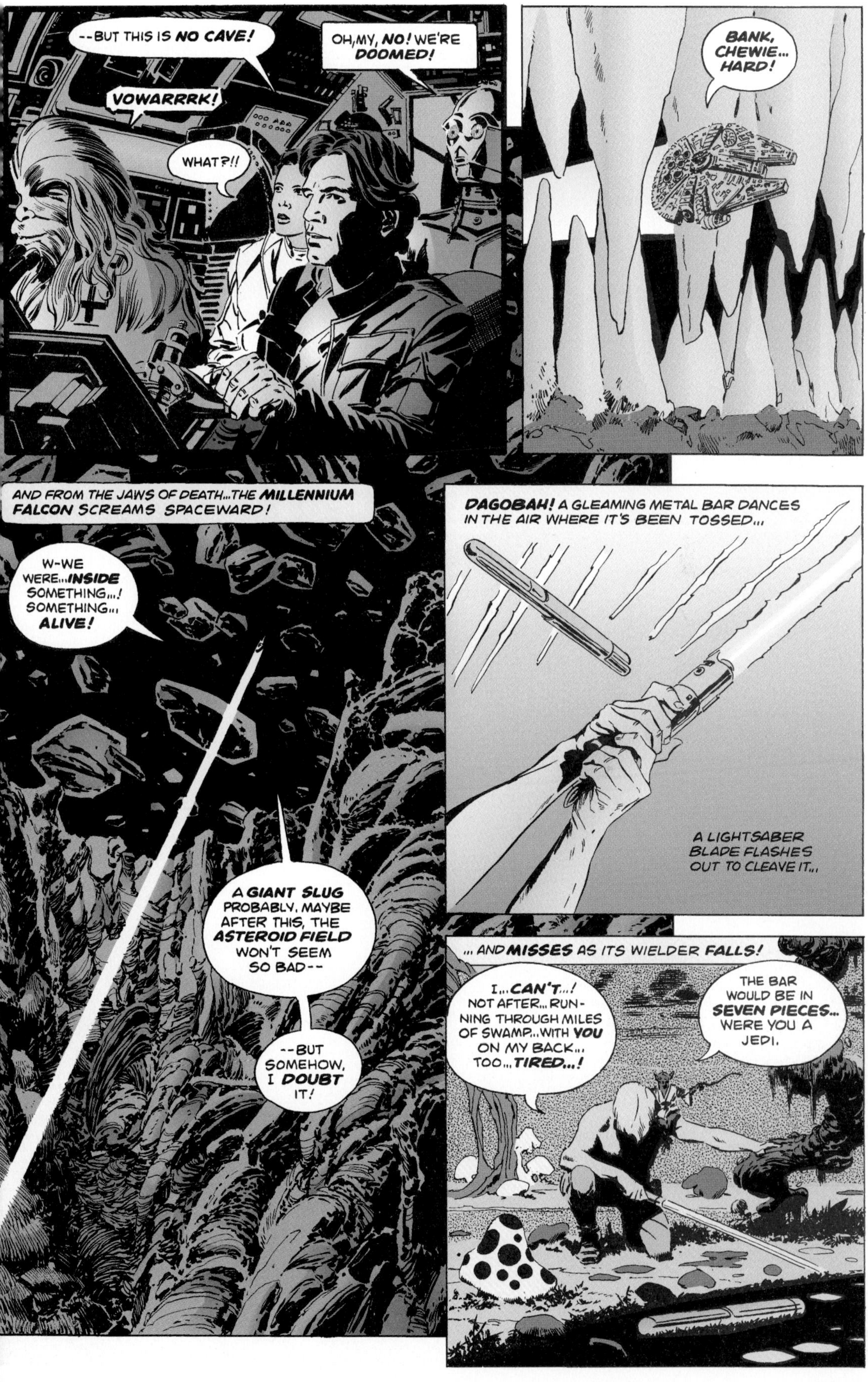
--BUT THIS IS NO CAVE!
OH, MY, NO! WE'RE DOOMED!
VOWARRRK!
WHAT?!!
BANK, CHEWIE... HARD!
AND FROM THE JAWS OF DEATH... THE MILLENNIUM FALCON SCREAMS SPACEWARD!
W-WE WERE... INSIDE SOMETHING...! SOMETHING... ALIVE!
A GIANT SLUG PROBABLY. MAYBE AFTER THIS, THE ASTEROID FIELD WON'T SEEM SO BAD--
--BUT SOMEHOW, I DOUBT IT!
DAGOBAH! A GLEAMING METAL BAR DANCES IN THE AIR WHERE IT'S BEEN TOSSED...
A LIGHTSABER BLADE FLASHES OUT TO CLEAVE IT...
... AND MISSES AS ITS WIELDER FALLS!
I... CAN'T...! NOT AFTER... RUNNING THROUGH MILES OF SWAMP... WITH YOU ON MY BACK... TOO... TIRED...!
THE BAR WOULD BE IN SEVEN PIECES... WERE YOU A JEDI.

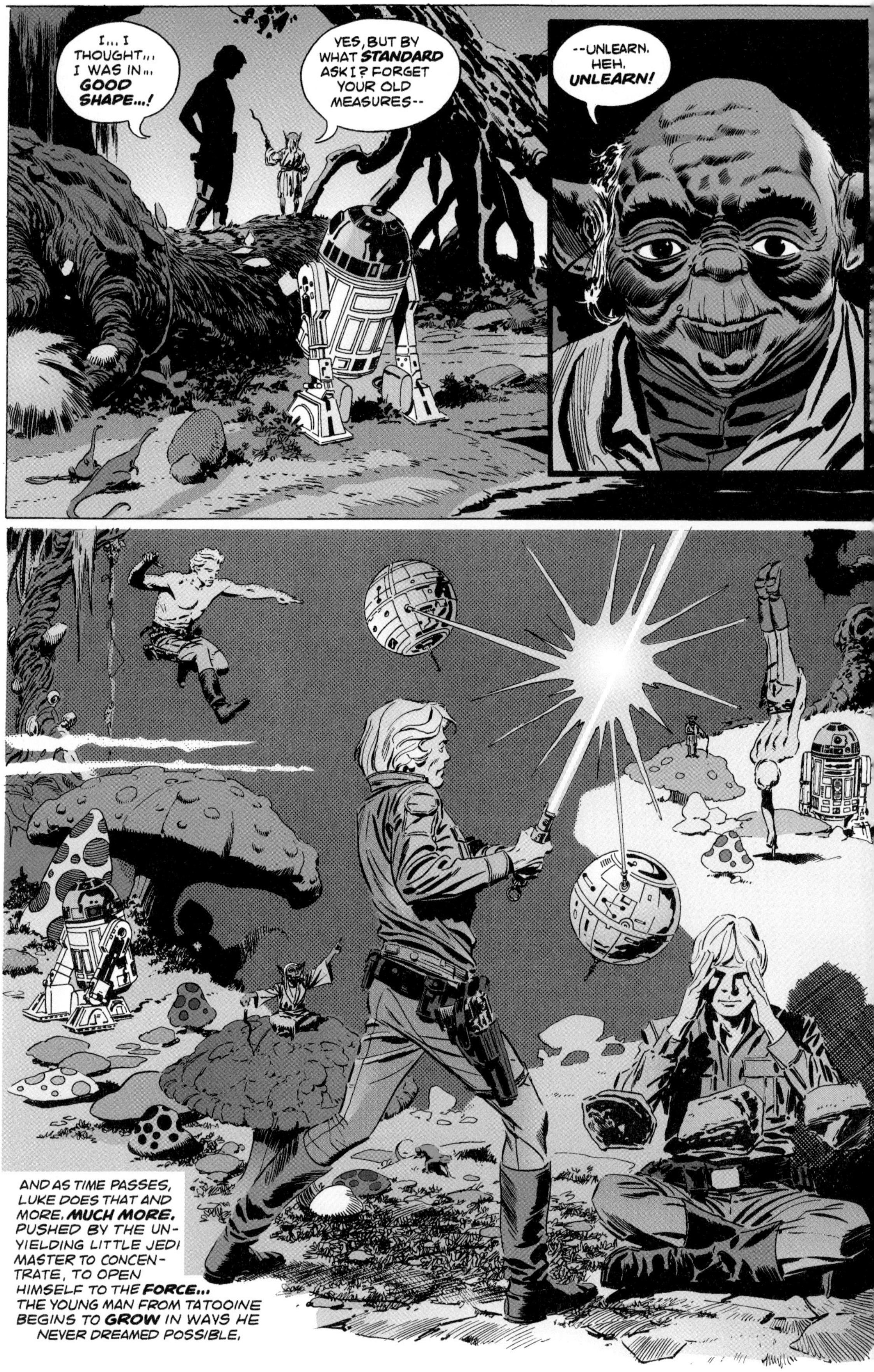
I... I THOUGHT... I WAS IN... GOOD SHAPE...!
YES, BUT BY WHAT STANDARD ASK I? FORGET YOUR OLD MEASURES--
--UNLEARN. HEH. UNLEARN!
AND AS TIME PASSES, LUKE DOES THAT AND MORE. MUCH MORE. PUSHED BY THE UNYIELDING LITTLE JEDI MASTER TO CONCENTRATE, TO OPEN HIMSELF TO THE FORCE... THE YOUNG MAN FROM TATOOINE BEGINS TO GROW IN WAYS HE NEVER DREAMED POSSIBLE.

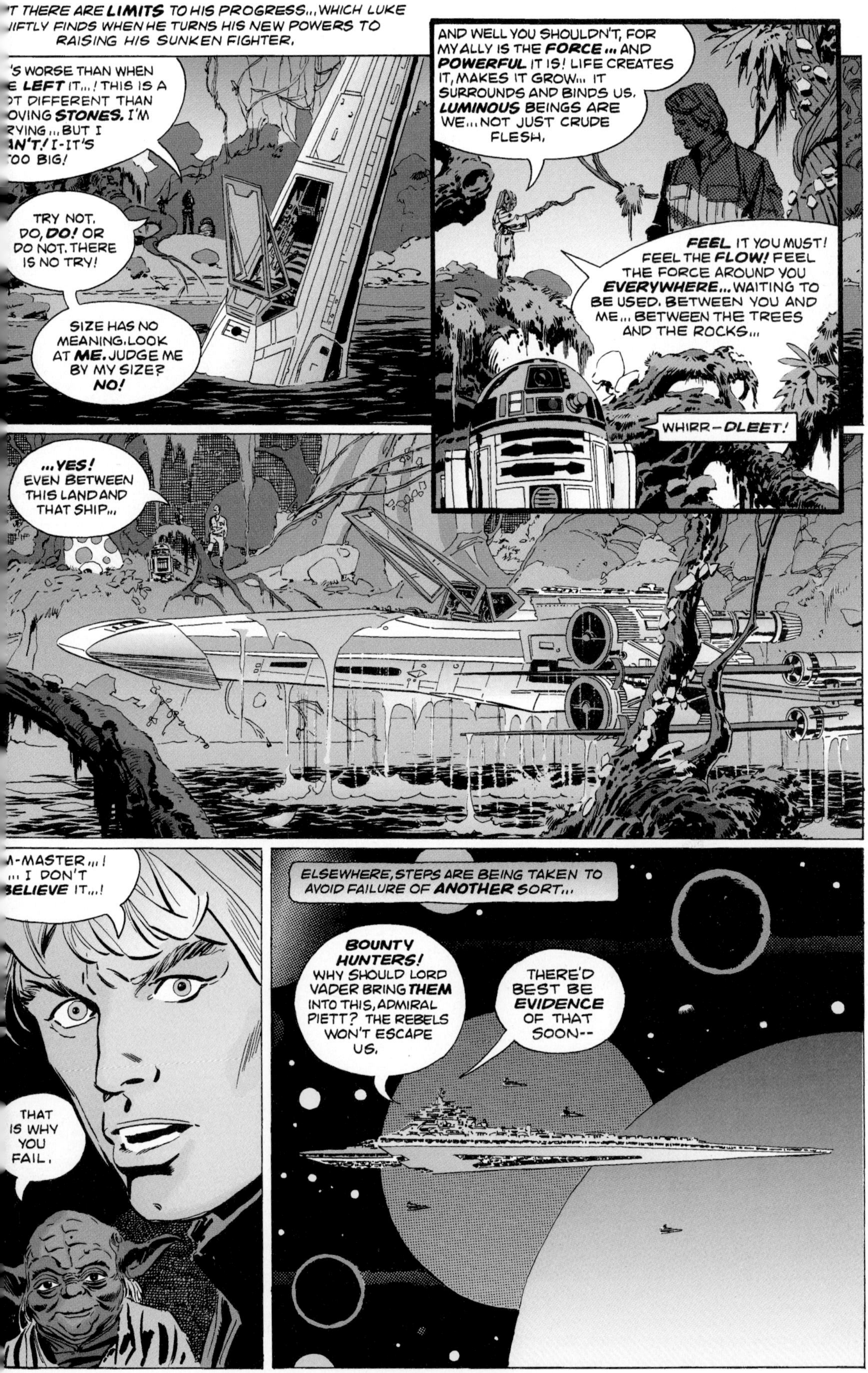

'T THERE ARE LIMITS TO HIS PROGRESS... WHICH LUKE
IIFTLY FINDS WHEN HE TURNS HIS NEW POWERS TO
RAISING HIS SUNKEN FIGHTER.
'S WORSE THAN WHEN
E LEFT IT...! THIS IS A
OT DIFFERENT THAN
OVING STONES. I'M
RYING... BUT I
AN'T! I-IT'S
OO BIG!
TRY NOT. DO, DO! OR DO NOT. THERE IS NO TRY!
SIZE HAS NO MEANING. LOOK AT ME. JUDGE ME BY MY SIZE? NO!
AND WELL YOU SHOULDN'T, FOR MY ALLY IS THE FORCE... AND POWERFUL IT IS! LIFE CREATES IT, MAKES IT GROW... IT SURROUNDS AND BINDS US. LUMINOUS BEINGS ARE WE... NOT JUST CRUDE FLESH.
FEEL IT YOU MUST! FEEL THE FLOW! FEEL THE FORCE AROUND YOU EVERYWHERE... WAITING TO BE USED. BETWEEN YOU AND ME... BETWEEN THE TREES AND THE ROCKS...
WHIRR-DLEET!
...YES! EVEN BETWEEN THIS LAND AND THAT SHIP...
I-MASTER...!
... I DON'T
BELIEVE IT...!
THAT IS WHY YOU FAIL.
ELSEWHERE, STEPS ARE BEING TAKEN TO AVOID FAILURE OF ANOTHER SORT...
BOUNTY HUNTERS! WHY SHOULD LORD VADER BRING THEM INTO THIS, ADMIRAL PIETT? THE REBELS WON'T ESCAPE US.
THERE'D BEST BE EVIDENCE OF THAT SOON--

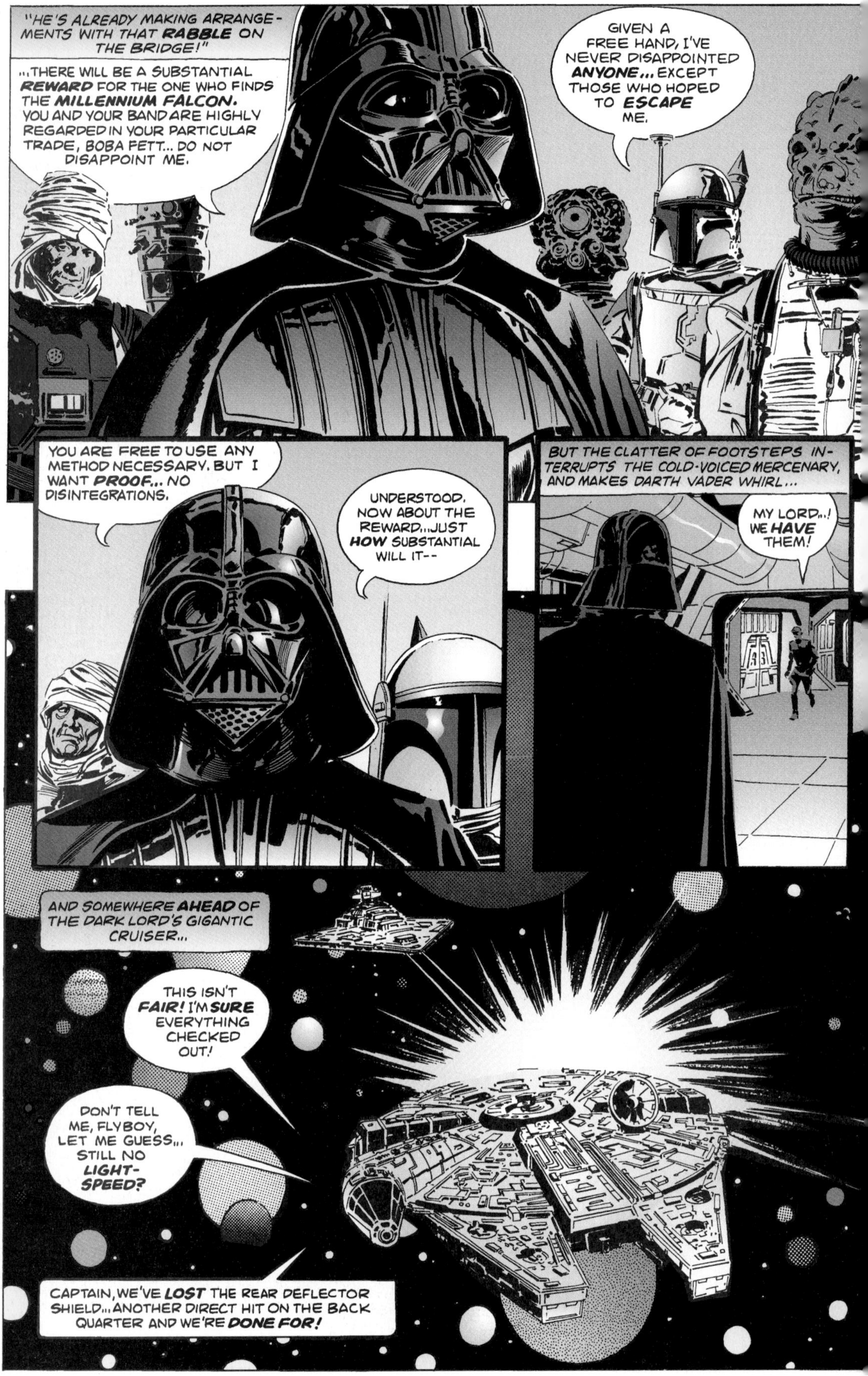

"HE'S ALREADY MAKING ARRANGEMENTS WITH THAT RABBLE ON THE BRIDGE!"
...THERE WILL BE A SUBSTANTIAL REWARD FOR THE ONE WHO FINDS THE MILLENNIUM FALCON. YOU AND YOUR BAND ARE HIGHLY REGARDED IN YOUR PARTICULAR TRADE, BOBA FETT... DO NOT DISAPPOINT ME.
GIVEN A FREE HAND, I'VE NEVER DISAPPOINTED ANYONE... EXCEPT THOSE WHO HOPED TO ESCAPE ME.
YOU ARE FREE TO USE ANY METHOD NECESSARY. BUT I WANT PROOF... NO DISINTEGRATIONS.
UNDERSTOOD. NOW ABOUT THE REWARD...JUST HOW SUBSTANTIAL WILL IT--
BUT THE CLATTER OF FOOTSTEPS INTERRUPTS THE COLD-VOICED MERCENARY, AND MAKES DARTH VADER WHIRL...
MY LORD...! WE HAVE THEM!
AND SOMEWHERE AHEAD OF THE DARK LORD'S GIGANTIC CRUISER...
THIS ISN'T FAIR! I'M SURE EVERYTHING CHECKED OUT!
DON'T TELL ME, FLYBOY, LET ME GUESS... STILL NO LIGHT-SPEED?
CAPTAIN, WE'VE LOST THE REAR DEFLECTOR SHIELD... ANOTHER DIRECT HIT ON THE BACK QUARTER AND WE'RE DONE FOR!

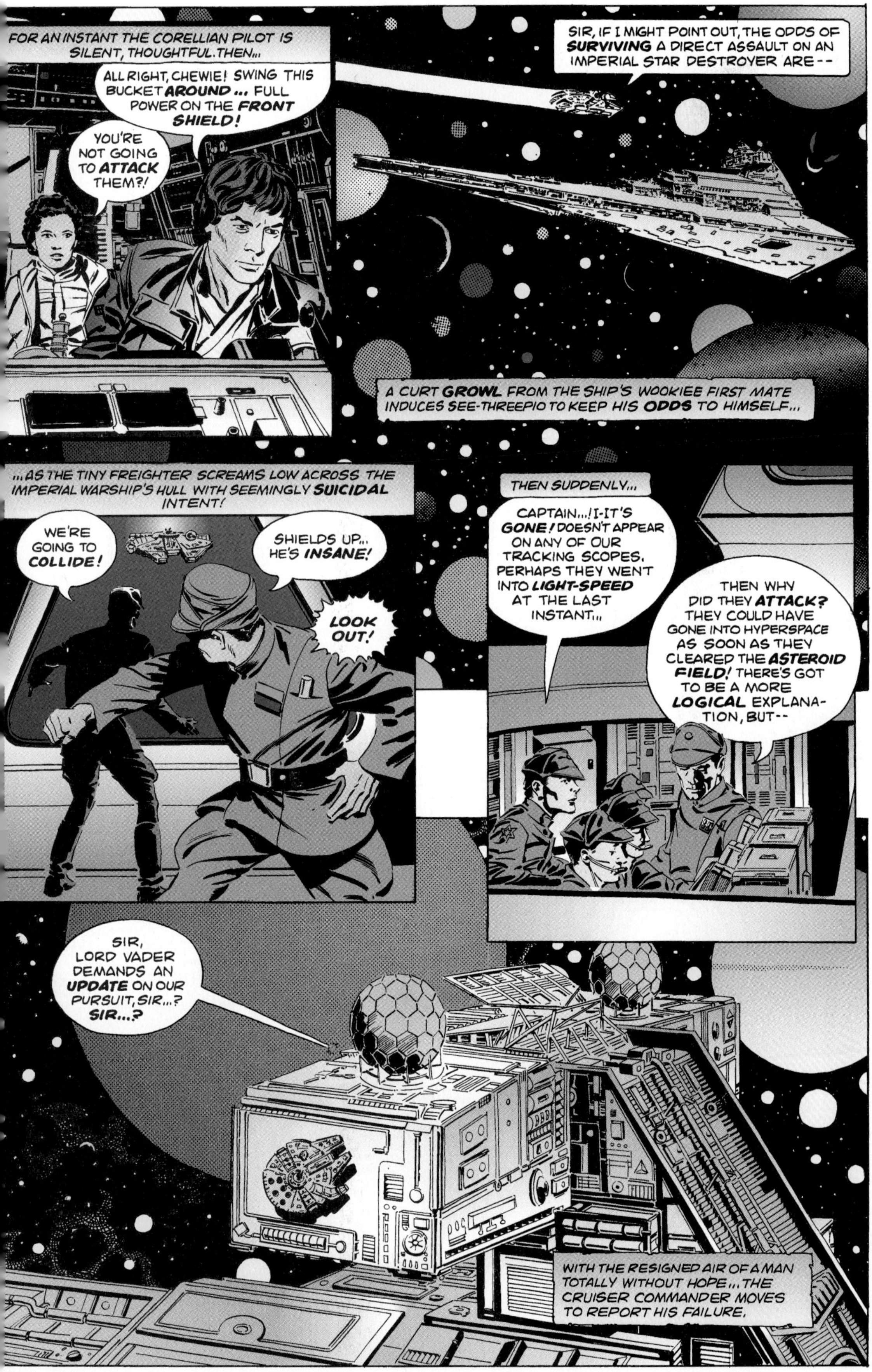
FOR AN INSTANT THE CORELLIAN PILOT IS SILENT, THOUGHTFUL. THEN...
ALL RIGHT, CHEWIE! SWING THIS BUCKET AROUND... FULL POWER ON THE FRONT SHIELD!
YOU'RE NOT GOING TO ATTACK THEM?!
SIR, IF I MIGHT POINT OUT, THE ODDS OF SURVIVING A DIRECT ASSAULT ON AN IMPERIAL STAR DESTROYER ARE--
A CURT GROWL FROM THE SHIP'S WOOKIEE FIRST MATE INDUCES SEE-THREEPIO TO KEEP HIS ODDS TO HIMSELF...
...AS THE TINY FREIGHTER SCREAMS LOW ACROSS THE IMPERIAL WARSHIP'S HULL WITH SEEMINGLY SUICIDAL INTENT!
WE'RE GOING TO COLLIDE!
SHIELDS UP... HE'S INSANE!
LOOK OUT!
THEN SUDDENLY...
CAPTAIN...! I-IT'S GONE! DOESN'T APPEAR ON ANY OF OUR TRACKING SCOPES. PERHAPS THEY WENT INTO LIGHT-SPEED AT THE LAST INSTANT...
THEN WHY DID THEY ATTACK? THEY COULD HAVE GONE INTO HYPERSPACE AS SOON AS THEY CLEARED THE ASTEROID FIELD! THERE'S GOT TO BE A MORE LOGICAL EXPLANATION, BUT--
SIR, LORD VADER DEMANDS AN UPDATE ON OUR PURSUIT, SIR...? SIR...?
WITH THE RESIGNED AIR OF A MAN TOTALLY WITHOUT HOPE... THE CRUISER COMMANDER MOVES TO REPORT HIS FAILURE.

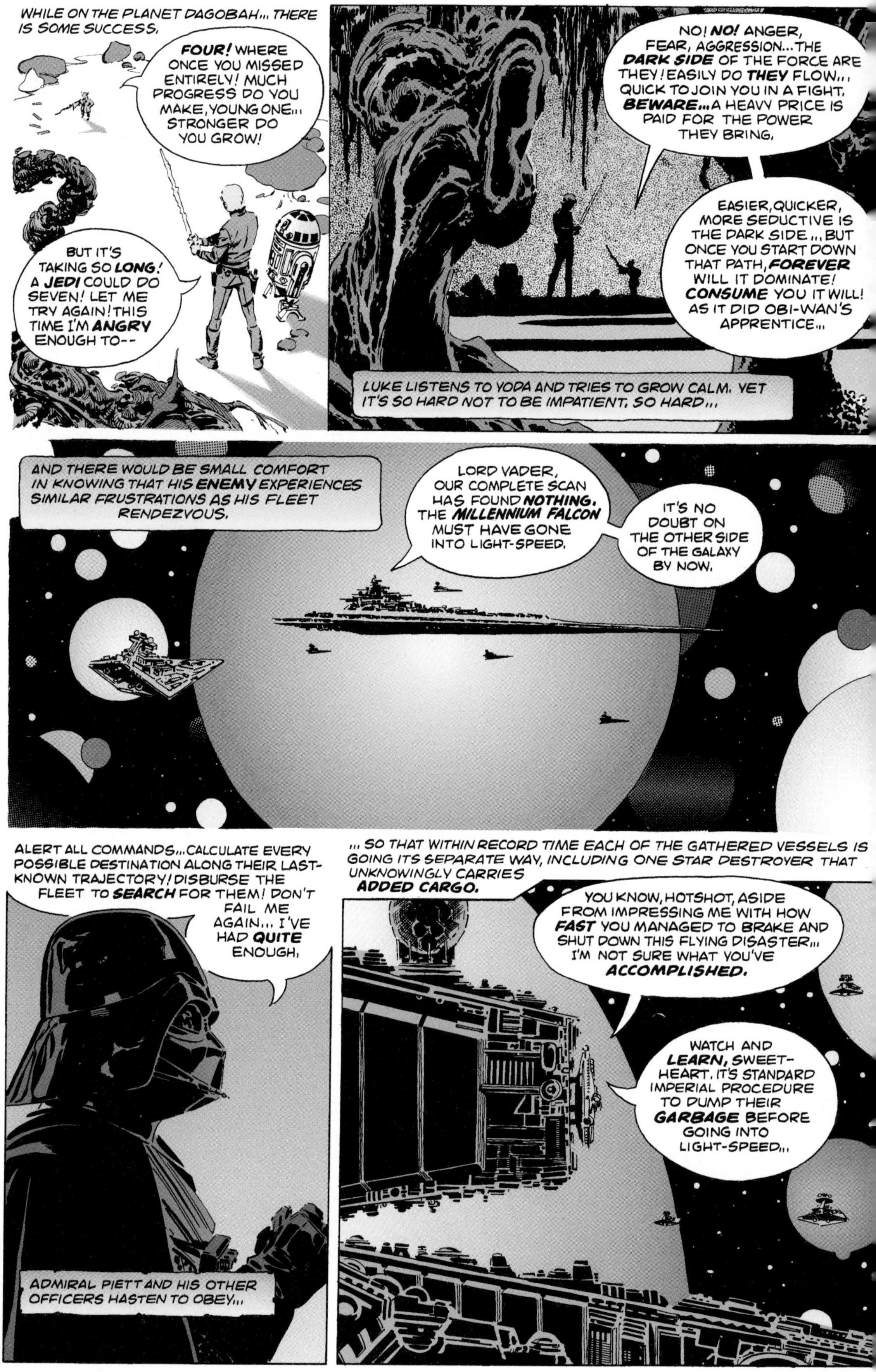
WHILE ON THE PLANET DAGOBAH... THERE IS SOME SUCCESS.
FOUR! WHERE ONCE YOU MISSED ENTIRELY! MUCH PROGRESS DO YOU MAKE, YOUNG ONE... STRONGER DO YOU GROW!
BUT IT'S TAKING SO LONG! A JEDI COULD DO SEVEN! LET ME TRY AGAIN! THIS TIME I'M ANGRY ENOUGH TO--
NO! NO! ANGER, FEAR, AGGRESSION...THE DARK SIDE OF THE FORCE ARE THEY! EASILY DO THEY FLOW... QUICK TO JOIN YOU IN A FIGHT. BEWARE...A HEAVY PRICE IS PAID FOR THE POWER THEY BRING.
EASIER, QUICKER, MORE SEDUCTIVE IS THE DARK SIDE... BUT ONCE YOU START DOWN THAT PATH, FOREVER WILL IT DOMINATE! CONSUME YOU IT WILL! AS IT DID OBI-WAN'S APPRENTICE...
LUKE LISTENS TO YODA AND TRIES TO GROW CALM. YET IT'S SO HARD NOT TO BE IMPATIENT. SO HARD...
AND THERE WOULD BE SMALL COMFORT IN KNOWING THAT HIS ENEMY EXPERIENCES SIMILAR FRUSTRATIONS AS HIS FLEET RENDEZVOUS.
LORD VADER, OUR COMPLETE SCAN HAS FOUND NOTHING. THE MILLENNIUM FALCON MUST HAVE GONE INTO LIGHT-SPEED.
IT'S NO DOUBT ON THE OTHER SIDE OF THE GALAXY BY NOW.
ALERT ALL COMMANDS...CALCULATE EVERY POSSIBLE DESTINATION ALONG THEIR LAST-KNOWN TRAJECTORY! DISBURSE THE FLEET TO SEARCH FOR THEM! DON'T FAIL ME AGAIN... I'VE HAD QUITE ENOUGH.
ADMIRAL PIETT AND HIS OTHER OFFICERS HASTEN TO OBEY...
... SO THAT WITHIN RECORD TIME EACH OF THE GATHERED VESSELS IS GOING ITS SEPARATE WAY, INCLUDING ONE STAR DESTROYER THAT UNKNOWINGLY CARRIES ADDED CARGO.
YOU KNOW, HOTSHOT, ASIDE FROM IMPRESSING ME WITH HOW FAST YOU MANAGED TO BRAKE AND SHUT DOWN THIS FLYING DISASTER... I'M NOT SURE WHAT YOU'VE ACCOMPLISHED.
WATCH AND LEARN, SWEET-HEART. IT'S STANDARD IMPERIAL PROCEDURE TO DUMP THEIR GARBAGE BEFORE GOING INTO LIGHT-SPEED...

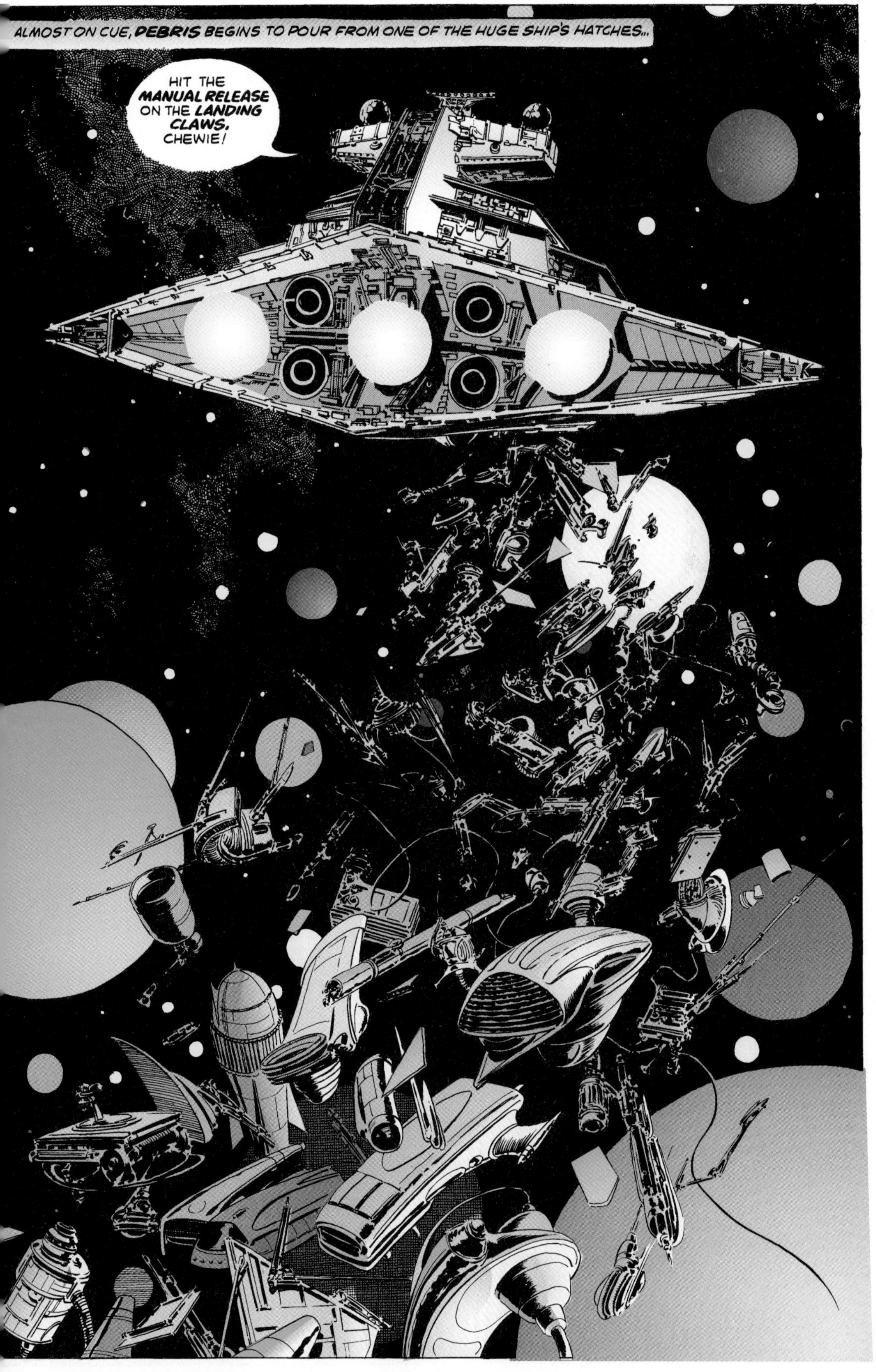
ALMOST ON CUE, DEBRIS BEGINS TO POUR FROM ONE OF THE HUGE SHIP'S HATCHES...
HIT THE MANUAL RELEASE ON THE LANDING CLAWS, CHEWIE!

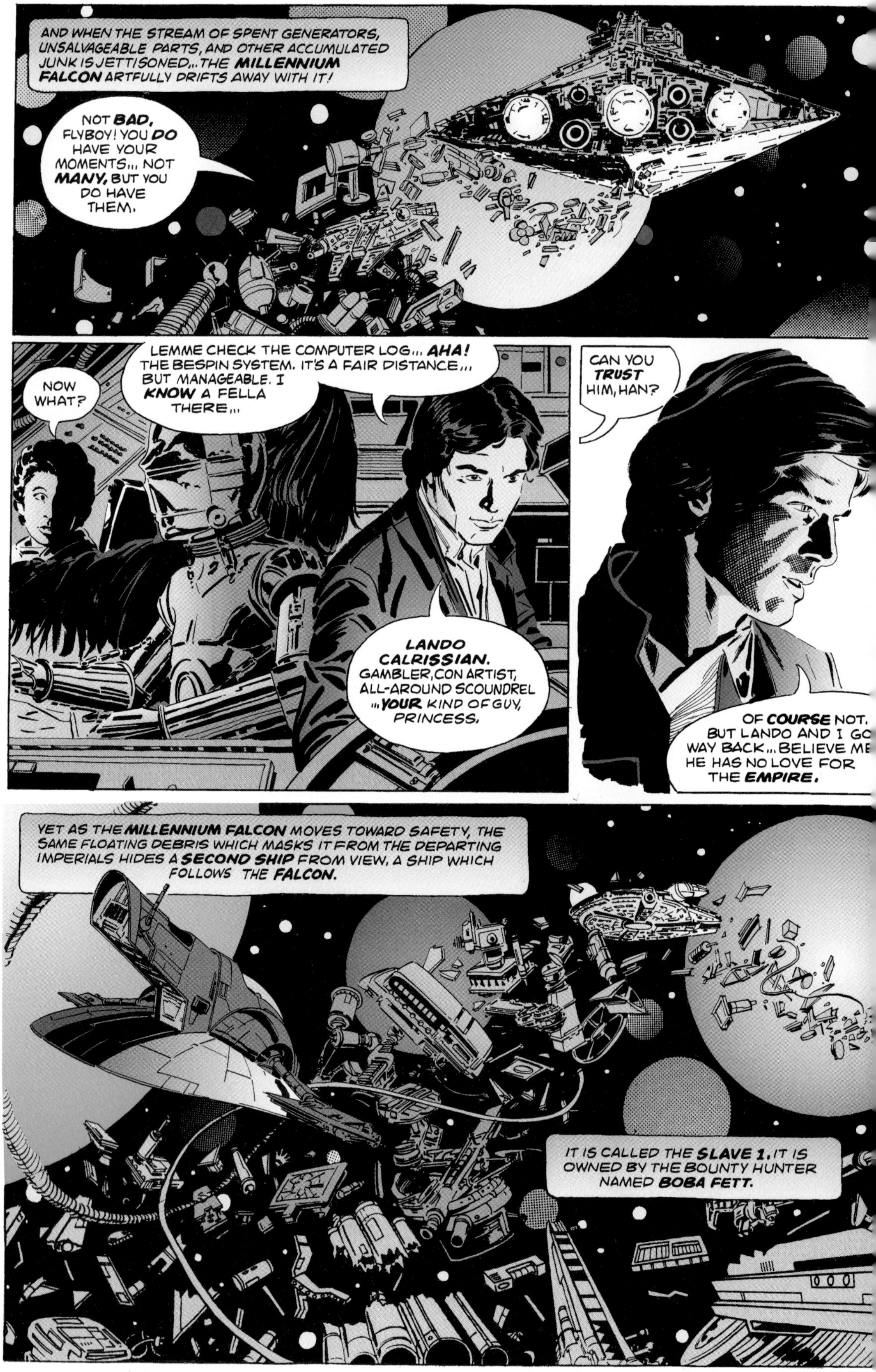
AND WHEN THE STREAM OF SPENT GENERATORS, UNSALVAGEABLE PARTS, AND OTHER ACCUMULATED JUNK IS JETTISONED... THE MILLENNIUM FALCON ARTFULLY DRIFTS AWAY WITH IT!
NOT BAD, FLYBOY! YOU DO HAVE YOUR MOMENTS... NOT MANY, BUT YOU DO HAVE THEM.
NOW WHAT?
LEMME CHECK THE COMPUTER LOG... AHA! THE BESPIN SYSTEM. IT'S A FAIR DISTANCE... BUT MANAGEABLE. I KNOW A FELLA THERE...
LANDO CALRISSIAN. GAMBLER, CON ARTIST, ALL-AROUND SCOUNDREL ...YOUR KIND OF GUY, PRINCESS.
CAN YOU TRUST HIM, HAN?
OF COURSE NOT. BUT LANDO AND I GO WAY BACK... BELIEVE ME HE HAS NO LOVE FOR THE EMPIRE.
YET AS THE MILLENNIUM FALCON MOVES TOWARD SAFETY, THE SAME FLOATING DEBRIS WHICH MASKS IT FROM THE DEPARTING IMPERIALS HIDES A SECOND SHIP FROM VIEW, A SHIP WHICH FOLLOWS THE FALCON.
IT IS CALLED THE SLAVE 1. IT IS OWNED BY THE BOUNTY HUNTER NAMED BOBA FETT.

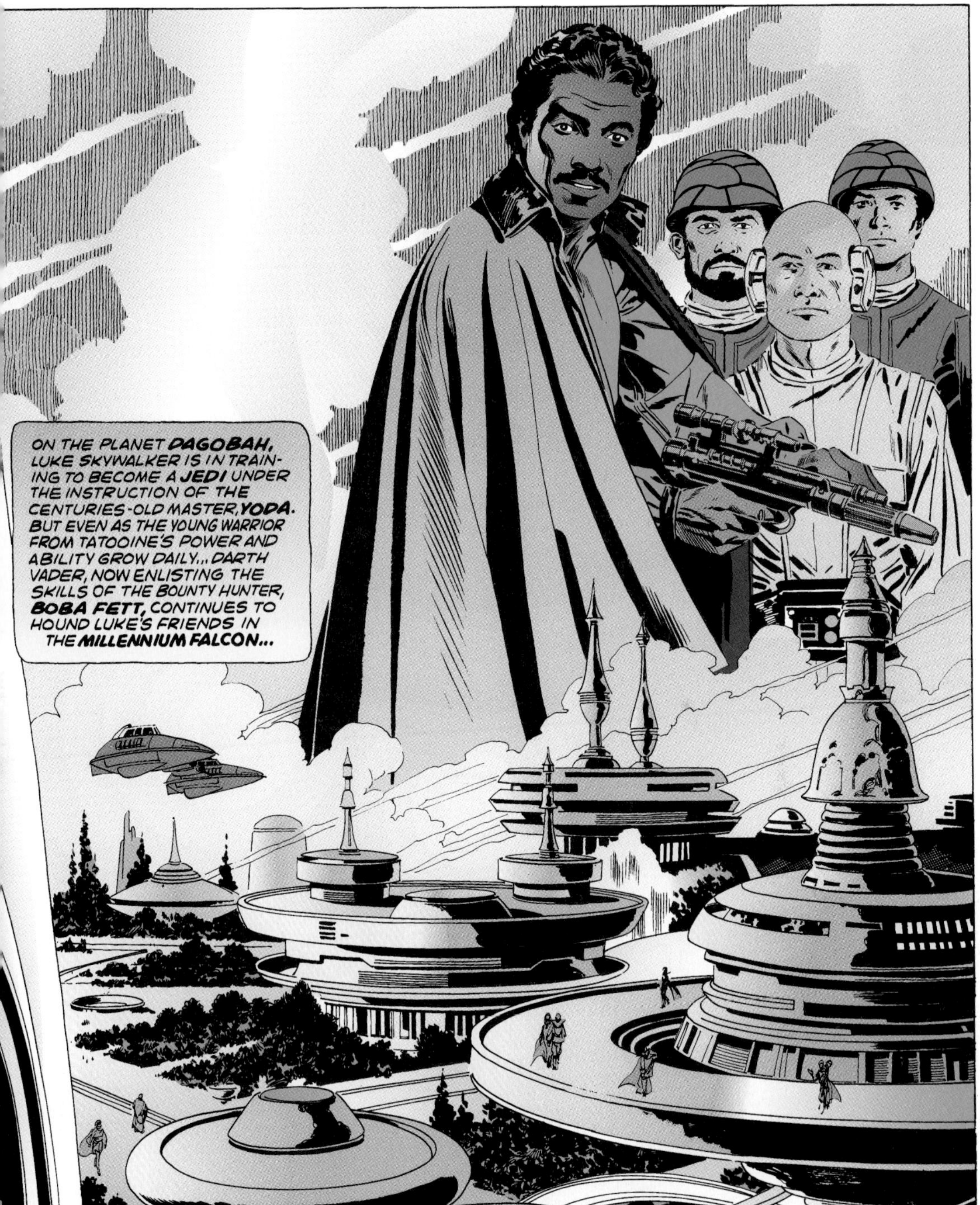
ON THE PLANET DAGOBAH, LUKE SKYWALKER IS IN TRAINING TO BECOME A JEDI UNDER THE INSTRUCTION OF THE CENTURIES-OLD MASTER, YODA. BUT EVEN AS THE YOUNG WARRIOR FROM TATOOINE'S POWER AND ABILITY GROW DAILY... DARTH VADER, NOW ENLISTING THE SKILLS OF THE BOUNTY HUNTER, BOBA FETT, CONTINUES TO HOUND LUKE'S FRIENDS IN THE MILLENNIUM FALCON...

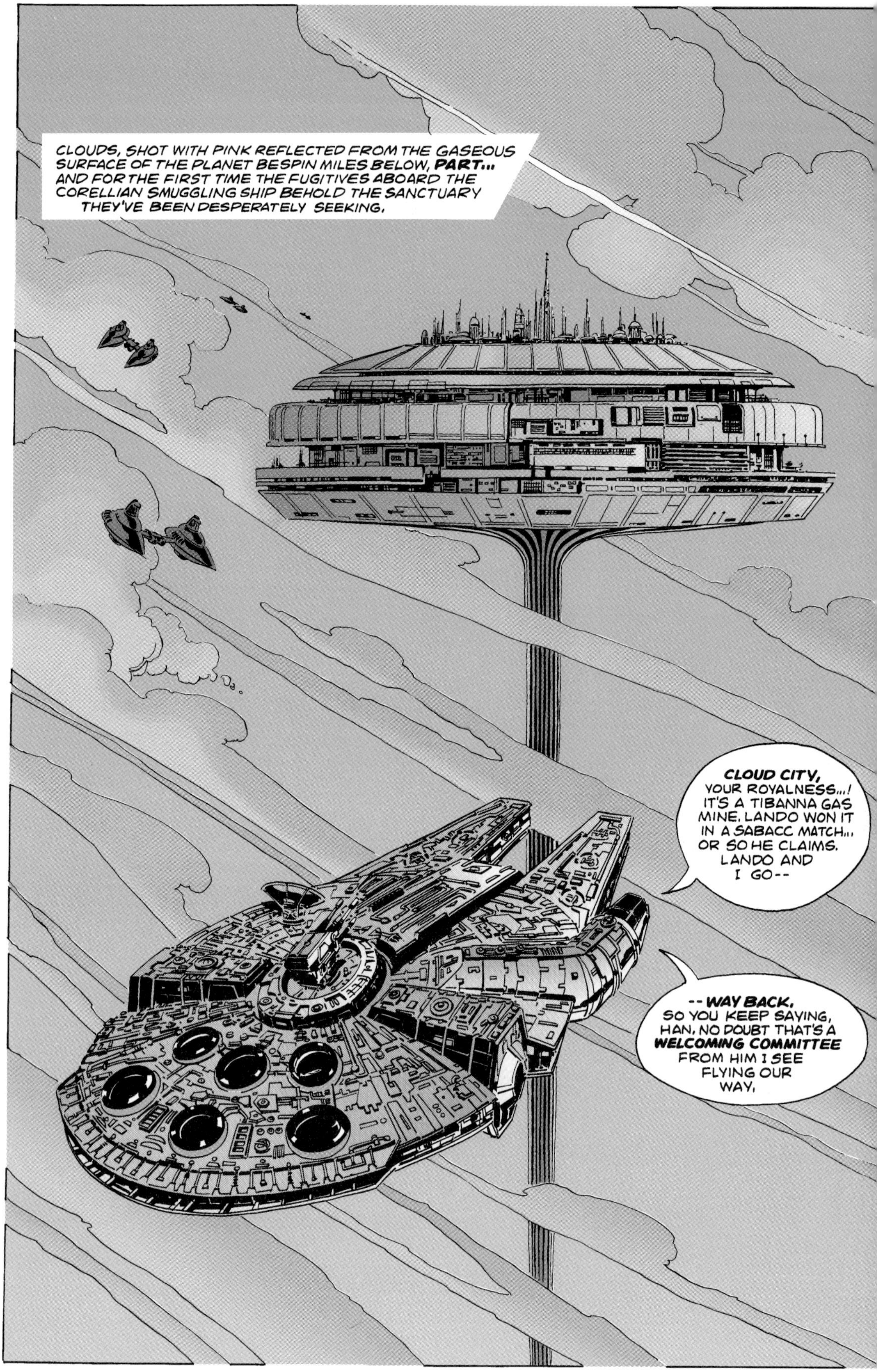
CLOUDS, SHOT WITH PINK REFLECTED FROM THE GASEOUS SURFACE OF THE PLANET BESPIN MILES BELOW, **PART...** AND FOR THE FIRST TIME THE FUGITIVES ABOARD THE CORELLIAN SMUGGLING SHIP BEHOLD THE SANCTUARY THEY'VE BEEN DESPERATELY SEEKING.
CLOUD CITY, YOUR ROYALNESS...! IT'S A TIBANNA GAS MINE. LANDO WON IT IN A SABACC MATCH... OR SO HE CLAIMS. LANDO AND I GO--
--WAY BACK. SO YOU KEEP SAYING, HAN. NO DOUBT THAT'S A **WELCOMING COMMITTEE** FROM HIM I SEE FLYING OUR WAY.

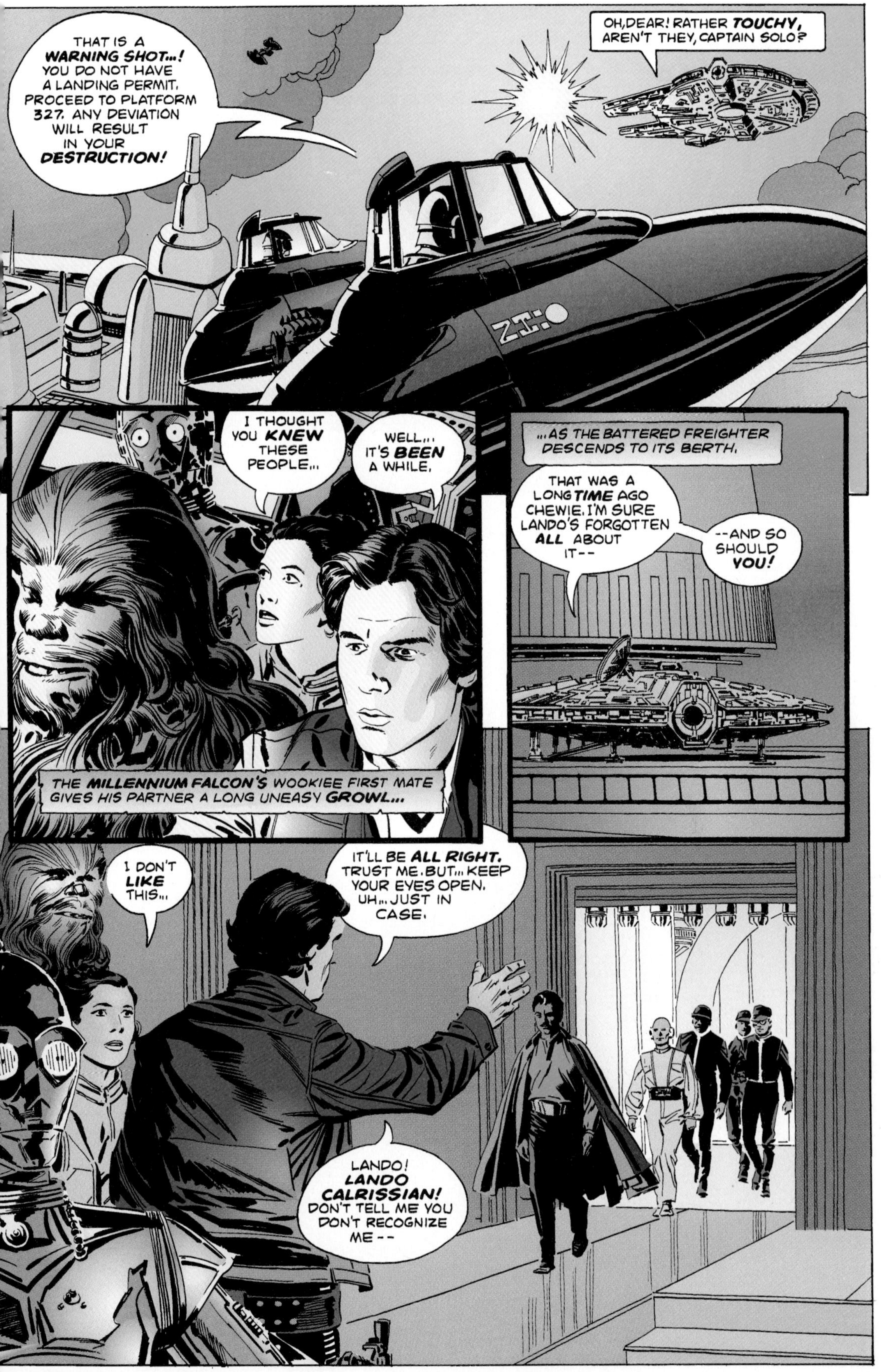
THAT IS A WARNING SHOT...! YOU DO NOT HAVE A LANDING PERMIT. PROCEED TO PLATFORM 327. ANY DEVIATION WILL RESULT IN YOUR DESTRUCTION!
OH, DEAR! RATHER TOUCHY, AREN'T THEY, CAPTAIN SOLO?
I THOUGHT YOU KNEW THESE PEOPLE...
WELL... IT'S BEEN A WHILE.
THE MILLENNIUM FALCON'S WOOKIEE FIRST MATE GIVES HIS PARTNER A LONG UNEASY GROWL...
...AS THE BATTERED FREIGHTER DESCENDS TO ITS BERTH.
THAT WAS A LONG TIME AGO CHEWIE. I'M SURE LANDO'S FORGOTTEN ALL ABOUT IT--
--AND SO SHOULD YOU!
I DON'T LIKE THIS...
IT'LL BE ALL RIGHT. TRUST ME. BUT... KEEP YOUR EYES OPEN. UH... JUST IN CASE.
LANDO! LANDO CALRISSIAN! DON'T TELL ME YOU DON'T RECOGNIZE ME --

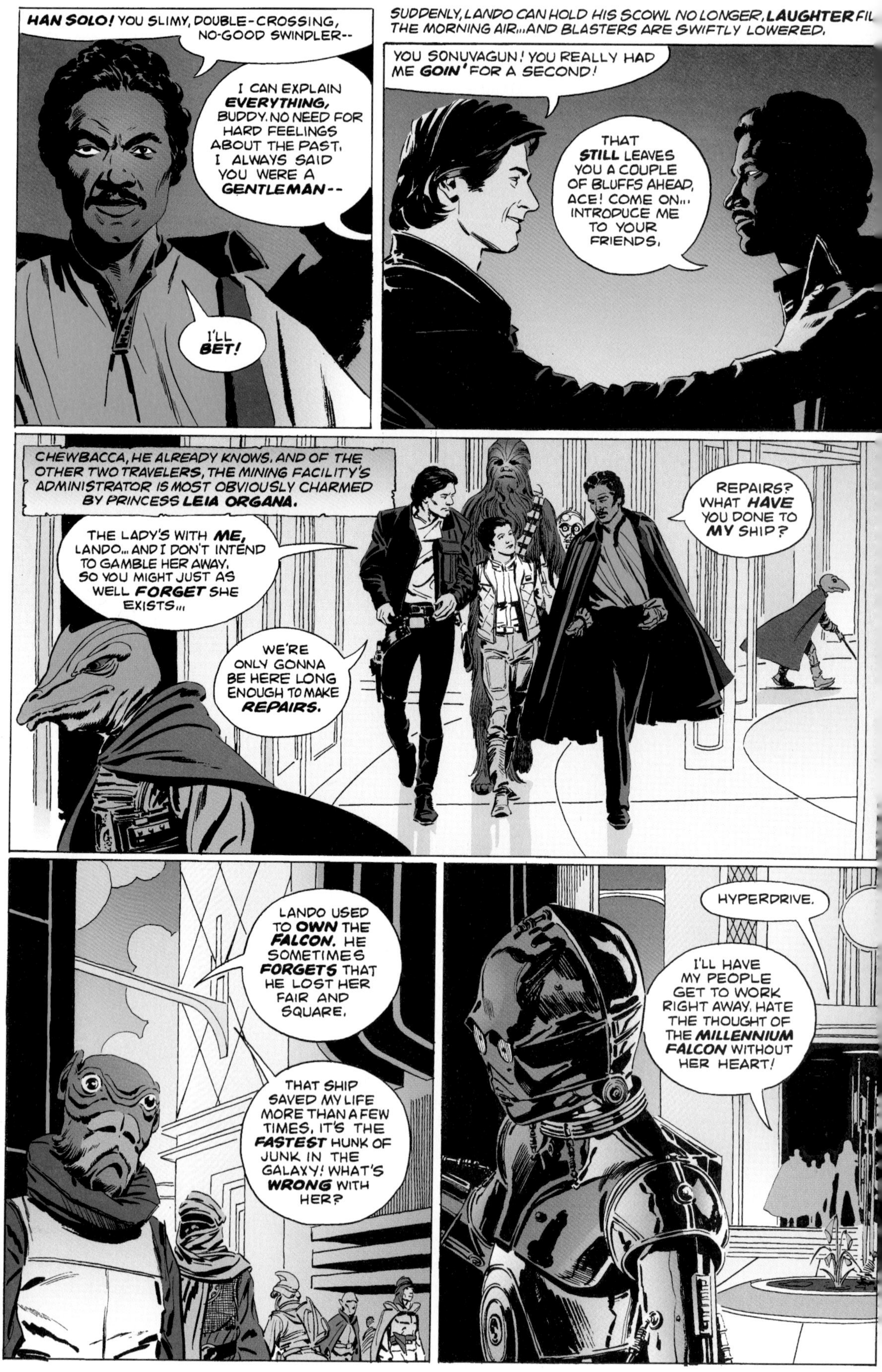
HAN SOLO! YOU SLIMY, DOUBLE-CROSSING, NO-GOOD SWINDLER--
I CAN EXPLAIN EVERYTHING, BUDDY. NO NEED FOR HARD FEELINGS ABOUT THE PAST. I ALWAYS SAID YOU WERE A GENTLEMAN--
I'LL BET!
SUDDENLY, LANDO CAN HOLD HIS SCOWL NO LONGER. LAUGHTER FIL
THE MORNING AIR...AND BLASTERS ARE SWIFTLY LOWERED.
YOU SONUVAGUN! YOU REALLY HAD ME GOIN' FOR A SECOND!
THAT STILL LEAVES YOU A COUPLE OF BLUFFS AHEAD, ACE! COME ON... INTRODUCE ME TO YOUR FRIENDS.
CHEWBACCA, HE ALREADY KNOWS. AND OF THE OTHER TWO TRAVELERS, THE MINING FACILITY'S ADMINISTRATOR IS MOST OBVIOUSLY CHARMED BY PRINCESS LEIA ORGANA.
THE LADY'S WITH ME, LANDO... AND I DON'T INTEND TO GAMBLE HER AWAY, SO YOU MIGHT JUST AS WELL FORGET SHE EXISTS...
WE'RE ONLY GONNA BE HERE LONG ENOUGH TO MAKE REPAIRS.
REPAIRS? WHAT HAVE YOU DONE TO MY SHIP?
LANDO USED TO OWN THE FALCON. HE SOMETIMES FORGETS THAT HE LOST HER FAIR AND SQUARE.
THAT SHIP SAVED MY LIFE MORE THAN A FEW TIMES. IT'S THE FASTEST HUNK OF JUNK IN THE GALAXY! WHAT'S WRONG WITH HER?
HYPERDRIVE.
I'LL HAVE MY PEOPLE GET TO WORK RIGHT AWAY. HATE THE THOUGHT OF THE MILLENNIUM FALCON WITHOUT HER HEART!

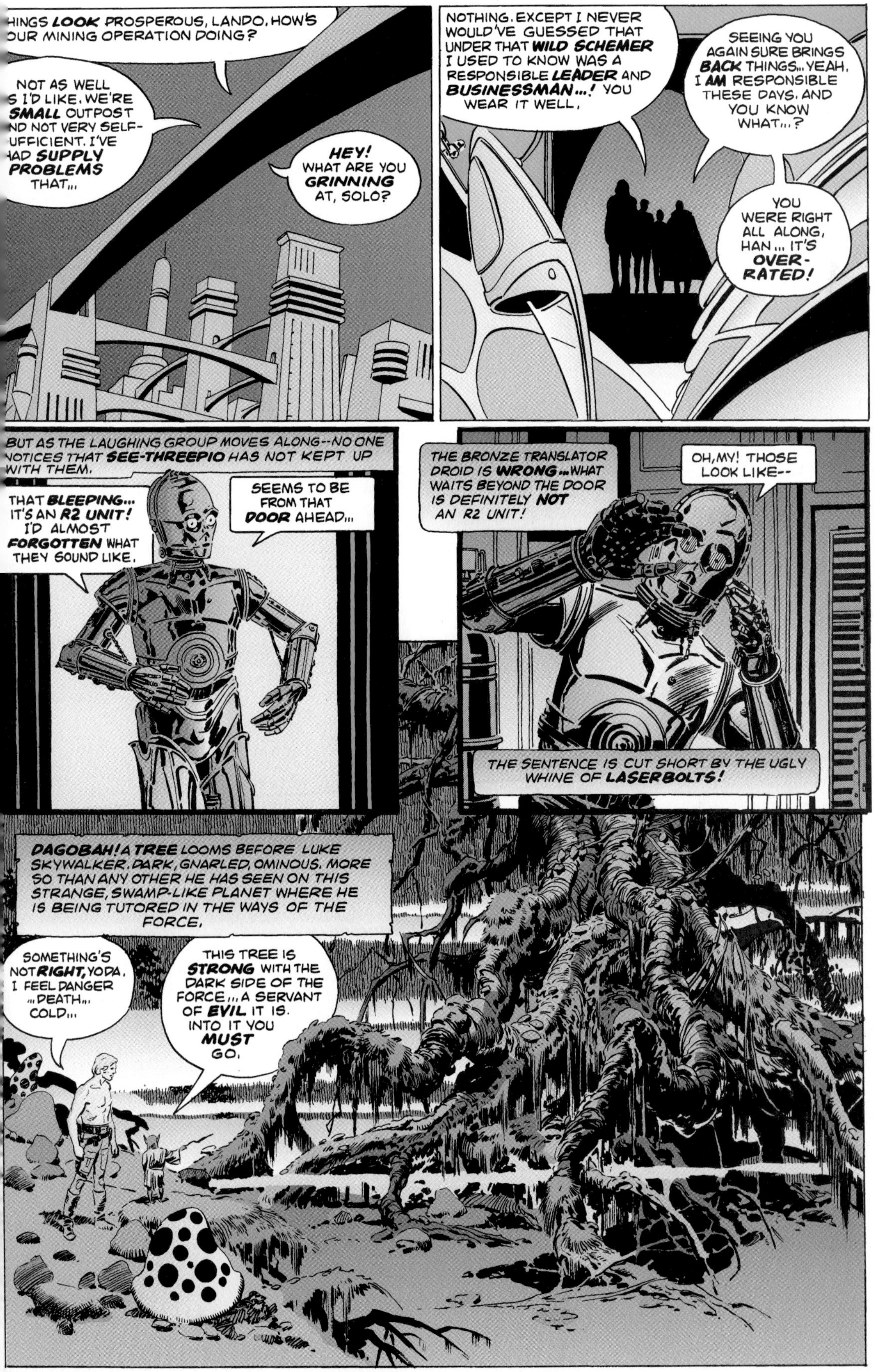
HINGS LOOK PROSPEROUS, LANDO. HOW'S OUR MINING OPERATION DOING?
NOT AS WELL S I'D LIKE. WE'RE SMALL OUTPOST ND NOT VERY SELF-UFFICIENT. I'VE HAD SUPPLY PROBLEMS THAT...
HEY! WHAT ARE YOU GRINNING AT, SOLO?
NOTHING. EXCEPT I NEVER WOULD'VE GUESSED THAT UNDER THAT WILD SCHEMER I USED TO KNOW WAS A RESPONSIBLE LEADER AND BUSINESSMAN...! YOU WEAR IT WELL.
SEEING YOU AGAIN SURE BRINGS BACK THINGS... YEAH, I AM RESPONSIBLE THESE DAYS. AND YOU KNOW WHAT...?
YOU WERE RIGHT ALL ALONG, HAN... IT'S OVER-RATED!
BUT AS THE LAUGHING GROUP MOVES ALONG--NO ONE NOTICES THAT SEE-THREEPIO HAS NOT KEPT UP WITH THEM.
THAT BLEEPING... IT'S AN R2 UNIT! I'D ALMOST FORGOTTEN WHAT THEY SOUND LIKE.
SEEMS TO BE FROM THAT DOOR AHEAD...
THE BRONZE TRANSLATOR DROID IS WRONG... WHAT WAITS BEYOND THE DOOR IS DEFINITELY NOT AN R2 UNIT!
OH, MY! THOSE LOOK LIKE--
THE SENTENCE IS CUT SHORT BY THE UGLY WHINE OF LASERBOLTS!
DAGOBAH! A TREE LOOMS BEFORE LUKE SKYWALKER. DARK, GNARLED, OMINOUS. MORE SO THAN ANY OTHER HE HAS SEEN ON THIS STRANGE, SWAMP-LIKE PLANET WHERE HE IS BEING TUTORED IN THE WAYS OF THE FORCE.
SOMETHING'S NOT RIGHT, YODA. I FEEL DANGER ...DEATH... COLD...
THIS TREE IS STRONG WITH THE DARK SIDE OF THE FORCE... A SERVANT OF EVIL IT IS. INTO IT YOU MUST GO.

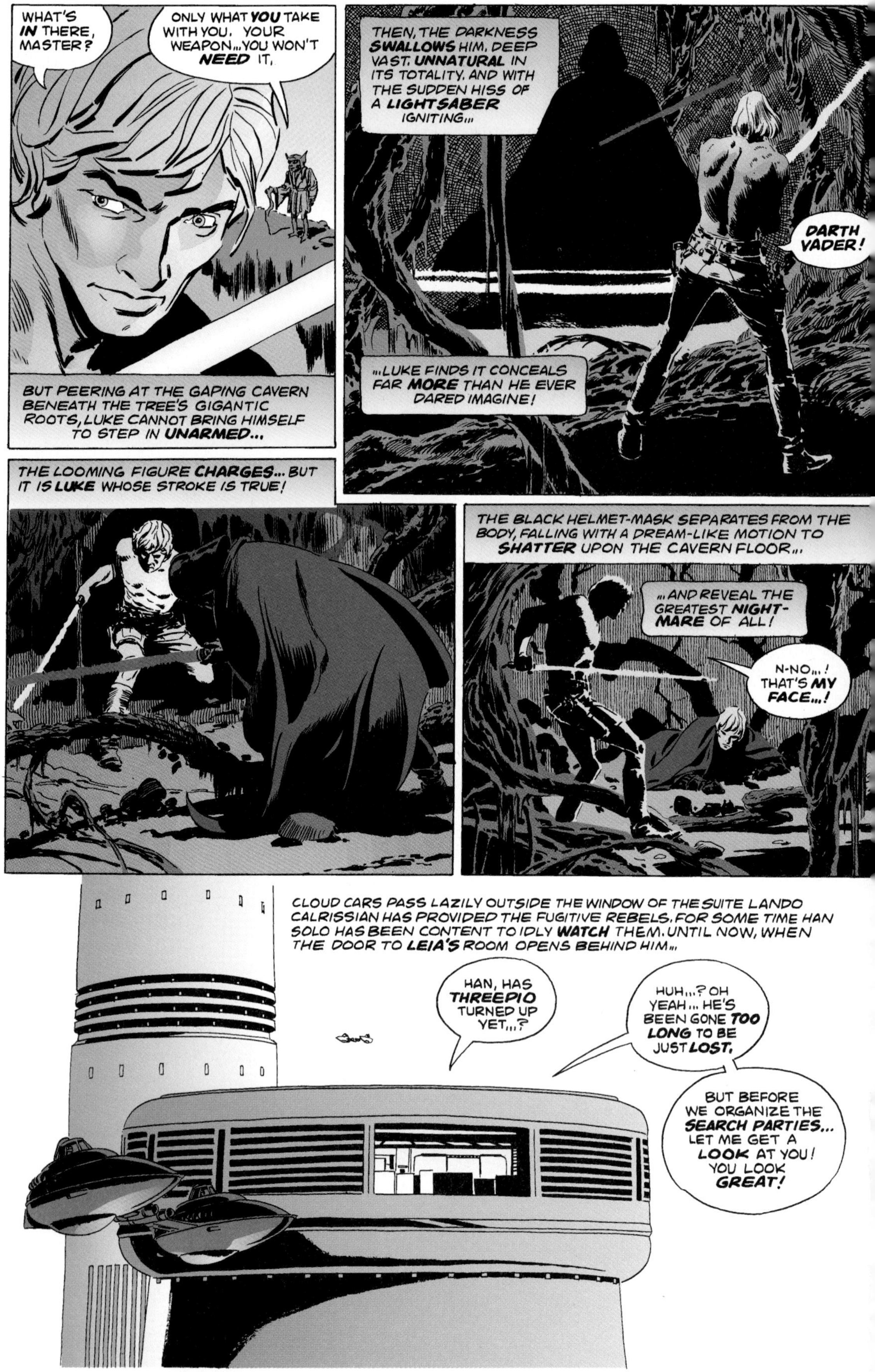
WHAT'S IN THERE, MASTER?
ONLY WHAT YOU TAKE WITH YOU. YOUR WEAPON... YOU WON'T NEED IT.
BUT PEERING AT THE GAPING CAVERN BENEATH THE TREE'S GIGANTIC ROOTS, LUKE CANNOT BRING HIMSELF TO STEP IN UNARMED...
THEN, THE DARKNESS SWALLOWS HIM. DEEP VAST. UNNATURAL IN ITS TOTALITY. AND WITH THE SUDDEN HISS OF A LIGHTSABER IGNITING...
...LUKE FINDS IT CONCEALS FAR MORE THAN HE EVER DARED IMAGINE!
DARTH VADER!
THE LOOMING FIGURE CHARGES... BUT IT IS LUKE WHOSE STROKE IS TRUE!
THE BLACK HELMET-MASK SEPARATES FROM THE BODY, FALLING WITH A DREAM-LIKE MOTION TO SHATTER UPON THE CAVERN FLOOR...
...AND REVEAL THE GREATEST NIGHT-MARE OF ALL!
N-NO...! THAT'S MY FACE...!
CLOUD CARS PASS LAZILY OUTSIDE THE WINDOW OF THE SUITE LANDO CALRISSIAN HAS PROVIDED THE FUGITIVE REBELS. FOR SOME TIME HAN SOLO HAS BEEN CONTENT TO IDLY WATCH THEM. UNTIL NOW, WHEN THE DOOR TO LEIA'S ROOM OPENS BEHIND HIM...
HAN, HAS THREEPIO TURNED UP YET...?
HUH...? OH YEAH... HE'S BEEN GONE TOO LONG TO BE JUST LOST.
BUT BEFORE WE ORGANIZE THE SEARCH PARTIES... LET ME GET A LOOK AT YOU! YOU LOOK GREAT!

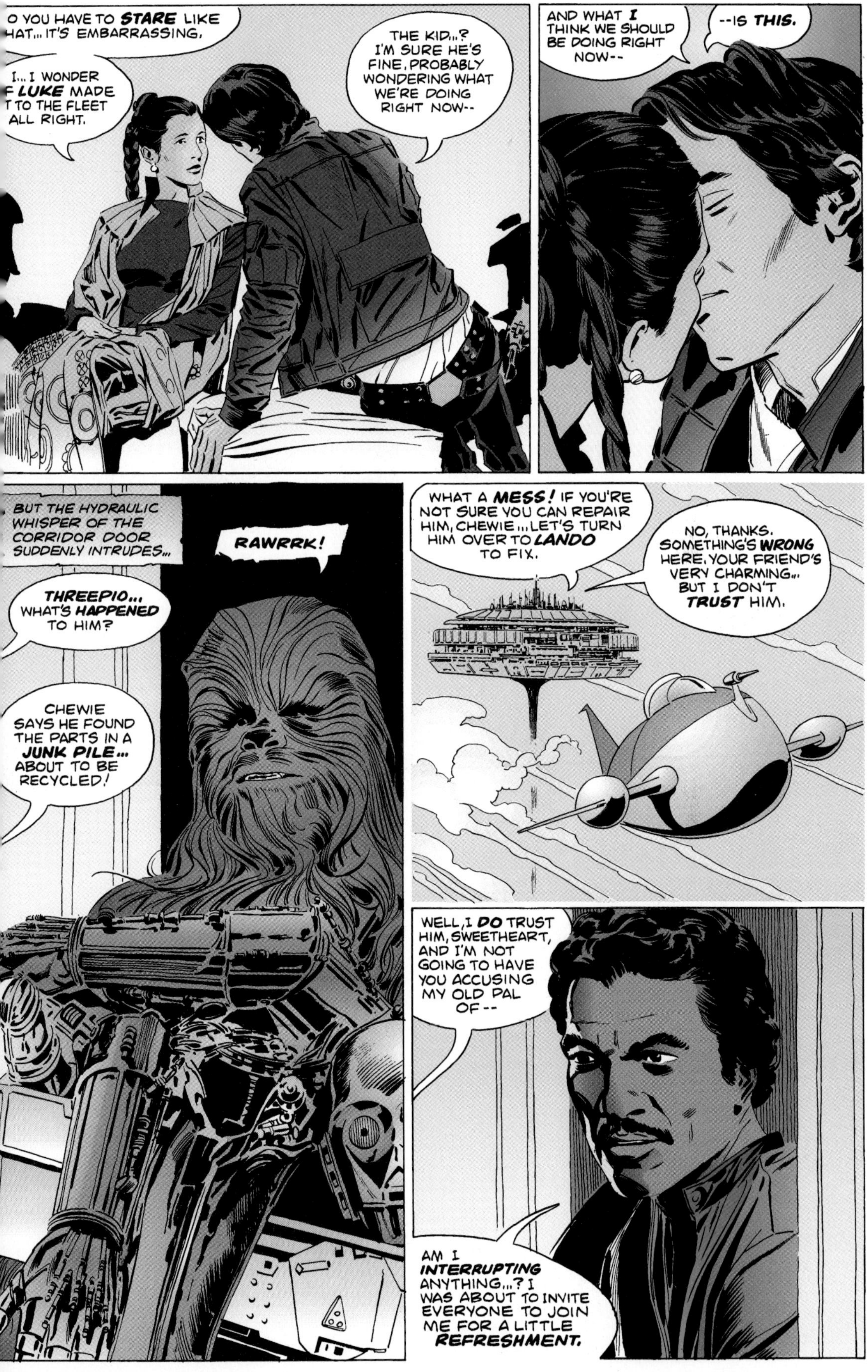

O YOU HAVE TO STARE LIKE HAT... IT'S EMBARRASSING.
I... I WONDER F LUKE MADE T TO THE FLEET ALL RIGHT.
THE KID...? I'M SURE HE'S FINE, PROBABLY WONDERING WHAT WE'RE DOING RIGHT NOW--
AND WHAT I THINK WE SHOULD BE DOING RIGHT NOW--
--IS THIS.
BUT THE HYDRAULIC WHISPER OF THE CORRIDOR DOOR SUDDENLY INTRUDES...
RAWRRK!
THREEPIO... WHAT'S HAPPENED TO HIM?
CHEWIE SAYS HE FOUND THE PARTS IN A JUNK PILE... ABOUT TO BE RECYCLED!
WHAT A MESS! IF YOU'RE NOT SURE YOU CAN REPAIR HIM, CHEWIE... LET'S TURN HIM OVER TO LANDO TO FIX.
NO, THANKS. SOMETHING'S WRONG HERE. YOUR FRIEND'S VERY CHARMING... BUT I DON'T TRUST HIM.
WELL, I DO TRUST HIM, SWEETHEART, AND I'M NOT GOING TO HAVE YOU ACCUSING MY OLD PAL OF--
AM I INTERRUPTING ANYTHING...? I WAS ABOUT TO INVITE EVERYONE TO JOIN ME FOR A LITTLE REFRESHMENT.

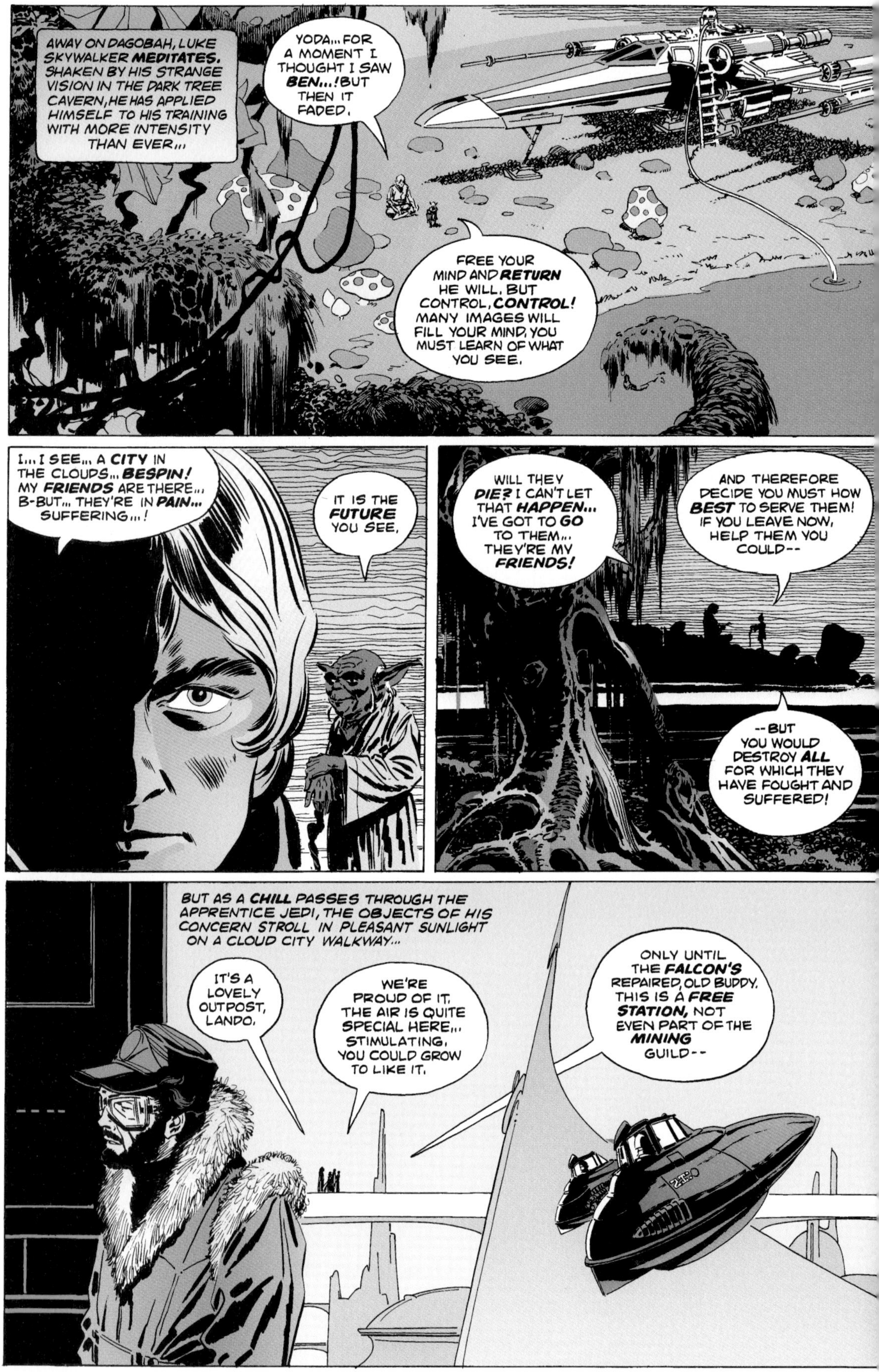
AWAY ON DAGOBAH, LUKE SKYWALKER MEDITATES. SHAKEN BY HIS STRANGE VISION IN THE DARK TREE CAVERN, HE HAS APPLIED HIMSELF TO HIS TRAINING WITH MORE INTENSITY THAN EVER...
YODA... FOR A MOMENT I THOUGHT I SAW BEN...! BUT THEN IT FADED.
FREE YOUR MIND AND RETURN HE WILL. BUT CONTROL, CONTROL! MANY IMAGES WILL FILL YOUR MIND, YOU MUST LEARN OF WHAT YOU SEE.
I... I SEE... A CITY IN THE CLOUDS... BESPIN! MY FRIENDS ARE THERE... B-BUT... THEY'RE IN PAIN... SUFFERING...!
IT IS THE FUTURE YOU SEE.
WILL THEY DIE? I CAN'T LET THAT HAPPEN... I'VE GOT TO GO TO THEM... THEY'RE MY FRIENDS!
AND THEREFORE DECIDE YOU MUST HOW BEST TO SERVE THEM! IF YOU LEAVE NOW, HELP THEM YOU COULD--
--BUT YOU WOULD DESTROY ALL FOR WHICH THEY HAVE FOUGHT AND SUFFERED!
BUT AS A CHILL PASSES THROUGH THE APPRENTICE JEDI, THE OBJECTS OF HIS CONCERN STROLL IN PLEASANT SUNLIGHT ON A CLOUD CITY WALKWAY...
IT'S A LOVELY OUTPOST, LANDO.
WE'RE PROUD OF IT. THE AIR IS QUITE SPECIAL HERE... STIMULATING. YOU COULD GROW TO LIKE IT.
ONLY UNTIL THE FALCON'S REPAIRED, OLD BUDDY. THIS IS A FREE STATION, NOT EVEN PART OF THE MINING GUILD--

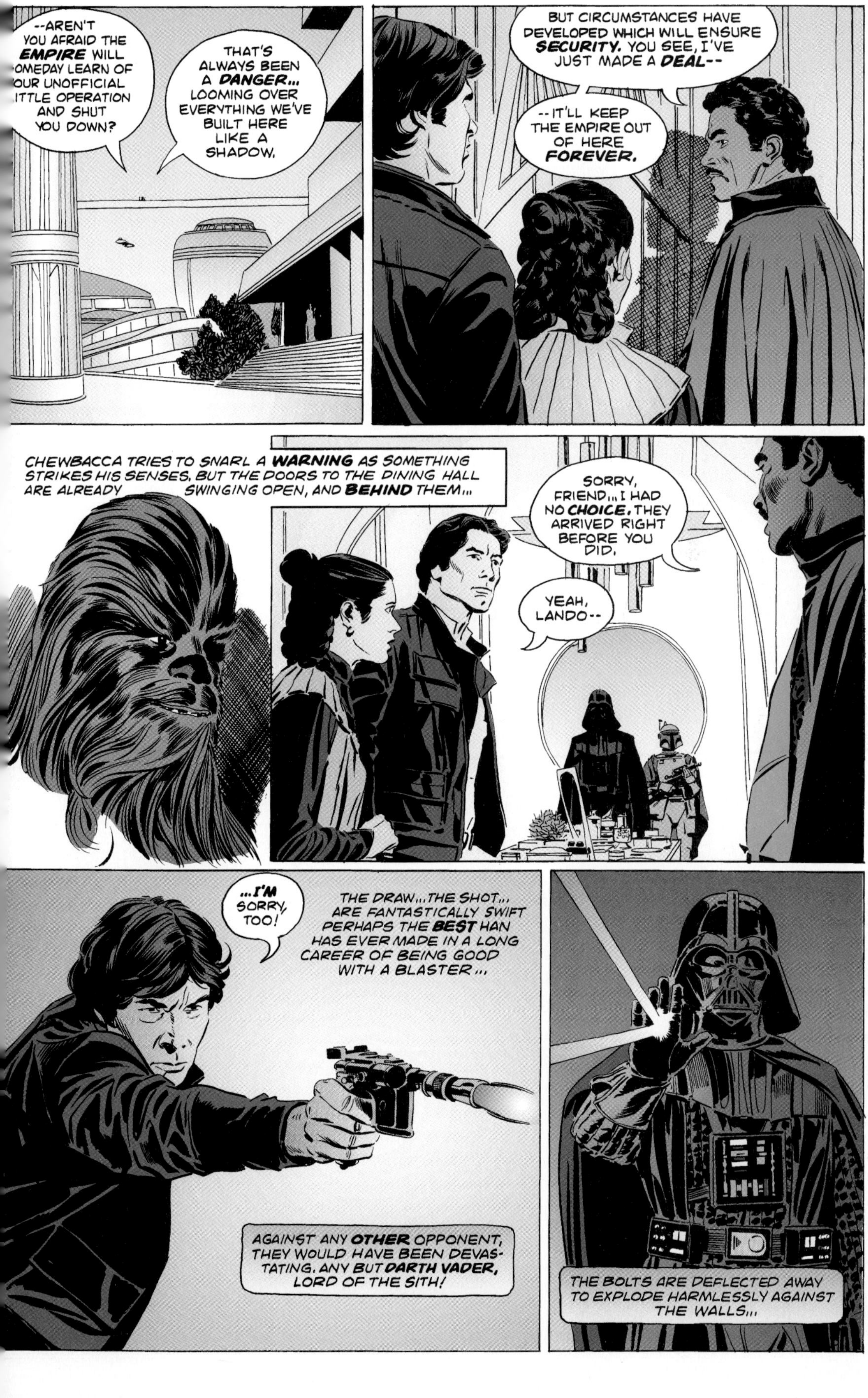
--AREN'T YOU AFRAID THE EMPIRE WILL SOMEDAY LEARN OF YOUR UNOFFICIAL LITTLE OPERATION AND SHUT YOU DOWN?
THAT'S ALWAYS BEEN A DANGER... LOOMING OVER EVERYTHING WE'VE BUILT HERE LIKE A SHADOW.
BUT CIRCUMSTANCES HAVE DEVELOPED WHICH WILL ENSURE SECURITY. YOU SEE, I'VE JUST MADE A DEAL--
--IT'LL KEEP THE EMPIRE OUT OF HERE FOREVER.
CHEWBACCA TRIES TO SNARL A WARNING AS SOMETHING STRIKES HIS SENSES, BUT THE DOORS TO THE DINING HALL ARE ALREADY SWINGING OPEN, AND BEHIND THEM...
SORRY, FRIEND... I HAD NO CHOICE. THEY ARRIVED RIGHT BEFORE YOU DID.
YEAH, LANDO--
...I'M SORRY, TOO!
THE DRAW...THE SHOT... ARE FANTASTICALLY SWIFT PERHAPS THE BEST HAN HAS EVER MADE IN A LONG CAREER OF BEING GOOD WITH A BLASTER...
AGAINST ANY OTHER OPPONENT, THEY WOULD HAVE BEEN DEVASTATING. ANY BUT DARTH VADER, LORD OF THE SITH!
THE BOLTS ARE DEFLECTED AWAY TO EXPLODE HARMLESSLY AGAINST THE WALLS...

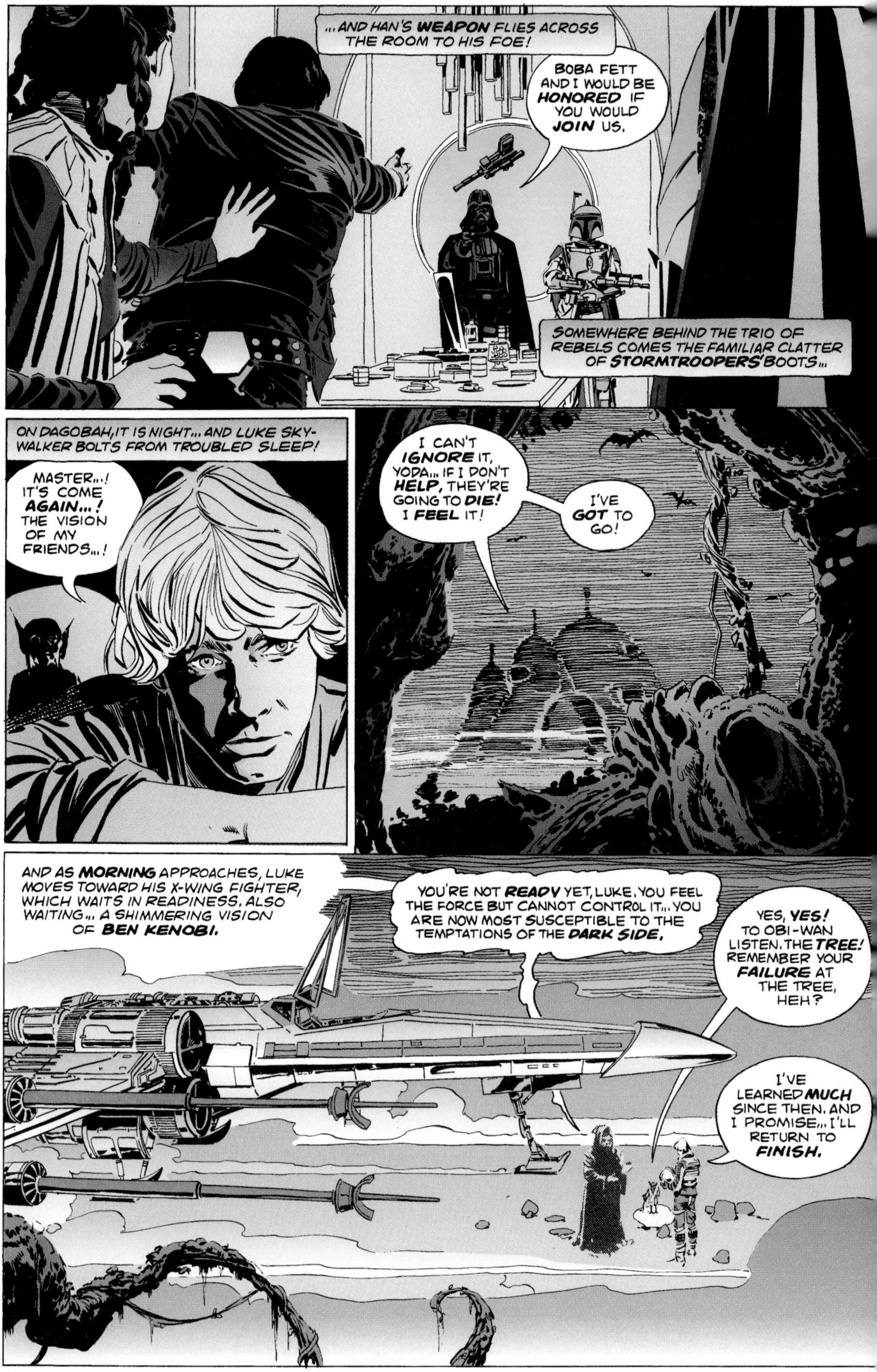
...AND HAN'S WEAPON FLIES ACROSS THE ROOM TO HIS FOE!
BOBA FETT AND I WOULD BE HONORED IF YOU WOULD JOIN US.
SOMEWHERE BEHIND THE TRIO OF REBELS COMES THE FAMILIAR CLATTER OF STORMTROOPERS' BOOTS...
ON DAGOBAH, IT IS NIGHT... AND LUKE SKYWALKER BOLTS FROM TROUBLED SLEEP!
MASTER...! IT'S COME AGAIN...! THE VISION OF MY FRIENDS...!
I CAN'T IGNORE IT, YODA... IF I DON'T HELP, THEY'RE GOING TO DIE! I FEEL IT!
I'VE GOT TO GO!
AND AS MORNING APPROACHES, LUKE MOVES TOWARD HIS X-WING FIGHTER, WHICH WAITS IN READINESS, ALSO WAITING... A SHIMMERING VISION OF BEN KENOBI.
YOU'RE NOT READY YET, LUKE. YOU FEEL THE FORCE BUT CANNOT CONTROL IT... YOU ARE NOW MOST SUSCEPTIBLE TO THE TEMPTATIONS OF THE DARK SIDE.
YES, YES! TO OBI-WAN LISTEN. THE TREE! REMEMBER YOUR FAILURE AT THE TREE, HEH?
I'VE LEARNED MUCH SINCE THEN. AND I PROMISE... I'LL RETURN TO FINISH.

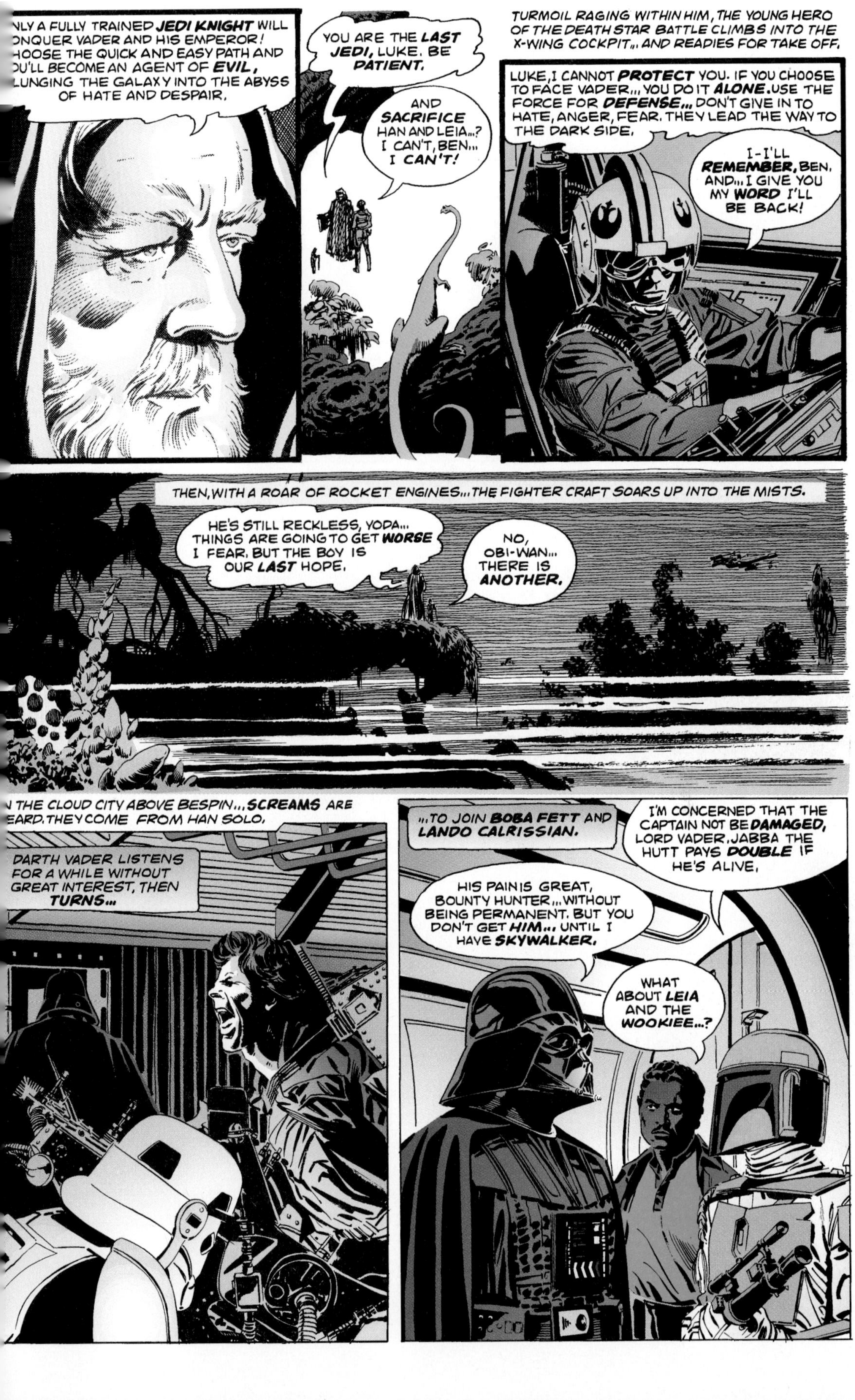

NLY A FULLY TRAINED JEDI KNIGHT WILL
ONQUER VADER AND HIS EMPEROR!
HOOSE THE QUICK AND EASY PATH AND
OU'LL BECOME AN AGENT OF EVIL,
LUNGING THE GALAXY INTO THE ABYSS
OF HATE AND DESPAIR.
YOU ARE THE LAST JEDI, LUKE. BE PATIENT.
AND SACRIFICE HAN AND LEIA...? I CAN'T, BEN... I CAN'T!
TURMOIL RAGING WITHIN HIM, THE YOUNG HERO OF THE DEATH STAR BATTLE CLIMBS INTO THE X-WING COCKPIT... AND READIES FOR TAKE OFF.
LUKE, I CANNOT PROTECT YOU. IF YOU CHOOSE TO FACE VADER... YOU DO IT ALONE. USE THE FORCE FOR DEFENSE... DON'T GIVE IN TO HATE, ANGER, FEAR. THEY LEAD THE WAY TO THE DARK SIDE.
I-I'LL REMEMBER, BEN. AND... I GIVE YOU MY WORD I'LL BE BACK!
THEN, WITH A ROAR OF ROCKET ENGINES... THE FIGHTER CRAFT SOARS UP INTO THE MISTS.
HE'S STILL RECKLESS, YODA... THINGS ARE GOING TO GET WORSE I FEAR. BUT THE BOY IS OUR LAST HOPE.
NO, OBI-WAN... THERE IS ANOTHER.
N THE CLOUD CITY ABOVE BESPIN... SCREAMS ARE
EARD. THEY COME FROM HAN SOLO.
DARTH VADER LISTENS FOR A WHILE WITHOUT GREAT INTEREST, THEN TURNS...
...TO JOIN BOBA FETT AND LANDO CALRISSIAN.
I'M CONCERNED THAT THE CAPTAIN NOT BE DAMAGED, LORD VADER. JABBA THE HUTT PAYS DOUBLE IF HE'S ALIVE.
HIS PAIN IS GREAT, BOUNTY HUNTER... WITHOUT BEING PERMANENT. BUT YOU DON'T GET HIM... UNTIL I HAVE SKYWALKER.
WHAT ABOUT LEIA AND THE WOOKIEE...?

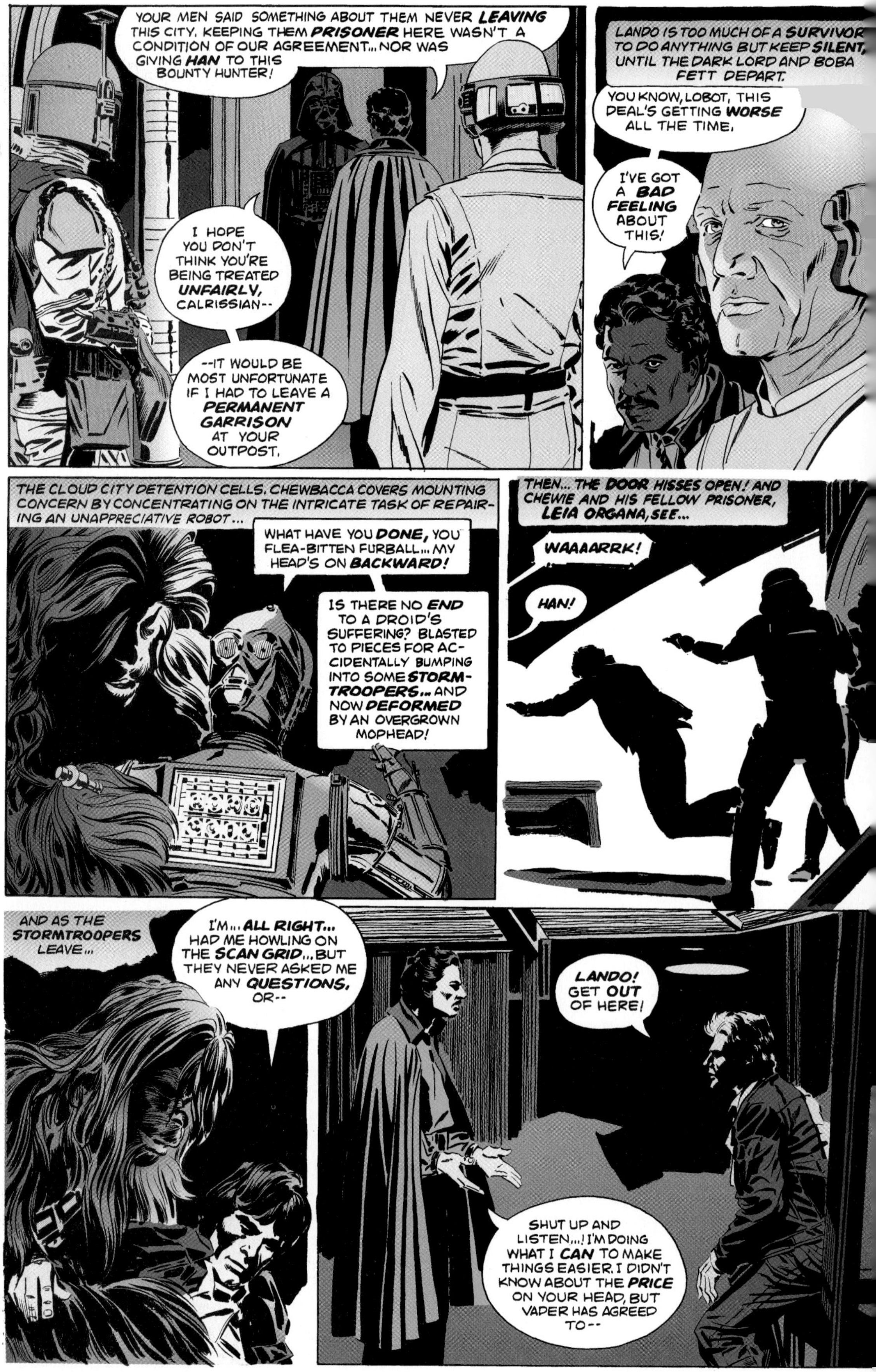
YOUR MEN SAID SOMETHING ABOUT THEM NEVER LEAVING THIS CITY. KEEPING THEM PRISONER HERE WASN'T A CONDITION OF OUR AGREEMENT... NOR WAS GIVING HAN TO THIS BOUNTY HUNTER!
I HOPE YOU DON'T THINK YOU'RE BEING TREATED UNFAIRLY, CALRISSIAN--
--IT WOULD BE MOST UNFORTUNATE IF I HAD TO LEAVE A PERMANENT GARRISON AT YOUR OUTPOST.
LANDO IS TOO MUCH OF A SURVIVOR TO DO ANYTHING BUT KEEP SILENT, UNTIL THE DARK LORD AND BOBA FETT DEPART.
YOU KNOW, LOBOT, THIS DEAL'S GETTING WORSE ALL THE TIME.
I'VE GOT A BAD FEELING ABOUT THIS!
THE CLOUD CITY DETENTION CELLS. CHEWBACCA COVERS MOUNTING CONCERN BY CONCENTRATING ON THE INTRICATE TASK OF REPAIRING AN UNAPPRECIATIVE ROBOT...
WHAT HAVE YOU DONE, YOU FLEA-BITTEN FURBALL... MY HEAD'S ON BACKWARD!
IS THERE NO END TO A DROID'S SUFFERING? BLASTED TO PIECES FOR ACCIDENTALLY BUMPING INTO SOME STORMTROOPERS... AND NOW DEFORMED BY AN OVERGROWN MOPHEAD!
THEN... THE DOOR HISSES OPEN! AND CHEWIE AND HIS FELLOW PRISONER, LEIA ORGANA, SEE...
WAAAARRK!
HAN!
AND AS THE STORMTROOPERS LEAVE...
I'M... ALL RIGHT... HAD ME HOWLING ON THE SCAN GRID... BUT THEY NEVER ASKED ME ANY QUESTIONS, OR--
LANDO! GET OUT OF HERE!
SHUT UP AND LISTEN...! I'M DOING WHAT I CAN TO MAKE THINGS EASIER. I DIDN'T KNOW ABOUT THE PRICE ON YOUR HEAD, BUT VADER HAS AGREED TO--

YOU DON'T *KNOW* MUCH IF YOU THINK DARTH VADER WANTS ALL OF US ANYTHING BUT *DEAD* BEFORE THIS THING IS OVER!

HE DOESN'T WANT YOU AT *ALL*, HAN! HE'S SETTING A *TRAP* FOR SOME YOUNG REBEL NAMED *SKYWALKER...* YOU PEOPLE ARE THE *BAIT.*

I DON'T KNOW WHAT'S SO *IMPORTANT* ABOUT THE KID, BUT THE IMPERIALS HAVE PINPOINTED THAT HE'S ON HIS *WAY...*

LUKE'S COMING *HERE*...? YOU FIXED US *ALL* PRETTY GOOD--

-- *FRIEND!*

FOR A MOMENT IT'S *A FIGHT...* UNTIL LANDO'S GUARDS MOVE IN, CLUBBING WITH THEIR BLASTERS!

OKAY... *ENOUGH!* I'VE DONE AS MUCH AS I CAN, WISH IT WERE MORE... BUT I'VE GOT MY *OWN* PROBLEMS.

I'VE ALREADY STUCK MY *NECK* OUT FARTHER THAN I SHOULD.

YEAH, YEAH, LANDO ... YOU'RE A REAL *HERO!*

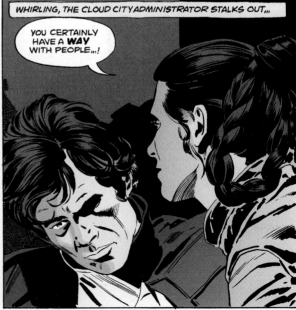

WHIRLING, THE CLOUD CITY ADMINISTRATOR STALKS OUT...

YOU CERTAINLY HAVE A *WAY* WITH PEOPLE ...!

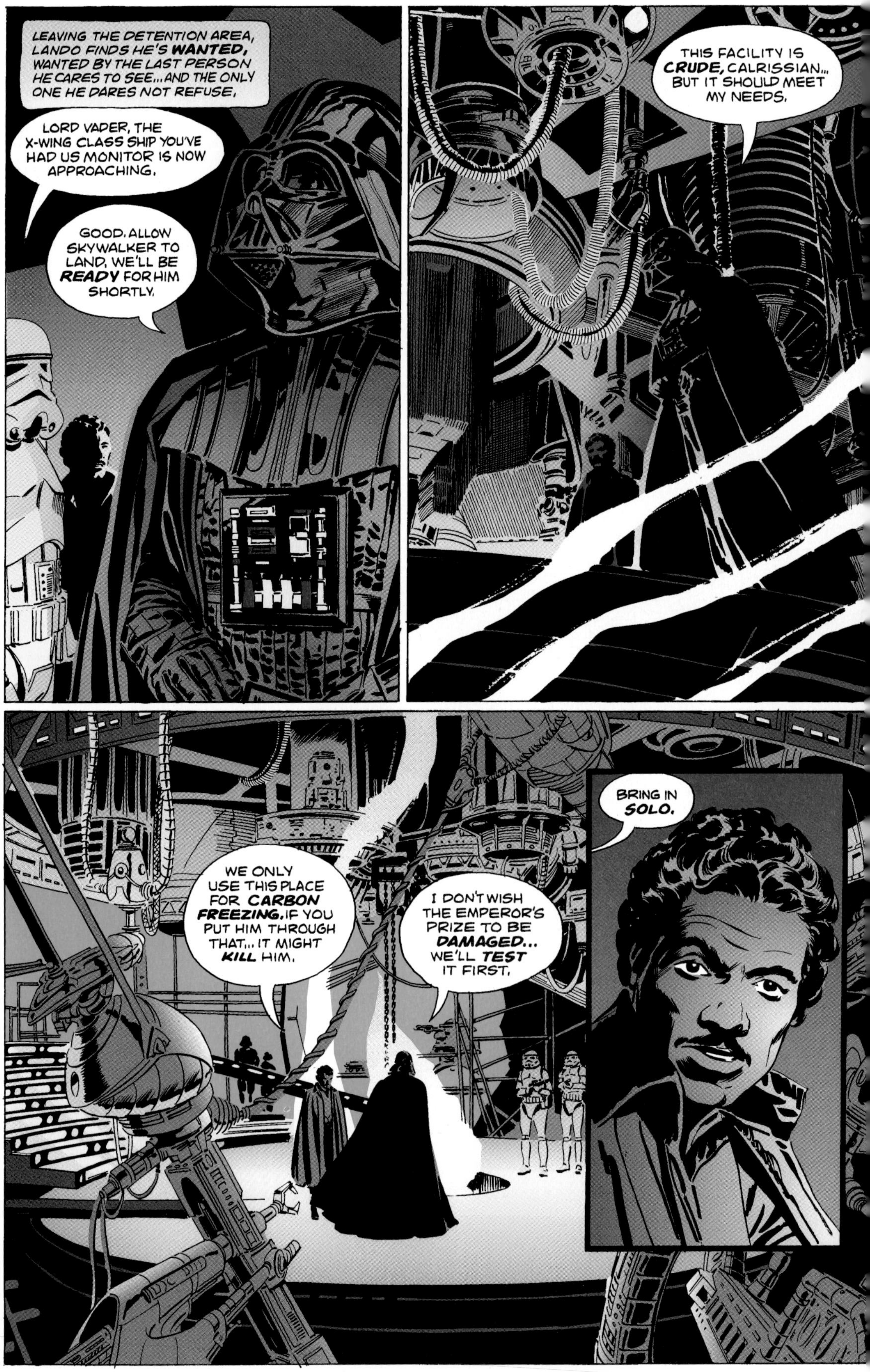
LEAVING THE DETENTION AREA, LANDO FINDS HE'S WANTED, WANTED BY THE LAST PERSON HE CARES TO SEE... AND THE ONLY ONE HE DARES NOT REFUSE.
LORD VADER, THE X-WING CLASS SHIP YOU'VE HAD US MONITOR IS NOW APPROACHING.
GOOD. ALLOW SKYWALKER TO LAND. WE'LL BE READY FOR HIM SHORTLY.
THIS FACILITY IS CRUDE, CALRISSIAN... BUT IT SHOULD MEET MY NEEDS.
WE ONLY USE THIS PLACE FOR CARBON FREEZING. IF YOU PUT HIM THROUGH THAT... IT MIGHT KILL HIM.
I DON'T WISH THE EMPEROR'S PRIZE TO BE DAMAGED... WE'LL TEST IT FIRST.
BRING IN SOLO.

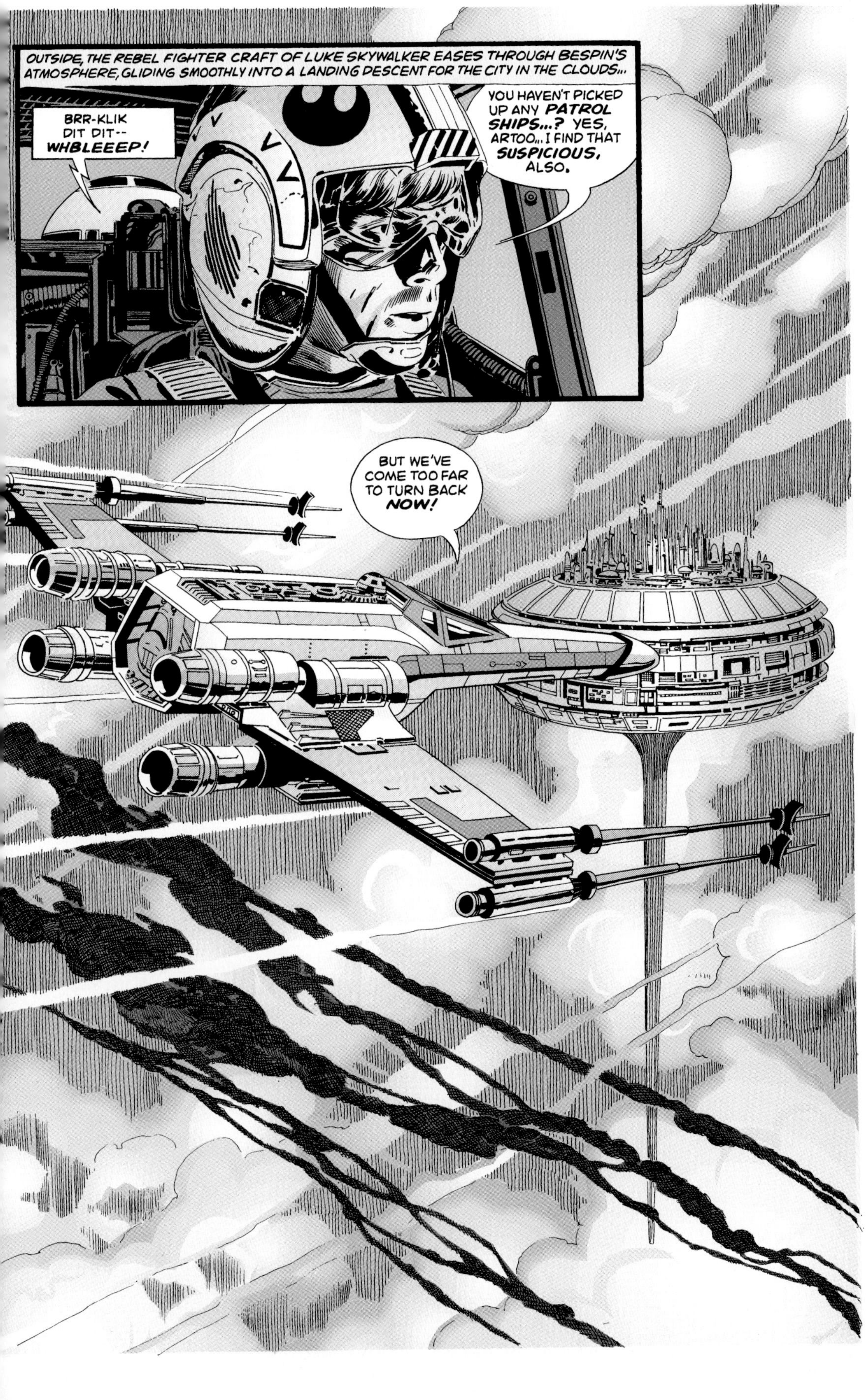
OUTSIDE, THE REBEL FIGHTER CRAFT OF LUKE SKYWALKER EASES THROUGH BESPIN'S ATMOSPHERE, GLIDING SMOOTHLY INTO A LANDING DESCENT FOR THE CITY IN THE CLOUDS...
BRR-KLIK DIT DIT-- WHBLEEEP!
YOU HAVEN'T PICKED UP ANY PATROL SHIPS...? YES, ARTOO... I FIND THAT SUSPICIOUS, ALSO.
BUT WE'VE COME TOO FAR TO TURN BACK NOW!

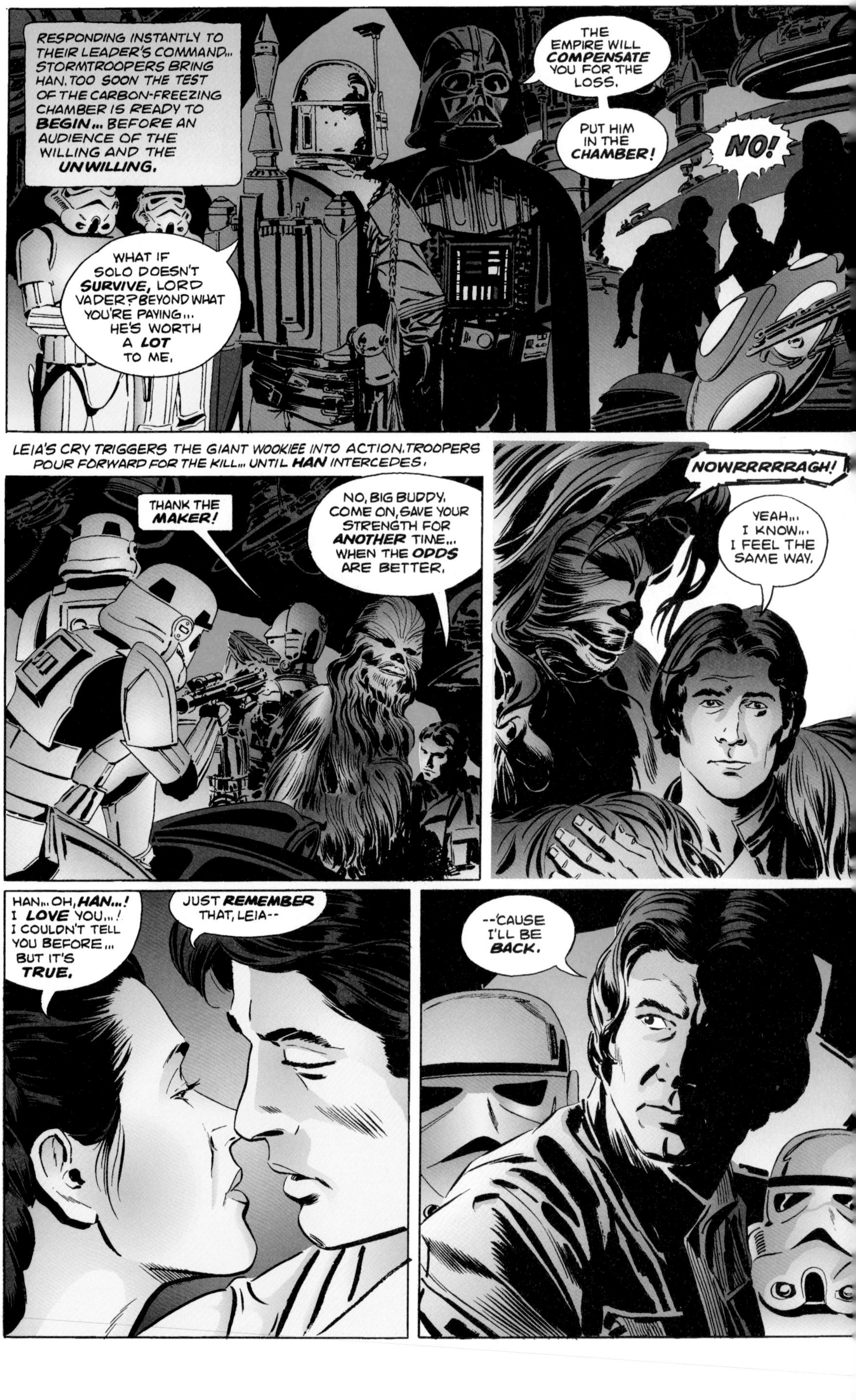
RESPONDING INSTANTLY TO THEIR LEADER'S COMMAND... STORMTROOPERS BRING HAN. TOO SOON THE TEST OF THE CARBON-FREEZING CHAMBER IS READY TO BEGIN... BEFORE AN AUDIENCE OF THE WILLING AND THE UNWILLING.
WHAT IF SOLO DOESN'T SURVIVE, LORD VADER? BEYOND WHAT YOU'RE PAYING... HE'S WORTH A LOT TO ME.
THE EMPIRE WILL COMPENSATE YOU FOR THE LOSS.
PUT HIM IN THE CHAMBER!
NO!
LEIA'S CRY TRIGGERS THE GIANT WOOKIEE INTO ACTION. TROOPERS POUR FORWARD FOR THE KILL... UNTIL HAN INTERCEDES.
THANK THE MAKER!
NO, BIG BUDDY. COME ON, SAVE YOUR STRENGTH FOR ANOTHER TIME... WHEN THE ODDS ARE BETTER.
NOWRRRRRRAGH!
YEAH... I KNOW... I FEEL THE SAME WAY.
HAN... OH, HAN...! I LOVE YOU...! I COULDN'T TELL YOU BEFORE... BUT IT'S TRUE.
JUST REMEMBER THAT, LEIA--
--'CAUSE I'LL BE BACK.

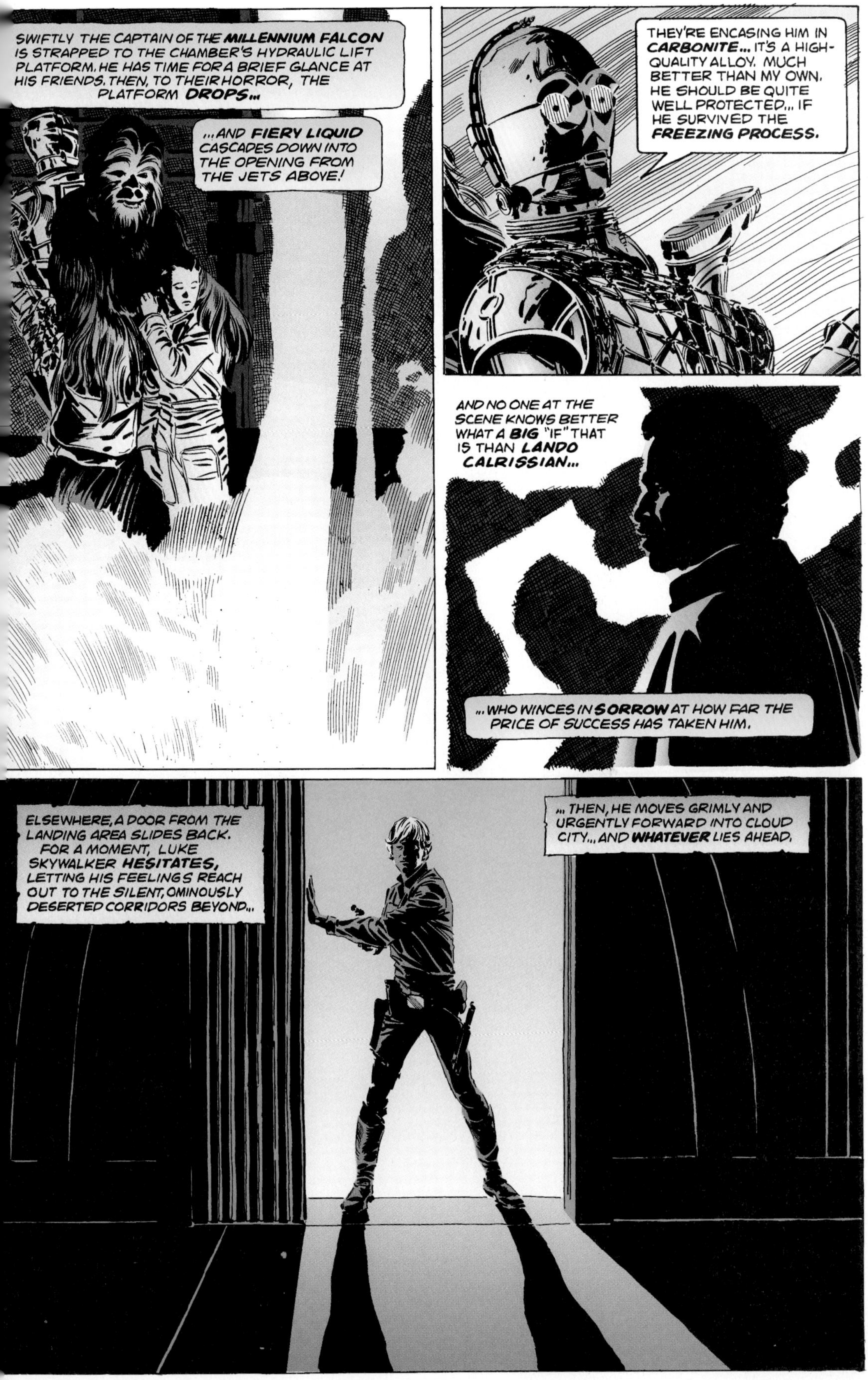
SWIFTLY THE CAPTAIN OF THE MILLENNIUM FALCON IS STRAPPED TO THE CHAMBER'S HYDRAULIC LIFT PLATFORM. HE HAS TIME FOR A BRIEF GLANCE AT HIS FRIENDS. THEN, TO THEIR HORROR, THE PLATFORM DROPS...
...AND FIERY LIQUID CASCADES DOWN INTO THE OPENING FROM THE JETS ABOVE!
THEY'RE ENCASING HIM IN CARBONITE... IT'S A HIGH-QUALITY ALLOY. MUCH BETTER THAN MY OWN. HE SHOULD BE QUITE WELL PROTECTED... IF HE SURVIVED THE FREEZING PROCESS.
AND NO ONE AT THE SCENE KNOWS BETTER WHAT A BIG "IF" THAT IS THAN LANDO CALRISSIAN...
...WHO WINCES IN SORROW AT HOW FAR THE PRICE OF SUCCESS HAS TAKEN HIM.
ELSEWHERE, A DOOR FROM THE LANDING AREA SLIDES BACK. FOR A MOMENT, LUKE SKYWALKER HESITATES, LETTING HIS FEELINGS REACH OUT TO THE SILENT, OMINOUSLY DESERTED CORRIDORS BEYOND...
...THEN, HE MOVES GRIMLY AND URGENTLY FORWARD INTO CLOUD CITY... AND WHATEVER LIES AHEAD.

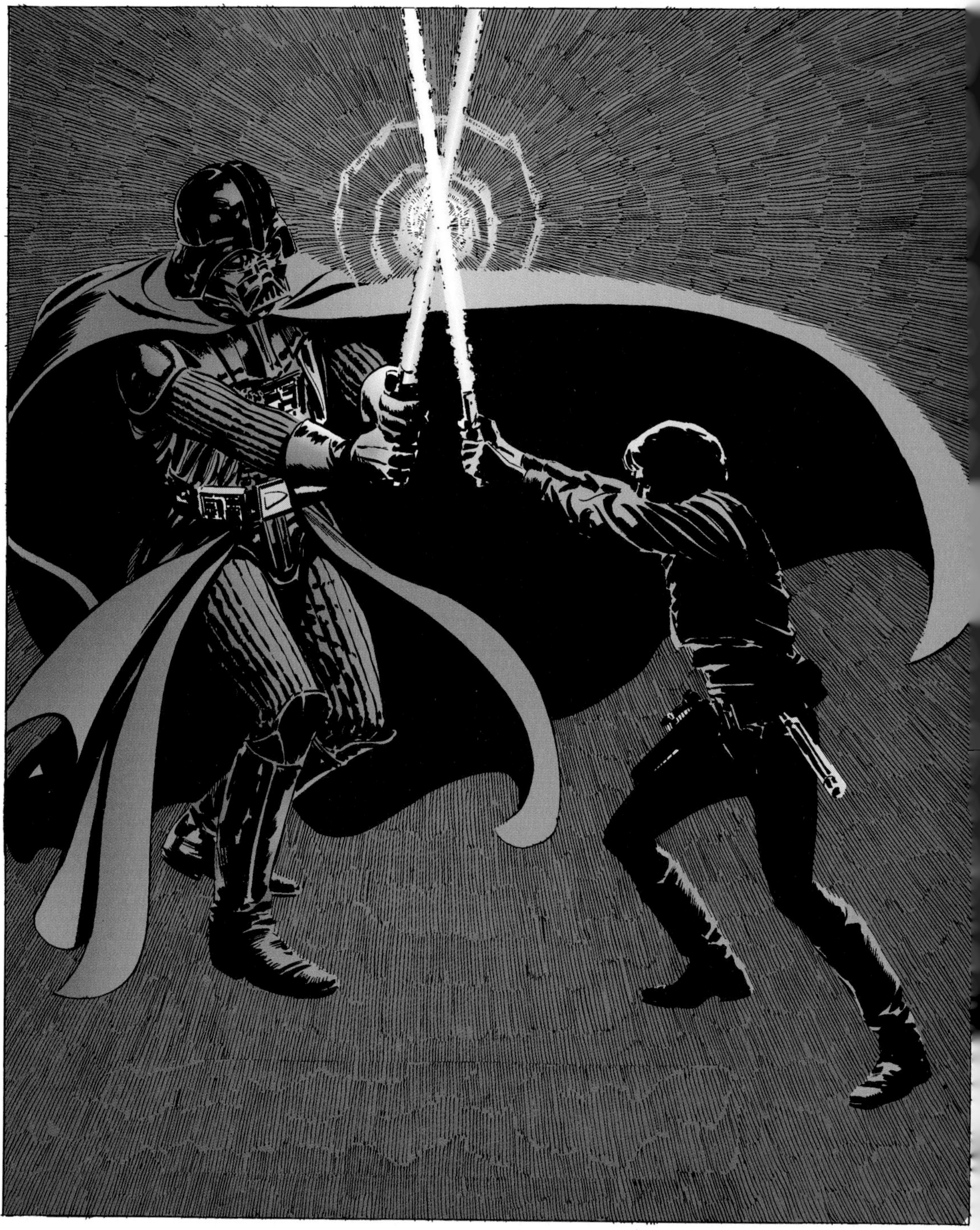

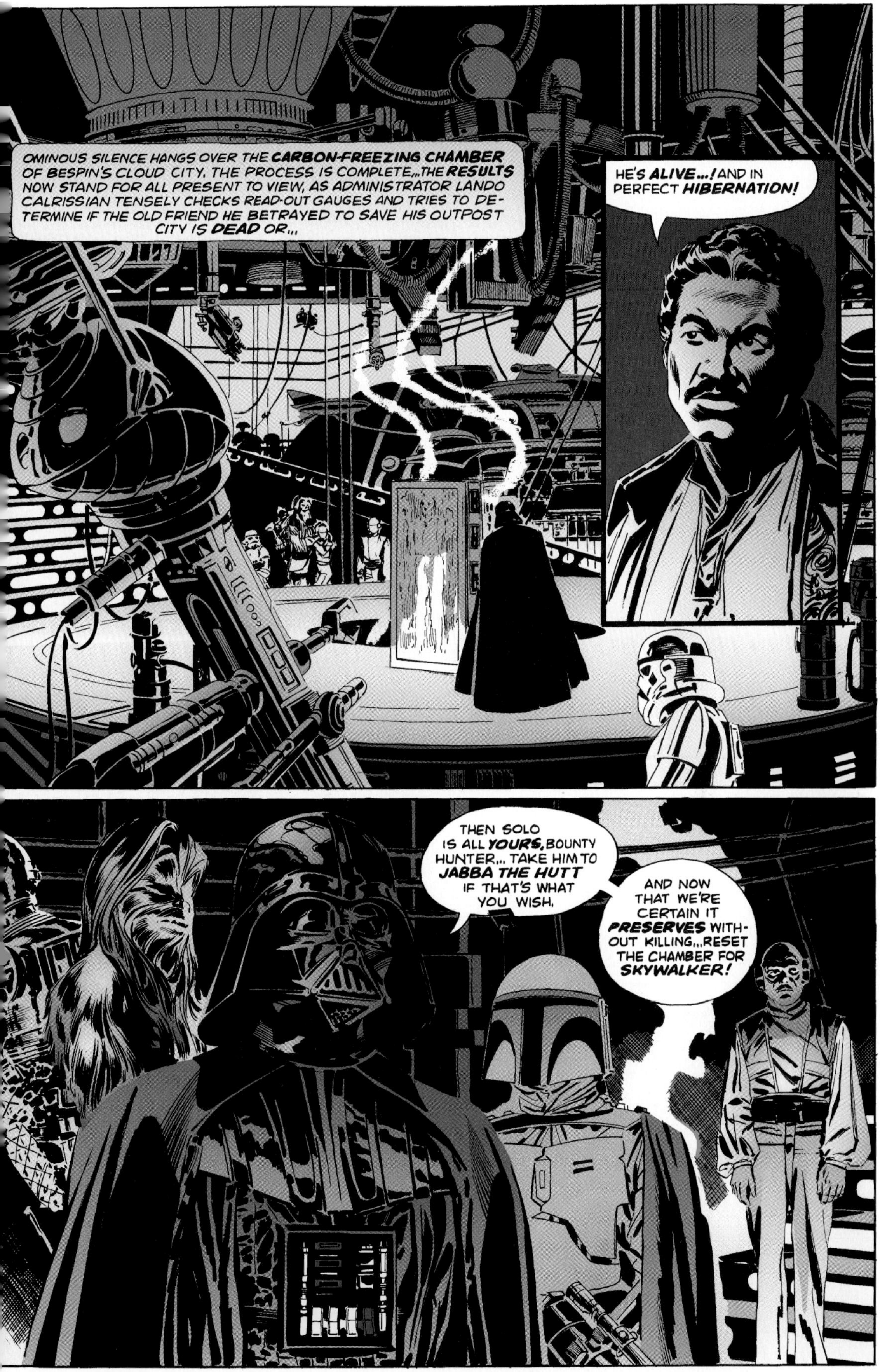
OMINOUS SILENCE HANGS OVER THE CARBON-FREEZING CHAMBER OF BESPIN'S CLOUD CITY. THE PROCESS IS COMPLETE... THE RESULTS NOW STAND FOR ALL PRESENT TO VIEW, AS ADMINISTRATOR LANDO CALRISSIAN TENSELY CHECKS READ-OUT GAUGES AND TRIES TO DETERMINE IF THE OLD FRIEND HE BETRAYED TO SAVE HIS OUTPOST CITY IS DEAD OR...
HE'S ALIVE...! AND IN PERFECT HIBERNATION!
THEN SOLO IS ALL YOURS, BOUNTY HUNTER... TAKE HIM TO JABBA THE HUTT IF THAT'S WHAT YOU WISH.
AND NOW THAT WE'RE CERTAIN IT PRESERVES WITHOUT KILLING... RESET THE CHAMBER FOR SKYWALKER!

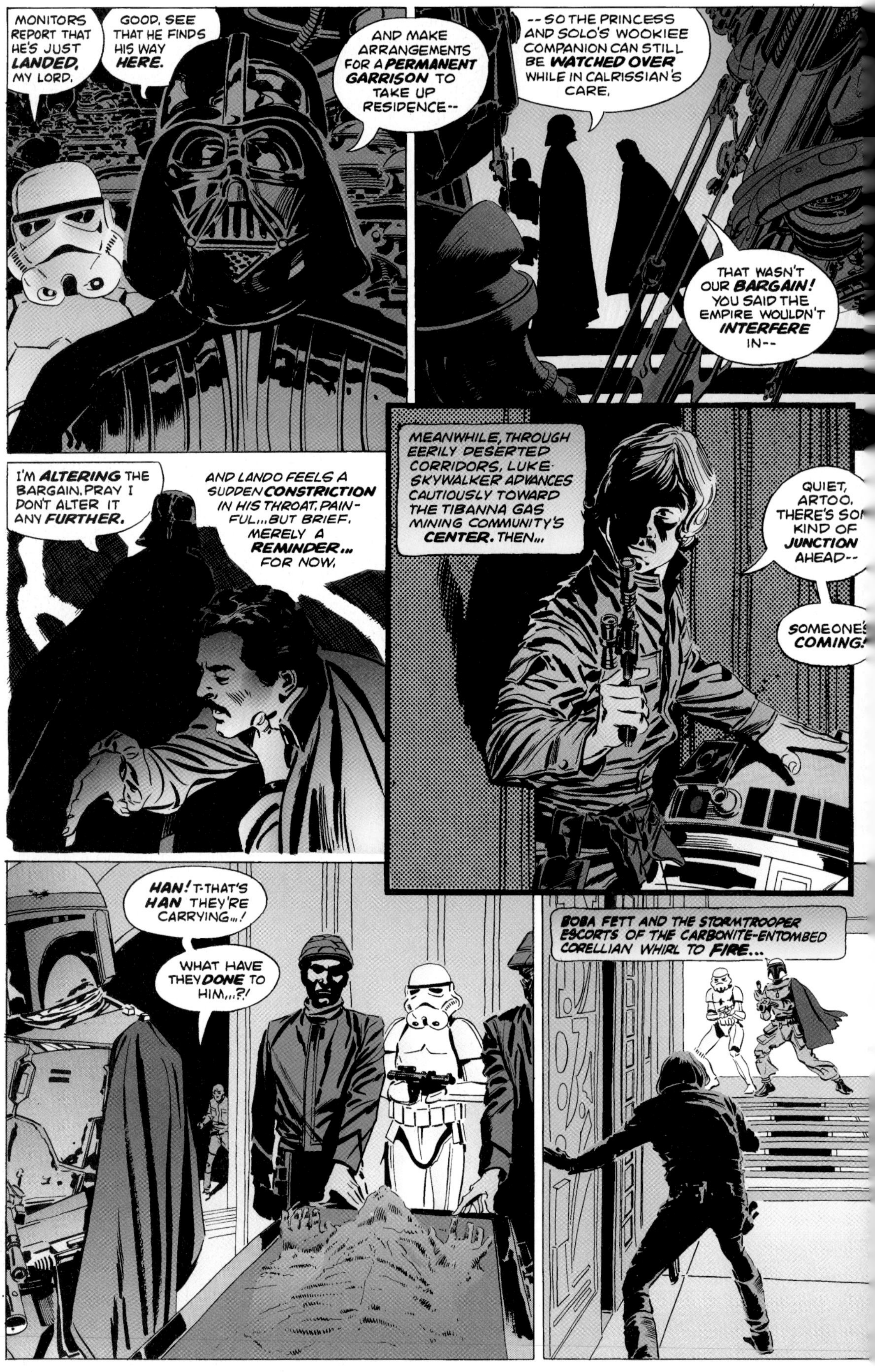
MONITORS REPORT THAT HE'S JUST LANDED, MY LORD.
GOOD, SEE THAT HE FINDS HIS WAY HERE.
AND MAKE ARRANGEMENTS FOR A PERMANENT GARRISON TO TAKE UP RESIDENCE--
-- SO THE PRINCESS AND SOLO'S WOOKIEE COMPANION CAN STILL BE WATCHED OVER WHILE IN CALRISSIAN'S CARE.
THAT WASN'T OUR BARGAIN! YOU SAID THE EMPIRE WOULDN'T INTERFERE IN--
I'M ALTERING THE BARGAIN. PRAY I DON'T ALTER IT ANY FURTHER.
AND LANDO FEELS A SUDDEN CONSTRICTION IN HIS THROAT. PAINFUL... BUT BRIEF. MERELY A REMINDER... FOR NOW.
MEANWHILE, THROUGH EERILY DESERTED CORRIDORS, LUKE SKYWALKER ADVANCES CAUTIOUSLY TOWARD THE TIBANNA GAS MINING COMMUNITY'S CENTER. THEN...
QUIET, ARTOO. THERE'S SOM KIND OF JUNCTION AHEAD--
SOMEONE'S COMING!
HAN! T-THAT'S HAN THEY'RE CARRYING...!
WHAT HAVE THEY DONE TO HIM...?!
BOBA FETT AND THE STORMTROOPER ESCORTS OF THE CARBONITE-ENTOMBED CORELLIAN WHIRL TO FIRE...

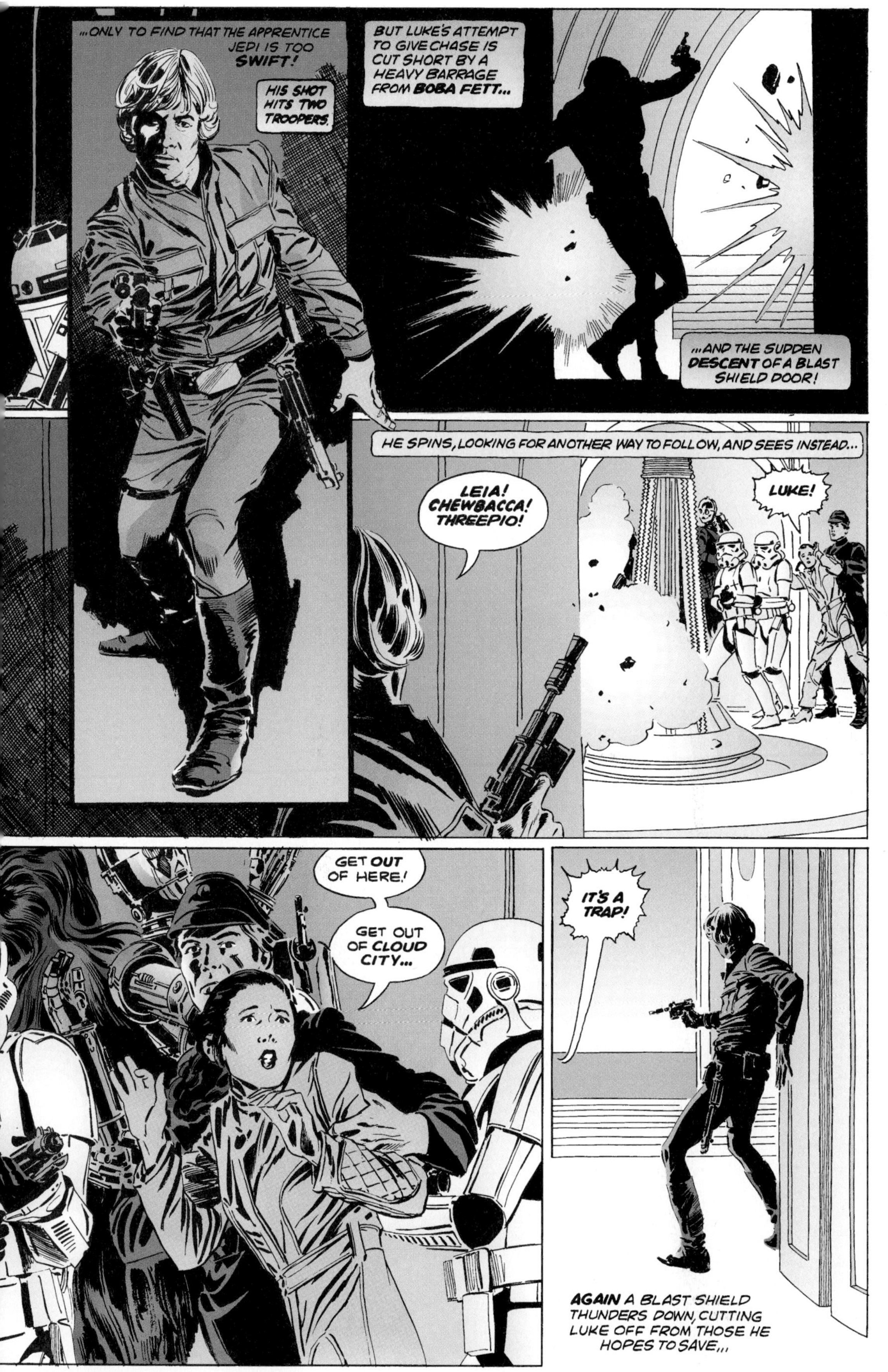
...ONLY TO FIND THAT THE APPRENTICE JEDI IS TOO SWIFT!
HIS SHOT HITS TWO TROOPERS.
BUT LUKE'S ATTEMPT TO GIVE CHASE IS CUT SHORT BY A HEAVY BARRAGE FROM BOBA FETT...
...AND THE SUDDEN DESCENT OF A BLAST SHIELD DOOR!
HE SPINS, LOOKING FOR ANOTHER WAY TO FOLLOW, AND SEES INSTEAD...
LEIA! CHEWBACCA! THREEPIO!
LUKE!
GET OUT OF HERE!
GET OUT OF CLOUD CITY...
IT'S A TRAP!
AGAIN A BLAST SHIELD THUNDERS DOWN, CUTTING LUKE OFF FROM THOSE HE HOPES TO SAVE...

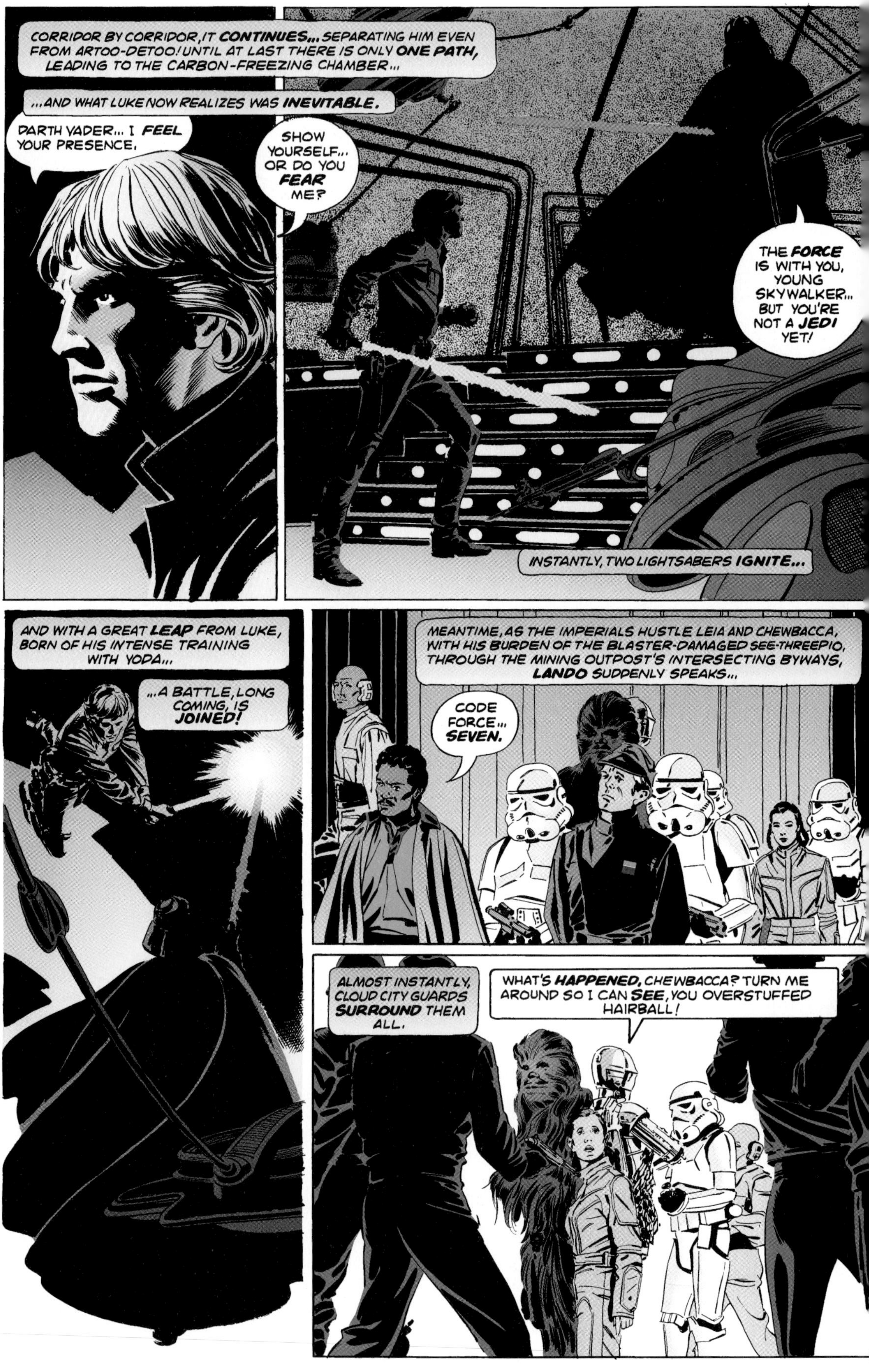
CORRIDOR BY CORRIDOR, IT CONTINUES... SEPARATING HIM EVEN FROM ARTOO-DETOO! UNTIL AT LAST THERE IS ONLY ONE PATH, LEADING TO THE CARBON-FREEZING CHAMBER...
...AND WHAT LUKE NOW REALIZES WAS INEVITABLE.
DARTH VADER... I FEEL YOUR PRESENCE.
SHOW YOURSELF... OR DO YOU FEAR ME?
THE FORCE IS WITH YOU, YOUNG SKYWALKER... BUT YOU'RE NOT A JEDI YET!
INSTANTLY, TWO LIGHTSABERS IGNITE...
AND WITH A GREAT LEAP FROM LUKE, BORN OF HIS INTENSE TRAINING WITH YODA...
...A BATTLE, LONG COMING, IS JOINED!
MEANTIME, AS THE IMPERIALS HUSTLE LEIA AND CHEWBACCA, WITH HIS BURDEN OF THE BLASTER-DAMAGED SEE-THREEPIO, THROUGH THE MINING OUTPOST'S INTERSECTING BYWAYS, LANDO SUDDENLY SPEAKS...
CODE FORCE... SEVEN.
ALMOST INSTANTLY, CLOUD CITY GUARDS SURROUND THEM ALL.
WHAT'S HAPPENED, CHEWBACCA? TURN ME AROUND SO I CAN SEE, YOU OVERSTUFFED HAIRBALL!

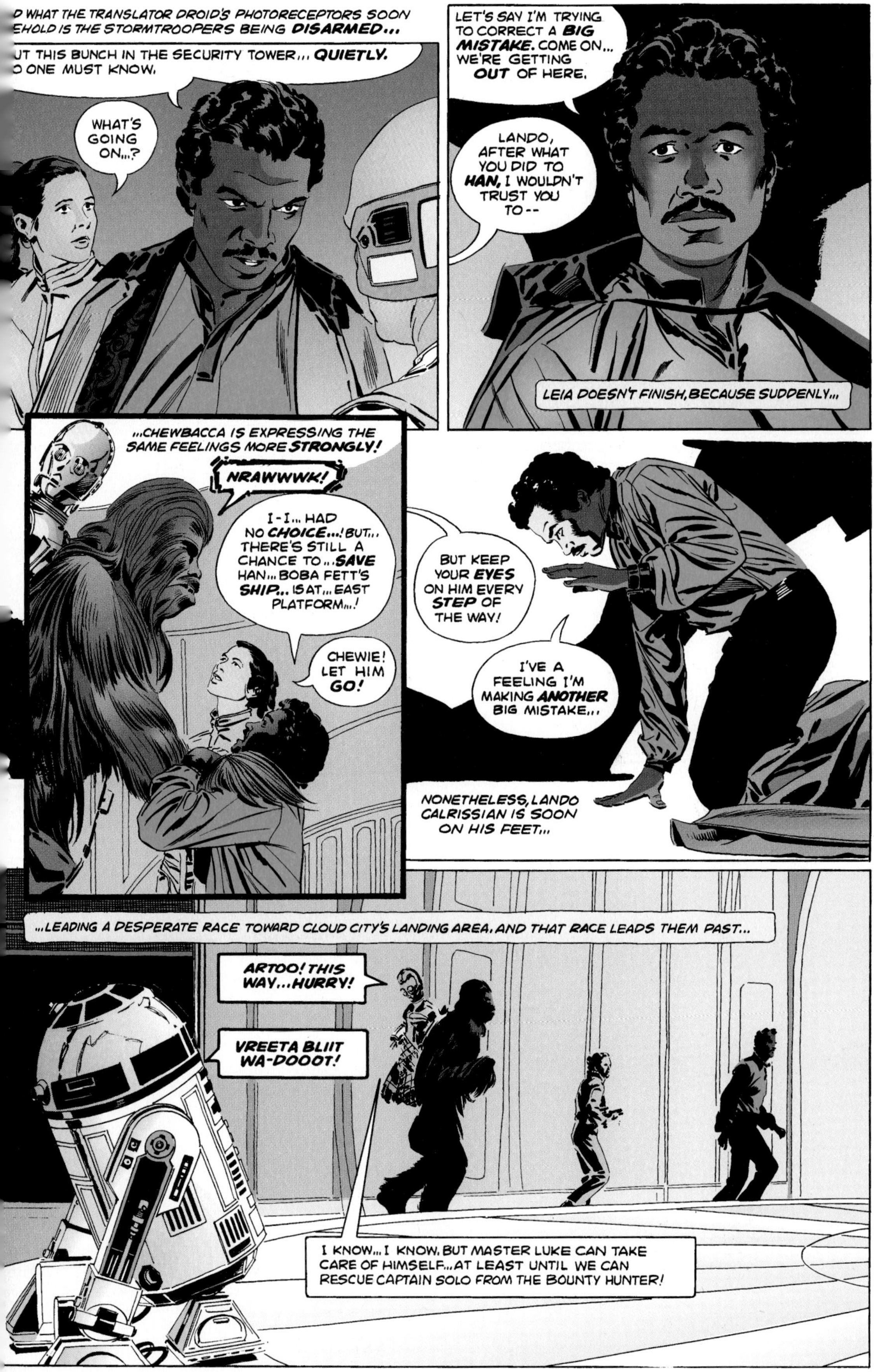

D WHAT THE TRANSLATOR DROID'S PHOTORECEPTORS SOON
EHOLD IS THE STORMTROOPERS BEING DISARMED...
UT THIS BUNCH IN THE SECURITY TOWER... QUIETLY.
O ONE MUST KNOW.
WHAT'S GOING ON...?
LET'S SAY I'M TRYING TO CORRECT A BIG MISTAKE. COME ON... WE'RE GETTING OUT OF HERE.
LANDO, AFTER WHAT YOU DID TO HAN, I WOULDN'T TRUST YOU TO--
LEIA DOESN'T FINISH, BECAUSE SUDDENLY...
...CHEWBACCA IS EXPRESSING THE SAME FEELINGS MORE STRONGLY!
NRAWWWK!
I-I... HAD NO CHOICE...! BUT... THERE'S STILL A CHANCE TO... SAVE HAN... BOBA FETT'S SHIP... IS AT... EAST PLATFORM...!
CHEWIE! LET HIM GO!
BUT KEEP YOUR EYES ON HIM EVERY STEP OF THE WAY!
I'VE A FEELING I'M MAKING ANOTHER BIG MISTAKE...
NONETHELESS, LANDO CALRISSIAN IS SOON ON HIS FEET...
...LEADING A DESPERATE RACE TOWARD CLOUD CITY'S LANDING AREA, AND THAT RACE LEADS THEM PAST...
ARTOO! THIS WAY... HURRY!
VREETA BLIIT WA-DOOOT!
I KNOW... I KNOW, BUT MASTER LUKE CAN TAKE CARE OF HIMSELF... AT LEAST UNTIL WE CAN RESCUE CAPTAIN SOLO FROM THE BOUNTY HUNTER!

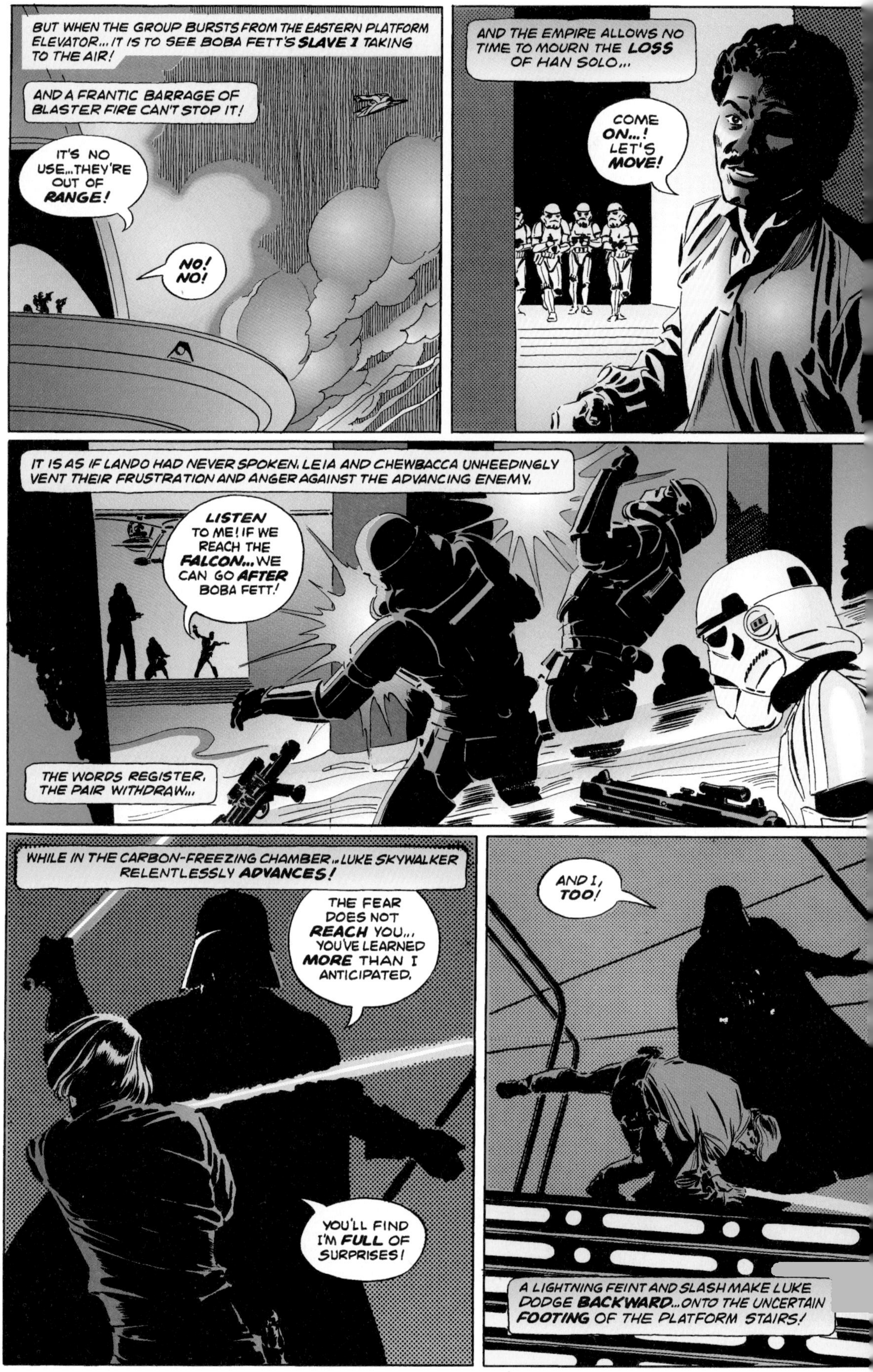
BUT WHEN THE GROUP BURSTS FROM THE EASTERN PLATFORM ELEVATOR... IT IS TO SEE BOBA FETT'S SLAVE 1 TAKING TO THE AIR!
AND A FRANTIC BARRAGE OF BLASTER FIRE CAN'T STOP IT!
IT'S NO USE...THEY'RE OUT OF RANGE!
NO! NO!
AND THE EMPIRE ALLOWS NO TIME TO MOURN THE LOSS OF HAN SOLO...
COME ON...! LET'S MOVE!
IT IS AS IF LANDO HAD NEVER SPOKEN. LEIA AND CHEWBACCA UNHEEDINGLY VENT THEIR FRUSTRATION AND ANGER AGAINST THE ADVANCING ENEMY.
LISTEN TO ME! IF WE REACH THE FALCON... WE CAN GO AFTER BOBA FETT!
THE WORDS REGISTER. THE PAIR WITHDRAW...
WHILE IN THE CARBON-FREEZING CHAMBER... LUKE SKYWALKER RELENTLESSLY ADVANCES!
THE FEAR DOES NOT REACH YOU... YOU'VE LEARNED MORE THAN I ANTICIPATED.
YOU'LL FIND I'M FULL OF SURPRISES!
AND I, TOO!
A LIGHTNING FEINT AND SLASH MAKE LUKE DODGE BACKWARD... ONTO THE UNCERTAIN FOOTING OF THE PLATFORM STAIRS!

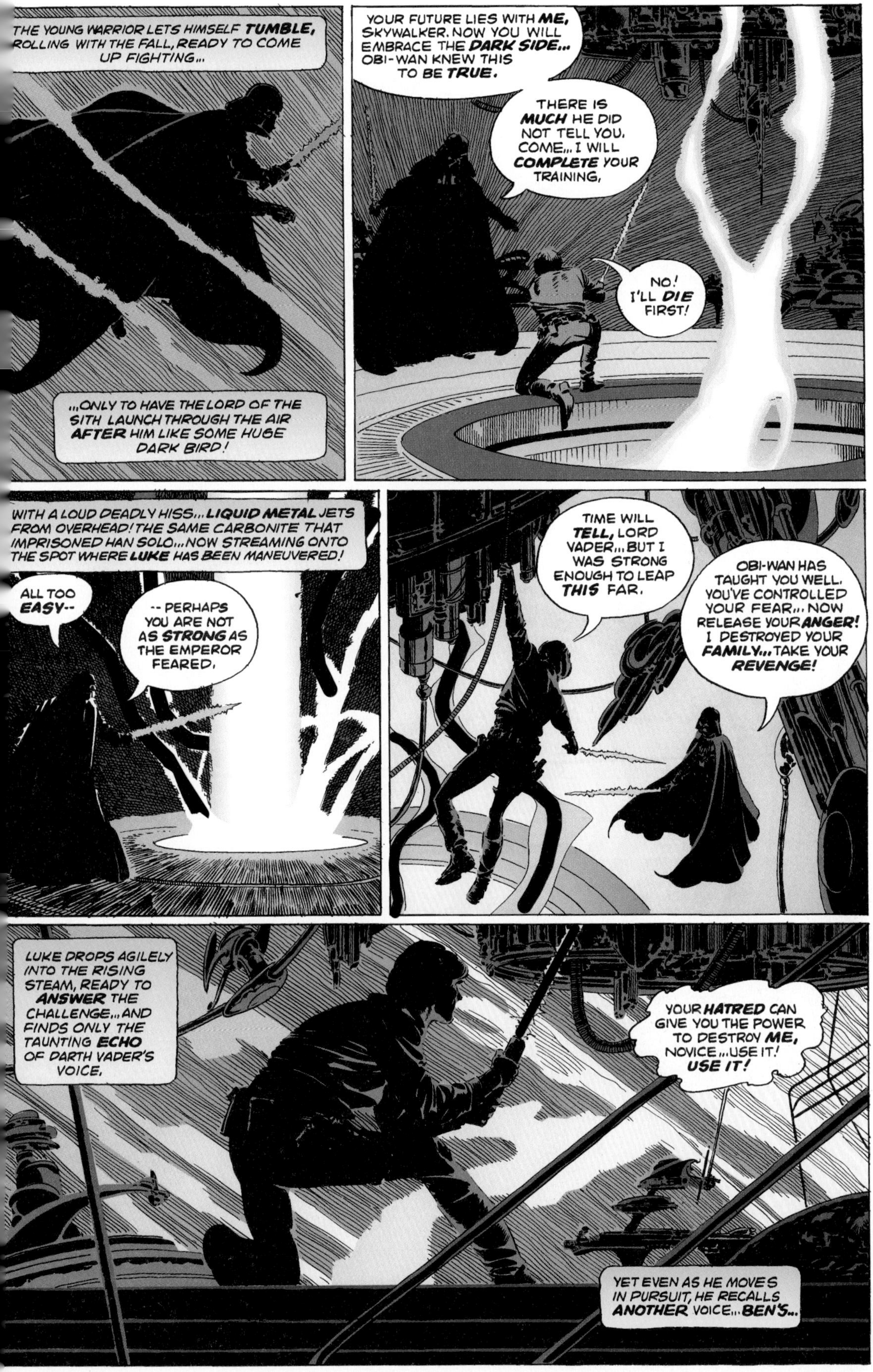
THE YOUNG WARRIOR LETS HIMSELF TUMBLE, ROLLING WITH THE FALL, READY TO COME UP FIGHTING...
...ONLY TO HAVE THE LORD OF THE SITH LAUNCH THROUGH THE AIR AFTER HIM LIKE SOME HUGE DARK BIRD!
YOUR FUTURE LIES WITH ME, SKYWALKER. NOW YOU WILL EMBRACE THE DARK SIDE... OBI-WAN KNEW THIS TO BE TRUE.
THERE IS MUCH HE DID NOT TELL YOU. COME... I WILL COMPLETE YOUR TRAINING.
NO! I'LL DIE FIRST!
WITH A LOUD DEADLY HISS... LIQUID METAL JETS FROM OVERHEAD! THE SAME CARBONITE THAT IMPRISONED HAN SOLO... NOW STREAMING ONTO THE SPOT WHERE LUKE HAS BEEN MANEUVERED!
ALL TOO EASY--
-- PERHAPS YOU ARE NOT AS STRONG AS THE EMPEROR FEARED.
TIME WILL TELL, LORD VADER... BUT I WAS STRONG ENOUGH TO LEAP THIS FAR.
OBI-WAN HAS TAUGHT YOU WELL. YOU'VE CONTROLLED YOUR FEAR... NOW RELEASE YOUR ANGER! I DESTROYED YOUR FAMILY... TAKE YOUR REVENGE!
LUKE DROPS AGILELY INTO THE RISING STEAM, READY TO ANSWER THE CHALLENGE... AND FINDS ONLY THE TAUNTING ECHO OF DARTH VADER'S VOICE.
YOUR HATRED CAN GIVE YOU THE POWER TO DESTROY ME, NOVICE... USE IT! USE IT!
YET EVEN AS HE MOVES IN PURSUIT, HE RECALLS ANOTHER VOICE... BEN'S...

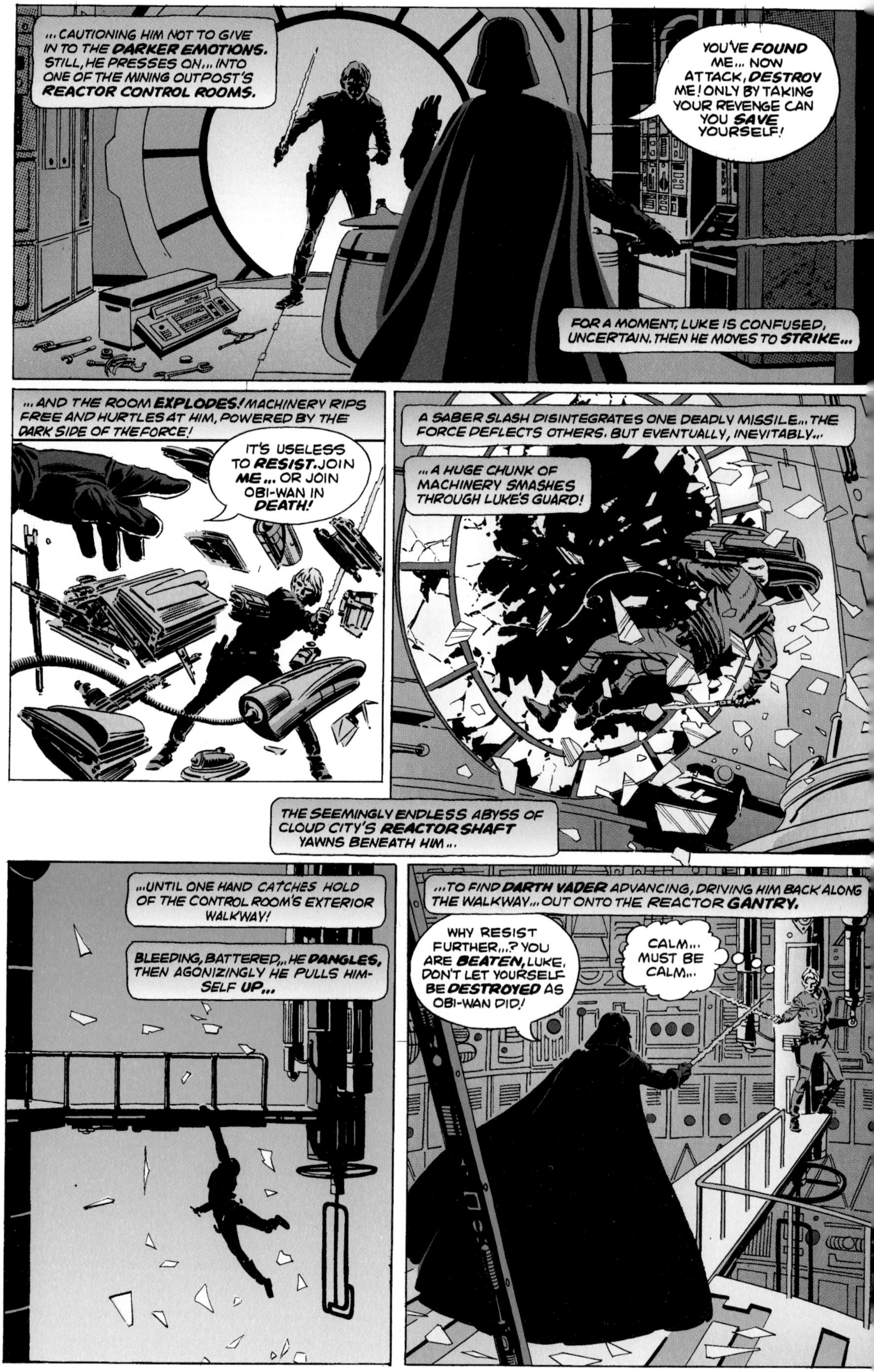
...CAUTIONING HIM NOT TO GIVE IN TO THE DARKER EMOTIONS. STILL, HE PRESSES ON... INTO ONE OF THE MINING OUTPOST'S REACTOR CONTROL ROOMS.
YOU'VE FOUND ME... NOW ATTACK, DESTROY ME! ONLY BY TAKING YOUR REVENGE CAN YOU SAVE YOURSELF!
FOR A MOMENT, LUKE IS CONFUSED, UNCERTAIN. THEN HE MOVES TO STRIKE...
...AND THE ROOM EXPLODES! MACHINERY RIPS FREE AND HURTLES AT HIM, POWERED BY THE DARK SIDE OF THE FORCE!
IT'S USELESS TO RESIST. JOIN ME... OR JOIN OBI-WAN IN DEATH!
A SABER SLASH DISINTEGRATES ONE DEADLY MISSILE... THE FORCE DEFLECTS OTHERS. BUT EVENTUALLY, INEVITABLY...
...A HUGE CHUNK OF MACHINERY SMASHES THROUGH LUKE'S GUARD!
THE SEEMINGLY ENDLESS ABYSS OF CLOUD CITY'S REACTOR SHAFT YAWNS BENEATH HIM...
...UNTIL ONE HAND CATCHES HOLD OF THE CONTROL ROOM'S EXTERIOR WALKWAY!
BLEEDING, BATTERED... HE DANGLES, THEN AGONIZINGLY HE PULLS HIMSELF UP...
...TO FIND DARTH VADER ADVANCING, DRIVING HIM BACK ALONG THE WALKWAY... OUT ONTO THE REACTOR GANTRY.
WHY RESIST FURTHER...? YOU ARE BEATEN, LUKE. DON'T LET YOURSELF BE DESTROYED AS OBI-WAN DID!
CALM... MUST BE CALM...

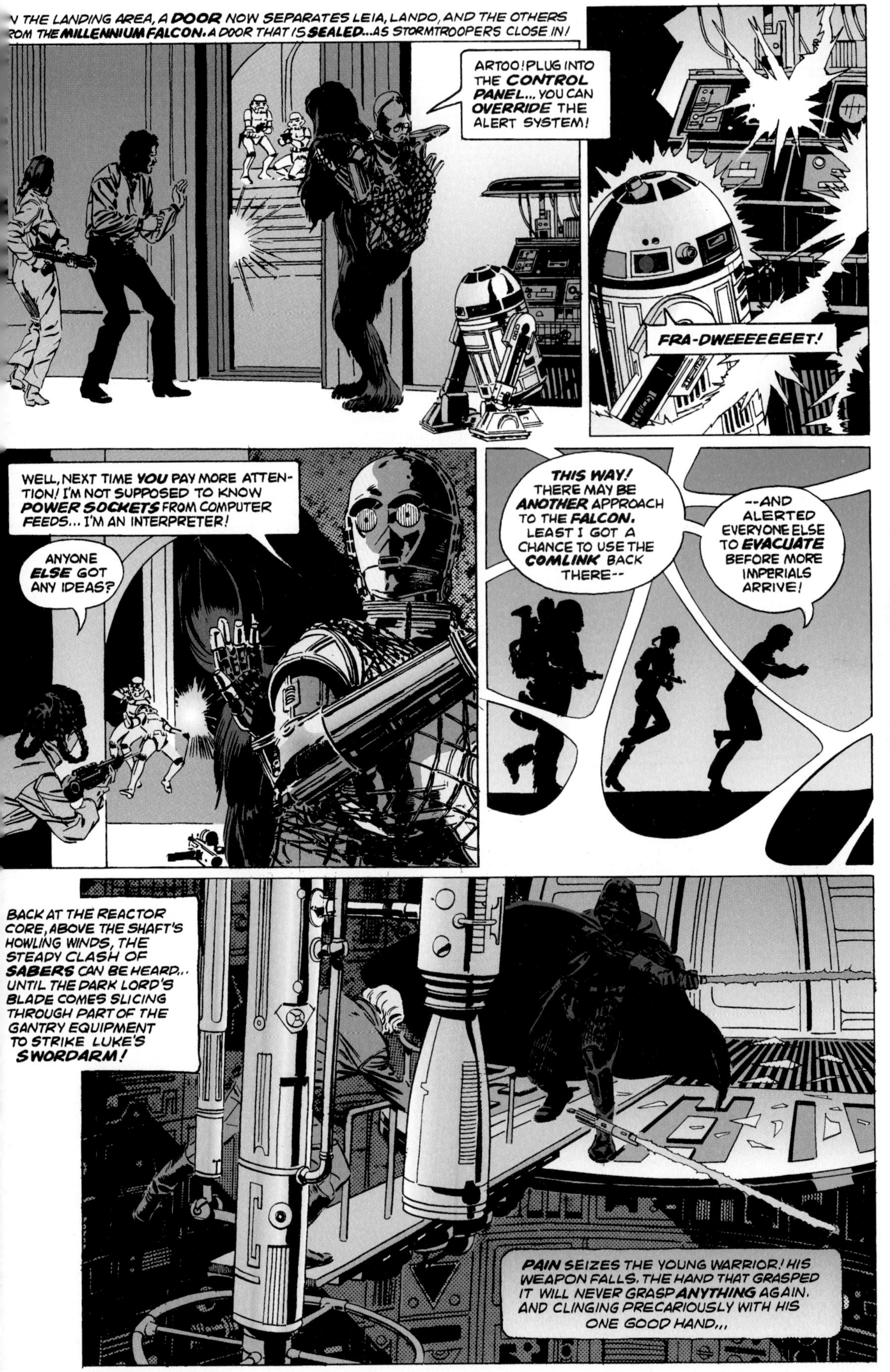

N THE LANDING AREA, A DOOR NOW SEPARATES LEIA, LANDO, AND THE OTHERS ROM THE MILLENNIUM FALCON. A DOOR THAT IS SEALED... AS STORMTROOPERS CLOSE IN!
ARTOO! PLUG INTO THE CONTROL PANEL... YOU CAN OVERRIDE THE ALERT SYSTEM!
FRA-DWEEEEEEET!
WELL, NEXT TIME YOU PAY MORE ATTENTION! I'M NOT SUPPOSED TO KNOW POWER SOCKETS FROM COMPUTER FEEDS... I'M AN INTERPRETER!
ANYONE ELSE GOT ANY IDEAS?
THIS WAY! THERE MAY BE ANOTHER APPROACH TO THE FALCON. LEAST I GOT A CHANCE TO USE THE COMLINK BACK THERE--
--AND ALERTED EVERYONE ELSE TO EVACUATE BEFORE MORE IMPERIALS ARRIVE!
BACK AT THE REACTOR CORE, ABOVE THE SHAFT'S HOWLING WINDS, THE STEADY CLASH OF SABERS CAN BE HEARD... UNTIL THE DARK LORD'S BLADE COMES SLICING THROUGH PART OF THE GANTRY EQUIPMENT TO STRIKE LUKE'S SWORDARM!
PAIN SEIZES THE YOUNG WARRIOR! HIS WEAPON FALLS. THE HAND THAT GRASPED IT WILL NEVER GRASP ANYTHING AGAIN. AND CLINGING PRECARIOUSLY WITH HIS ONE GOOD HAND...

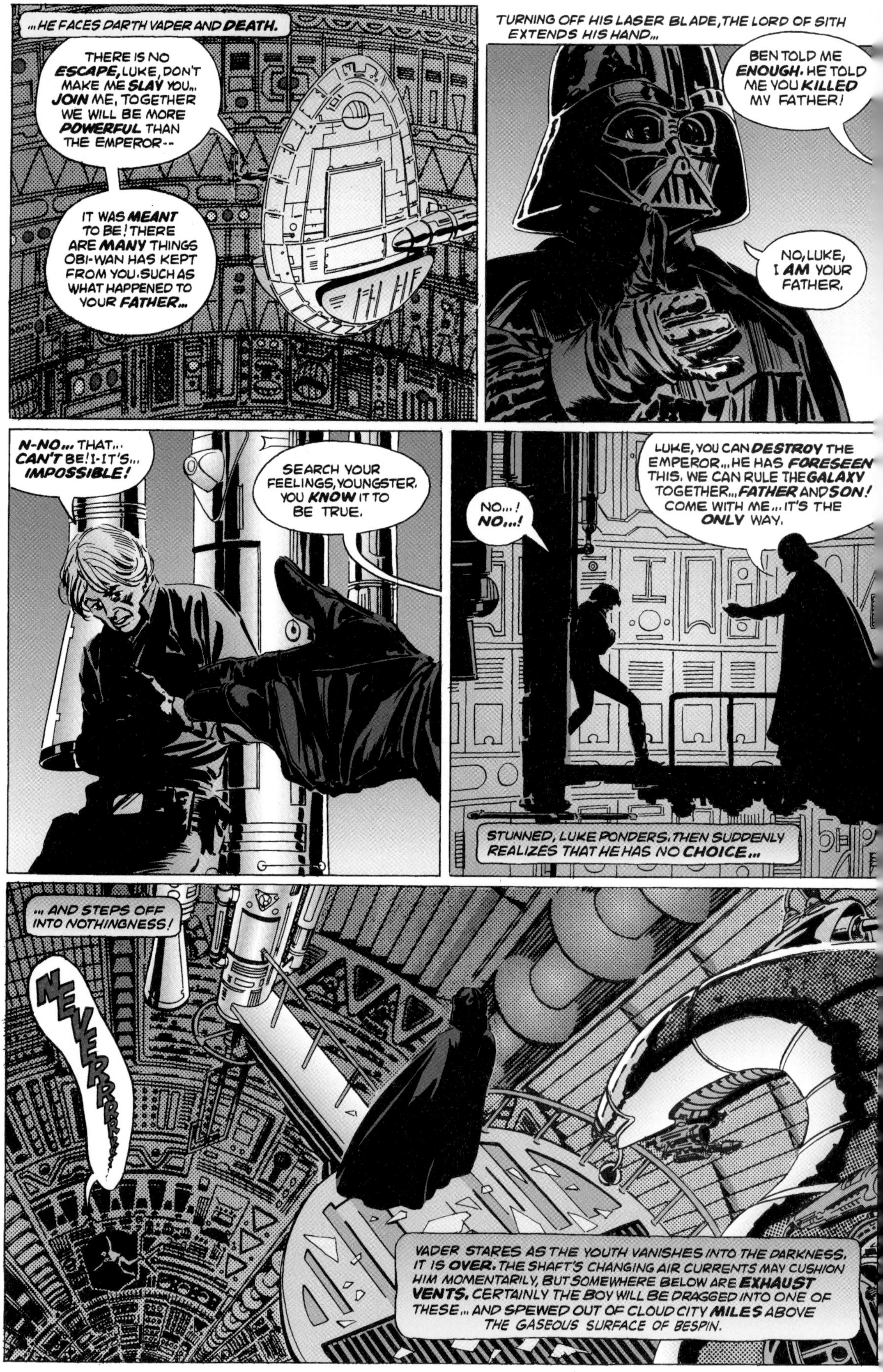
...HE FACES DARTH VADER AND DEATH.
THERE IS NO ESCAPE, LUKE, DON'T MAKE ME SLAY YOU... JOIN ME, TOGETHER WE WILL BE MORE POWERFUL THAN THE EMPEROR--
IT WAS MEANT TO BE! THERE ARE MANY THINGS OBI-WAN HAS KEPT FROM YOU. SUCH AS WHAT HAPPENED TO YOUR FATHER...
TURNING OFF HIS LASER BLADE, THE LORD OF SITH EXTENDS HIS HAND...
BEN TOLD ME ENOUGH. HE TOLD ME YOU KILLED MY FATHER!
NO, LUKE, I AM YOUR FATHER.
N-NO... THAT... CAN'T BE! I-IT'S... IMPOSSIBLE!
SEARCH YOUR FEELINGS, YOUNGSTER. YOU KNOW IT TO BE TRUE.
NO...! NO...!
LUKE, YOU CAN DESTROY THE EMPEROR... HE HAS FORESEEN THIS. WE CAN RULE THE GALAXY TOGETHER... FATHER AND SON! COME WITH ME... IT'S THE ONLY WAY.
STUNNED, LUKE PONDERS. THEN SUDDENLY REALIZES THAT HE HAS NO CHOICE...
...AND STEPS OFF INTO NOTHINGNESS!
NEVERRRR
VADER STARES AS THE YOUTH VANISHES INTO THE DARKNESS. IT IS OVER. THE SHAFT'S CHANGING AIR CURRENTS MAY CUSHION HIM MOMENTARILY, BUT SOMEWHERE BELOW ARE EXHAUST VENTS. CERTAINLY THE BOY WILL BE DRAGGED INTO ONE OF THESE... AND SPEWED OUT OF CLOUD CITY MILES ABOVE THE GASEOUS SURFACE OF BESPIN.

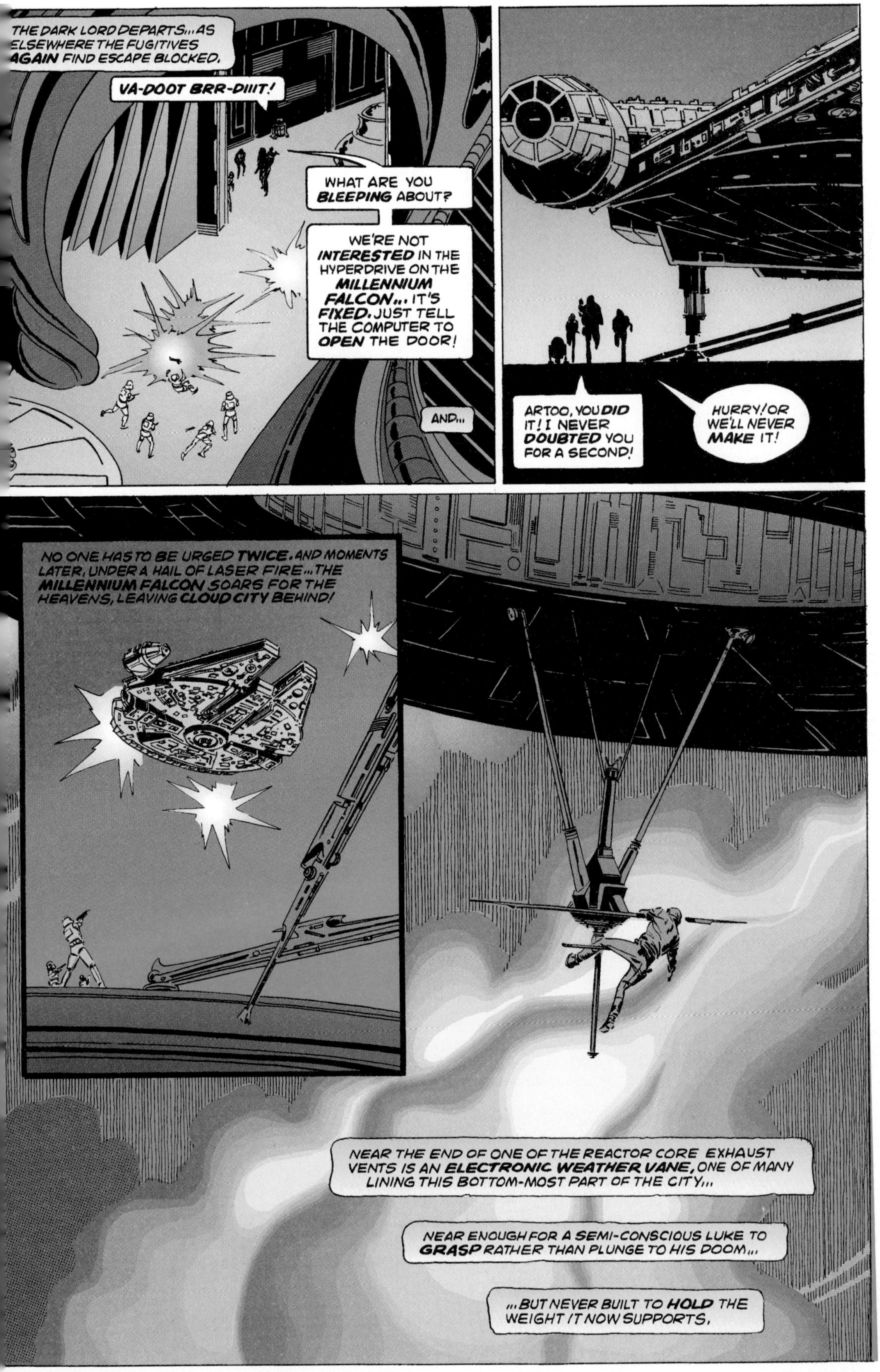
THE DARK LORD DEPARTS... AS ELSEWHERE THE FUGITIVES AGAIN FIND ESCAPE BLOCKED.
VA-DOOT BRR-DIIIT!
WHAT ARE YOU BLEEPING ABOUT?
WE'RE NOT INTERESTED IN THE HYPERDRIVE ON THE MILLENNIUM FALCON... IT'S FIXED. JUST TELL THE COMPUTER TO OPEN THE DOOR!
AND...
ARTOO, YOU DID IT! I NEVER DOUBTED YOU FOR A SECOND!
HURRY! OR WE'LL NEVER MAKE IT!
NO ONE HAS TO BE URGED TWICE. AND MOMENTS LATER, UNDER A HAIL OF LASER FIRE... THE MILLENNIUM FALCON SOARS FOR THE HEAVENS, LEAVING CLOUD CITY BEHIND!
NEAR THE END OF ONE OF THE REACTOR CORE EXHAUST VENTS IS AN ELECTRONIC WEATHER VANE, ONE OF MANY LINING THIS BOTTOM-MOST PART OF THE CITY...
NEAR ENOUGH FOR A SEMI-CONSCIOUS LUKE TO GRASP RATHER THAN PLUNGE TO HIS DOOM...
...BUT NEVER BUILT TO HOLD THE WEIGHT IT NOW SUPPORTS.

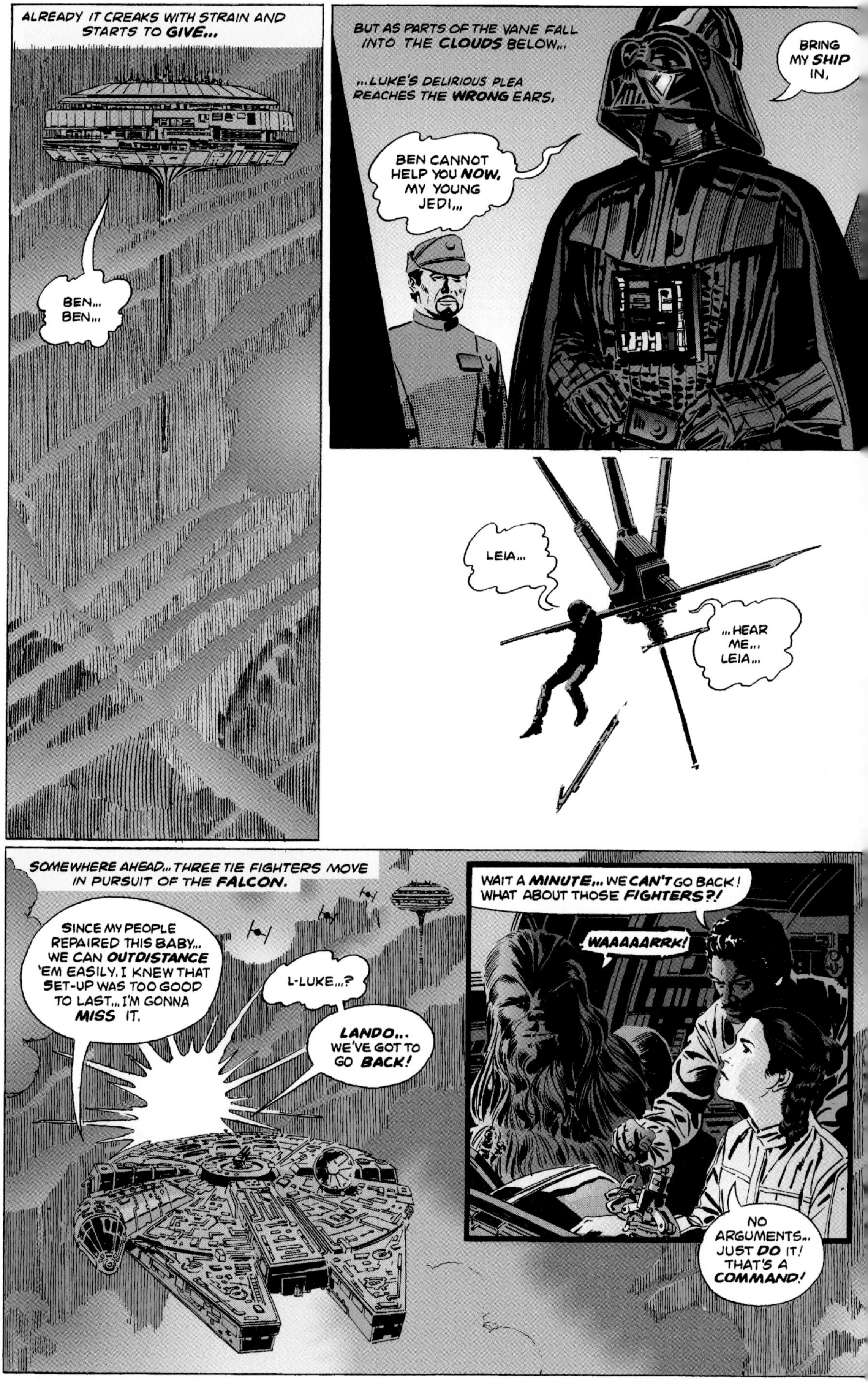
ALREADY IT CREAKS WITH STRAIN AND STARTS TO GIVE...
BEN... BEN...
BUT AS PARTS OF THE VANE FALL INTO THE CLOUDS BELOW...
...LUKE'S DELIRIOUS PLEA REACHES THE WRONG EARS.
BEN CANNOT HELP YOU NOW, MY YOUNG JEDI...
BRING MY SHIP IN.
LEIA...
...HEAR ME... LEIA...
SOMEWHERE AHEAD... THREE TIE FIGHTERS MOVE IN PURSUIT OF THE FALCON.
SINCE MY PEOPLE REPAIRED THIS BABY... WE CAN OUTDISTANCE 'EM EASILY. I KNEW THAT SET-UP WAS TOO GOOD TO LAST... I'M GONNA MISS IT.
L-LUKE...?
LANDO... WE'VE GOT TO GO BACK!
WAIT A MINUTE... WE CAN'T GO BACK! WHAT ABOUT THOSE FIGHTERS?!
WAAAAARRK!
NO ARGUMENTS... JUST DO IT! THAT'S A COMMAND!

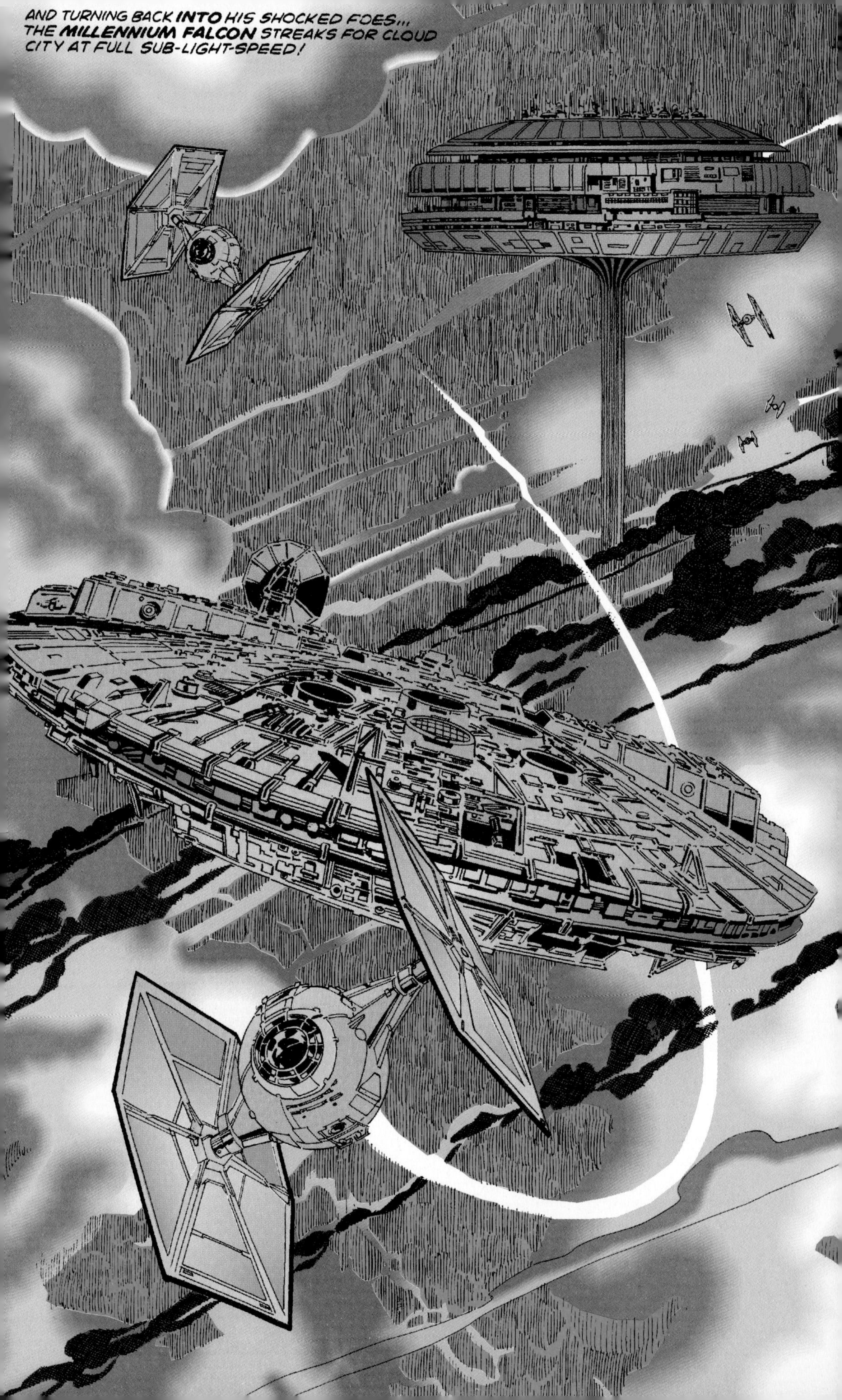
AND TURNING BACK INTO HIS SHOCKED FOES... THE MILLENNIUM FALCON STREAKS FOR CLOUD CITY AT FULL SUB-LIGHT-SPEED!

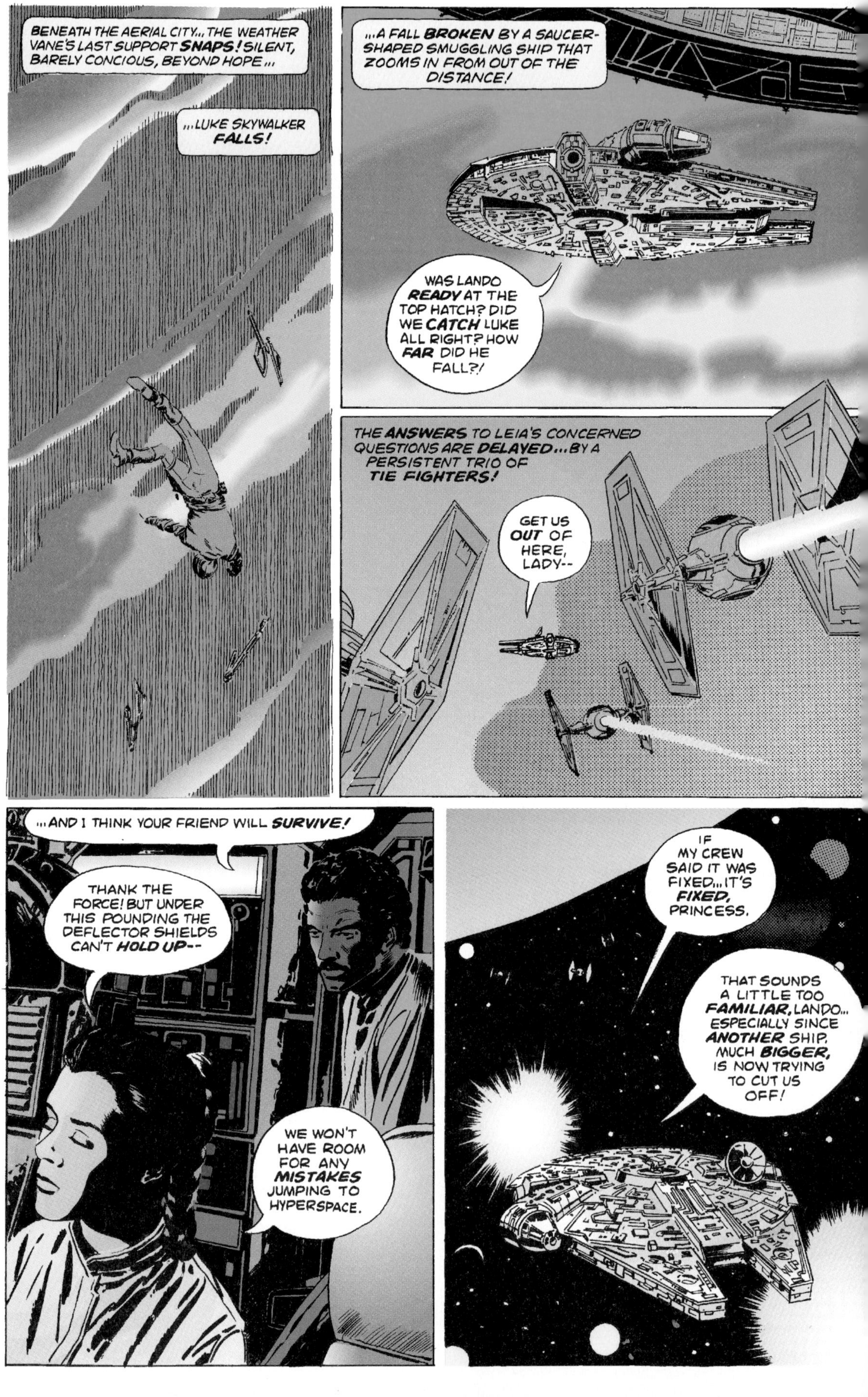

BENEATH THE AERIAL CITY... THE WEATHER VANE'S LAST SUPPORT SNAPS! SILENT, BARELY CONCIOUS, BEYOND HOPE...
...LUKE SKYWALKER FALLS!
...A FALL BROKEN BY A SAUCER-SHAPED SMUGGLING SHIP THAT ZOOMS IN FROM OUT OF THE DISTANCE!
WAS LANDO READY AT THE TOP HATCH? DID WE CATCH LUKE ALL RIGHT? HOW FAR DID HE FALL?!
THE ANSWERS TO LEIA'S CONCERNED QUESTIONS ARE DELAYED... BY A PERSISTENT TRIO OF TIE FIGHTERS!
GET US OUT OF HERE, LADY--
...AND I THINK YOUR FRIEND WILL SURVIVE!
THANK THE FORCE! BUT UNDER THIS POUNDING THE DEFLECTOR SHIELDS CAN'T HOLD UP--
WE WON'T HAVE ROOM FOR ANY MISTAKES JUMPING TO HYPERSPACE.
IF MY CREW SAID IT WAS FIXED... IT'S FIXED, PRINCESS.
THAT SOUNDS A LITTLE TOO FAMILIAR, LANDO... ESPECIALLY SINCE ANOTHER SHIP, MUCH BIGGER, IS NOW TRYING TO CUT US OFF!

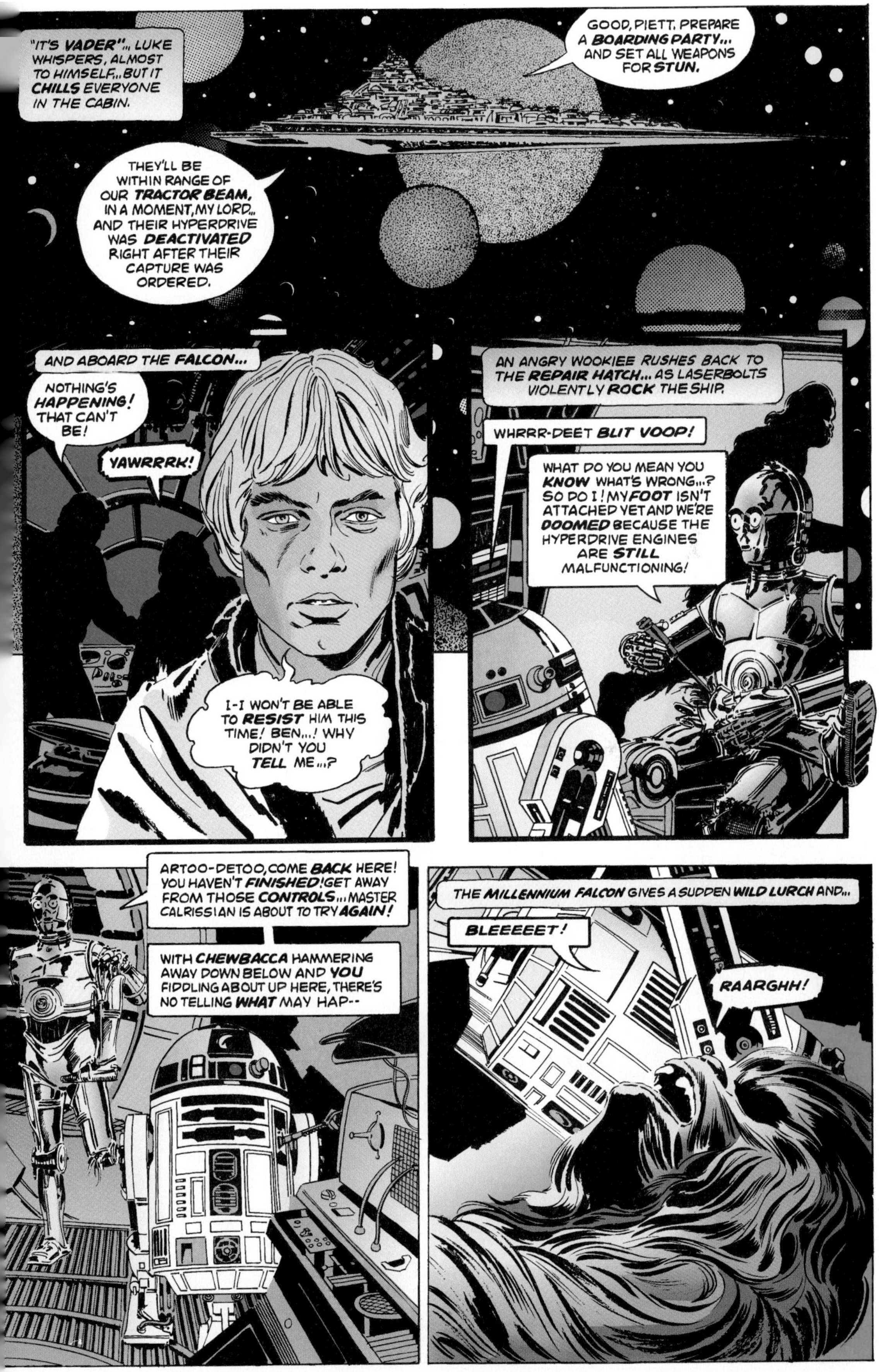

"IT'S VADER"... LUKE WHISPERS, ALMOST TO HIMSELF... BUT IT CHILLS EVERYONE IN THE CABIN.
GOOD, PIETT. PREPARE A BOARDING PARTY... AND SET ALL WEAPONS FOR STUN.
THEY'LL BE WITHIN RANGE OF OUR TRACTOR BEAM, IN A MOMENT, MY LORD... AND THEIR HYPERDRIVE WAS DEACTIVATED RIGHT AFTER THEIR CAPTURE WAS ORDERED.
AND ABOARD THE FALCON...
NOTHING'S HAPPENING! THAT CAN'T BE!
YAWRRRK!
I-I WON'T BE ABLE TO RESIST HIM THIS TIME! BEN...! WHY DIDN'T YOU TELL ME...?
AN ANGRY WOOKIEE RUSHES BACK TO THE REPAIR HATCH... AS LASERBOLTS VIOLENTLY ROCK THE SHIP.
WHRRR-DEET BLIT VOOP!
WHAT DO YOU MEAN YOU KNOW WHAT'S WRONG...? SO DO I! MY FOOT ISN'T ATTACHED YET AND WE'RE DOOMED BECAUSE THE HYPERDRIVE ENGINES ARE STILL MALFUNCTIONING!
ARTOO-DETOO, COME BACK HERE! YOU HAVEN'T FINISHED! GET AWAY FROM THOSE CONTROLS... MASTER CALRISSIAN IS ABOUT TO TRY AGAIN!
WITH CHEWBACCA HAMMERING AWAY DOWN BELOW AND YOU FIDDLING ABOUT UP HERE, THERE'S NO TELLING WHAT MAY HAP--
THE MILLENNIUM FALCON GIVES A SUDDEN WILD LURCH AND...
BLEEEEET!
RAARGHH!

THAT DID IT!

AND DESPITE AN INCREDIBLE **COMMOTION** IN THE REPAIR HATCH, HAN SOLO'S FREIGHTER SPEEDS AWAY INTO INFINITY... AND **SAFETY** AT LAST!

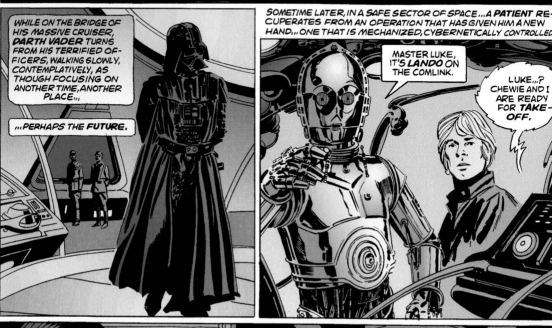

WHILE ON THE BRIDGE OF HIS **MASSIVE** CRUISER, **DARTH VADER** TURNS FROM HIS **TERRIFIED** OFFICERS, WALKING SLOWLY, CONTEMPLATIVELY, AS THOUGH FOCUSING ON ANOTHER TIME, ANOTHER PLACE...

...PERHAPS THE **FUTURE.**

SOMETIME LATER, IN A SAFE SECTOR OF SPACE... A **PATIENT** RECUPERATES FROM AN OPERATION THAT HAS GIVEN HIM A NEW HAND... ONE THAT IS MECHANIZED, CYBERNETICALLY CONTROLLED.

MASTER LUKE, IT'S **LANDO** ON THE COMLINK.

LUKE...? CHEWIE AND I ARE READY FOR **TAKE-OFF.**

I'LL SEE YOU ON **TATOOINE.**

AND DON'T **WORRY,** LEIA... WE'LL **FIND** HAN!

VAROWRK!

AND AS THE **MILLENNIUM FALCON** PULLS AWAY FROM THE REBEL BATTLE CRUISER THAT HAS BEEN A TEMPORARY REFUGE... THOSE LEFT **BEHIND** HAVE MANY THOUGHTS, MANY UNCERTAINTIES, BUT FOR THIS MOMENT...

...THEY ALSO HAVE **PEACE.**

TAKE **CARE,** MY FRIENDS... MAY THE **FORCE** BE WITH YOU!

END

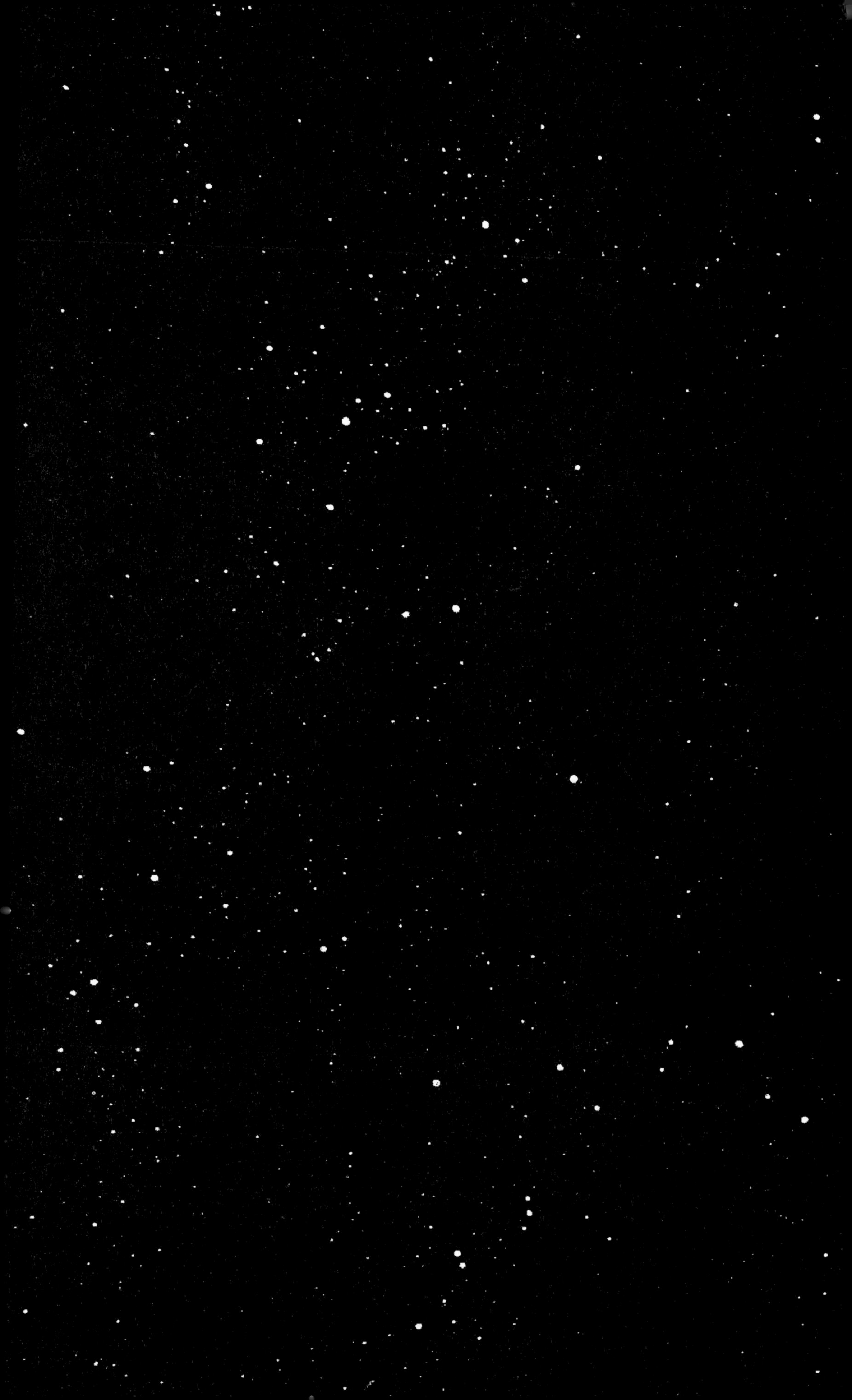